A Nation Within a Nation

A NATION WITHIN A NATION

---

*Organizing African-American
Communities Before the Civil War*

John Ernest

The American Ways Series

IVAN R. DEE   *Chicago*

www.ivanrdee.com

Library of Congress Cataloging-in-Publication Data:
Ernest, John.
  A nation within a nation : organizing African-American communities before the
Civil War / John Ernest.
      p. cm.
  Includes index.
  ISBN 978-1-56663-807-4 (cloth : alk. paper) — ISBN 978-1-56663-917-0
(electronic)
  1. African Americans—Societies, etc.—History—19th century. 2. African
American fraternal organizations—History—19th century. 3. African American
churches—History—19th century. 4. African Americans—Congresses—History—
19th century. 5. African American schools—History—19th century. 6. African
American press—History—19th century. 7. African Americans—Race identity—
History—19th century. 8. African Americans—Social conditions—19th century.
9. African Americans—Education—History—19th century. 10. Community
organization—United States—History—19th century. I. Title.
  E185.5.E76 2011
  973'.0496073—dc22
                                                              2010043409

Contents

Preface

AT THE 2008 Republican National Convention in Minneapolis-St. Paul, vice-presidential nominee Sarah Palin, defending her preparation for national leadership while taking a swipe at the Democratic presidential nominee, declared, "I guess a small-town mayor is sort of like a community organizer, except that you have actual responsibilities." Questions about Palin's experience would linger—she served as mayor of Wasilla, Alaska, from 1996 to 2002, and as the state's governor beginning in 2006—but her remarks successfully raised questions about Barack Obama's experience as a community organizer in Chicago from 1985 to 1988. Shortly after graduating with a B.A. from Columbia University in 1983, Obama accepted a position as director of the Developing Communities Project, a program formed in association with the Calumet Community Religious Conference, itself the result of a coalition of various churches looking to help laid-off workers in the area. Administrative titles and programs aside, Obama's early career in public service seemed to many beyond the scope of the usual political résumé. Even seasoned political commentators were at a loss to explain what exactly a "community organizer" does, as did Obama himself. In his memoir *Dreams from My Father*, Obama reports that he had trouble answering classmates who asked him about his position as a community organizer. Perhaps he best captures his sense of his work when he says in his memoir, simply, that he went to Chicago to "organize black folks."

What does it mean to "organize black folks"? To some extent, Obama's job was to establish a working coalition between the predominantly black residents of Chicago's southern neighborhoods and the working class residents of surrounding areas, including northeastern Indiana suburbs, who had been hard hit by the collapse of the steel industry in the 1970s. Black communities were suspicious of outsiders, and therefore of the Calumet Conference's white Catholic base, and Obama worked to help form interracial and Catholic-Protestant alliances. Organizing black folks, then, involved getting black Americans to recognize socioeconomic commonalities that trumped established lines of social difference. But Obama's actual work led him into the ways in which black folks were in fact already organized—through their churches, their schools, and the formal and informal ways that they had come to understand themselves as a community. Being a community organizer, that is, involved the work of organizing not just black folks but black communities.

This book explores the roots of that important distinction—between black folks and black communities—examining the process by which, from the late eighteenth century to the Civil War, black people reimagined and recreated themselves as vibrant, self-defining communities. For the most part I address the condition of black Americans who were not enslaved, those who could claim the relative (at times little more than the nominal) condition of freedom available to blacks in the nation's first half-century. By far the great majority of those of African origins living in the United States during these years were the many—by the time of the Civil War, nearly four million—who were enslaved. Theirs too is an inspiring story of community organization which includes, usually under the veil of secrecy, religious organization, networks of communication, rituals of social interaction, resistance to slavery, and the holistic immersion in and transcendence over their condition that is most powerfully preserved in the spirituals. But those other African Americans who had escaped or otherwise risen out of the horrors of slavery had a story to tell as well, a story they pieced together for themselves by piecing themselves together from the fragmented mass they were expected to remain. Most of these other African Americans lived in the urban regions of the North, where slavery was gradually abolished in the decades following the American Revolution, though some lived in tenuous circumstances in the slaveholding South and others looked for new opportunities and fortunes in the West. Wherever they lived, though, black people understood that opportunities would come only if they could establish working bonds of self-preservation and self-determination. They understood the difference between a significant concentration of black people and a black *community*. Circumstances demanded, in short, community organizers.

This book is devoted to those who responded to that call, and to the concept of community they promoted. Community, to these men and women, meant something more than a common condition determined by the laws and social customs that made black people, at best, second-class citizens in the United States, and something more than the bonds of a people who could claim a "common" heritage in the diverse cultures of Africa. Community required a common sense of history, shared goals for the future, and lives interconnected by religious, educational, economic, and political forums for mutual assistance and debate. Either excluded from or restricted in their participation in churches, political parties, and the economic marketplace, African Americans were largely left either to fend for themselves or to accept the degraded condition available to them in a deeply racist culture. To accept their condition was to allow themselves to be simply black people in white America, with blackness taken as a visible marker of an insurmountable handicap in life. To create themselves as black communities was the means by which they could work toward a more inclusive local, state, and national polity, with blackness functioning as a visible sign of a shared spiritual and intellectual determination. As in the biblical stories from which they often drew inspiration, the mark of degradation could be transformed into the mark of a blessed and determined people—not a proclamation of separatism but a reminder that full political and social inclusion begins with those who have been most fundamentally excluded.

When Obama entered Chicago's South Side to organize black folks, he encountered the legacy of the efforts that began in the years covered in this book. Those critical of Obama followed him into the black community in which he lived and worked to understand—or perhaps simply to expose—the significance of his status as an African American who was a serious contender for the nation's highest office. Many believed they found their answers in the radicalism that seemed to be at the heart of the kind of community organizing in which Obama was involved—a way of getting communities to insist on a hearing from the powers that be, those who too often seemed either hard of hearing or shut off from some members of the communities they had been elected to serve. Many believed, too, that they found the secret significance of Obama's blackness in the church he attended and in the form of liberation theology espoused by the church's pastor and Obama's spiritual mentor, the Reverend Jeremiah Wright. Obama himself, looking to present himself as a viable candidate for all Americans, sometimes seemed to struggle with the concept of blackness that emerged from the institutional centers and community leaders he had worked with. The story behind those centers and many of those leaders, the story of what distinguishes many black communities in the United States, is much more complicated than the one political commentators were prepared to tell. This book presents the early chapters of that story.

Acknowledgments

THIS IS A BOOK about community, and I could not have written it without the guidance and support of a dedicated community of scholars. I am deeply indebted to those who wrote the local, regional, and national studies that guided me through my own research for this project. John David Smith initiated this journey when he offered me the opportunity to write this book, and I appreciate his thoughtful suggestions and support along the way. In an impressively thoughtful and detailed reading of the original manuscript, Ivan Dee provided both a humbling and an encouraging critique that made this a much stronger book than it would otherwise have been. Such editors are rare, and I am fortunate to have had this chance to learn from one of the best. My research assistants—Sohinee Roy, Luminita M. Dragulescu, Jim Greene, and Cara Snider—provided substantial help at different stages of this project. Their attention to detail and their ability to find needles in haystacks are impressive, and I am grateful to them for their contributions. I'm indebted as well to the librarians at West Virginia University and the University of Virginia, and particularly to the interlibrary loan services at WVU. Early chapters of this book were first critiqued by the WVU English Department's faculty research group, and I am grateful for their careful and supportive readings of my work. I am fortunate to be a member of a department that includes such accomplished scholars who still manage to be generous with their time.

In writing this book I have been guided by mentors who never knew they were serving as such. The inspiration for this book came from the work of Leon F. Litwack, Frances Smith Foster, and Eric Gardner. I've written the book with many scholars in mind but with these three especially, hoping that my work might be a worthy response to the high standards of scholarship and of personal commitment to African-American history they have set.

I wrote much of this book during a difficult time personally. I'm grateful to Rebecca Mays Ernest for her faith in me, which made this period easier than it might have been. Thanks especially to Denise Eno Stewart for providing the time, the space, and the inspiration I needed to continue working on this project when the world pressed in around me. I could not have finished it without her.

J. E.

Wenonah, New Jersey
August 2010

A Nation Within a Nation

1

Cities on the Hill

Organizing Communities

IN ITS September 8, 1865, issue the *Liberator*, the most influential of the anti-slavery newspapers, published an "Address from the Colored Citizens of Norfolk, Va., to the People of the United States." With the ending of the Civil War, the abolitionists associated with the *Liberator* might well have felt that their work was nearly completed, but this message emphasized the work that remained. It noted the considerable contributions of black Americans to the nation's wealth and development, both in the nominally free North and in the South, where "the millions upon millions of acres, in its countless plantations, laden with precious crops, bear witness to the unrequited industry of our people." What amounted to another abolitionist movement lay ahead—the abolition of oppression and the granting of "the full enjoyment of those privileges of full citizenship which not only are our undoubted right, but are indispensable to that elevation and prosperity of our people which must be the desire of every patriot." The Address was signed—on June 20, 1865—"in behalf of the colored people of Norfolk and vicinity" by prominent black clergymen and citizens of the city, and by the great black abolitionist and "Honorary Member" of this community, Henry Highland Garnet, formerly of the North but then pastor of the Fifteenth Street Presbyterian Church of Washington, D.C.

The project set out in the appeal would extend throughout the twentieth century, but the progress made along the way depended heavily on the efforts of community organizations—in this case the process by which eight men could claim the authority of "the colored people of Norfolk and vicinity" so as to represent a collective mission and a unified voice. Such organizations proliferated after the Civil War, and historians have noted their importance in promoting the interests and even the existence of a conceptually coherent collective of people, the African-American community. Less appreciated are those many groups and associations created between the late eighteenth century and the Civil War, even though much of what we know about African-American history during that time is a result of the efforts of those organizations. This book will explore the importance of African-American attempts to organize themselves in various local settings and across the country.

In *Democracy in America* (1835–1840), Alexis de Tocqueville observed that "Americans of all ages, all conditions, and all dispositions, constantly form associations." Black Americans were no exception to this rule. Like other Americans, they formed associations, as Tocqueville said of the nation generally, "religious, moral, serious, futile, general or restricted, enormous or diminute." From the late eighteenth century to the Civil War, African Americans gathered in many associations designed to promote education, provide financial security, disseminate information, popularize anti-slavery sentiment, protect fragile privileges while arguing for full civil rights, worship freely, and promote stable communities in the face of harsh restrictions, prejudices, and outright oppression. The most basic of these associations were mutual benefit organizations, designed in part to provide insurance against financial loss in times of personal and family crisis, including funding for funerals and, in some cases, access to cemeteries in a time of segregated burials. But such associations both encouraged and overlapped with other organizations, including the formation of black fraternal groups, literary societies, churches and religious denominations, schools, and black-run and black-oriented periodicals and publishing venues. Some of these organizations were interracial, others were devoted specifically to claiming pride in an African heritage and piecing together an African-American history capable of encouraging a politically unified community. Many organizations were short-lived, but many others lasted through the years, often communicating with one another to form a web of relations that stretched across the nation, north and south, east and west.

Some sign of the success of such efforts is evident in the Address from the Colored Citizens of Norfolk. The affiliations and communications among black communities are evidenced in this Address by the signature of the Northern activist and minister Henry Highland Garnet but also in the rhetorical mode of the Address, including its history of African-American involvement in the formation and development of the United States, from Crispus Attucks at the Boston massacre to African-American service in the Civil War. Most notably it mentions "Andrew Jackson's famous appeal to the colored 'citizens' of Louisiana," a reference to two proclamations issued in 1814 by then General Andrew Jackson, in which he hailed black Americans as "fellow citizens." These documents were quoted frequently by the black leader Frederick Douglass in various speeches and articles, and by numerous other African-American writers as well, including Hosea Easton in 1837, Robert Benjamin Lewis in 1844, William C. Nell in 1851 and 1855, Martin R. Delany in 1852, William J. Watkins in 1853, William Wells Brown in 1867 and 1873, and George Washington Williams in 1883. A staple of African-American historical writing, Jackson's proclamations were used by black Americans (despite the fact that the slaveholding Jackson could hardly be viewed as a friend to their cause) as authoritative evidence that they should not have to argue for their right to citizenship. In its general contours as well as in its details, the Norfolk Address shows signs of the success of African-American associations and of the black press in promoting a national historical narrative that accounted for the experience of African Americans and argued for their rights.

What is impressive about the Norfolk association, with its overtones of a national collective, is that African-American communities faced an even more basic problem than arguing against white oppression—namely, the challenge of gathering together those of African heritage to form a potentially coherent community. To a great extent, scholarly and popular references to an African-American past engage in a convenient fiction: the assumption of a conceptually coherent community in the process of development. Throughout the early national period of the United States, such a community simply didn't exist, though the grounds and need for it were strongly recognized by black leaders and writers. Long after Africans were brought to America by force—people from different regions, often speaking different languages and shaped by different religious beliefs and cultural practices—they remained scattered and fragmented both geographically and ideologically, in terms of their living conditions and the possibilities they entertained for themselves. Hosea

Easton, an influential minister and community activist, declared in 1837 that African Americans "belong to no people, race, or nation; subjects of no government—citizens of no country—scattered surplus remnants of two races, and of different nations—severed into individuality—rendered a mass of broken fragments, thrown to and fro, by the boisterous passions of this and other ungodly nations." In 1848 Garnet, represented in the Norfolk Address, mourned the "children . . . scattered over the whole earth . . . tortured, taunted, and hurried out of life by unprecedented cruelty." Martin Delany, one of the most accomplished black leaders of his time, in 1852 referred to the imagined black community as "a *broken people*." As is emphasized even by the anguished and sometimes contentious disagreements over what name to use in even identifying this group—African, Negro, Colored, Anglo-African, and the like—this was a collective defined in part by a dominant culture and in part by their own variously organized efforts to understand themselves.

The confusion over identification was inevitable, given the absurd dynamics of racial classification in the nineteenth century. Over time and generations, the color line separating black and white Americans became harder to draw as mixed-race individuals increasingly populated all the nation's regions. While there was considerable disagreement among African Americans about the value or even the propriety of racial mixing, many agreed with Garnet when he observed in 1848 that "it is a stubborn fact, that it is impossible to separate the pale man and the man of color, and therefore the result which to them is so fearful, is inevitable." "*This Western World*," he asserted with emphasis, "*is destined to be filled with a mixed race*." But such racial mixing as occurred did little to shift the nation's emphasis on white privilege, leading instead to an increasingly complicated legal and social landscape. White people were kidnapped and held in slavery; enslaved people escaped from slavery by presenting themselves as white; and numerous juries faced court cases in which the central issue was to decide whether someone was white or black. Increasingly, many people found themselves living on the tenuous color line, where the visible markers of racial distinctions broke down and racial identity—in the courts and elsewhere—was often determined not simply by ancestry but by social affiliations: the people one knew, the places one went, the life one lived.

Such racial mixing often complicated African-American development, for many found their achievements ascribed to "their white blood," making even some blacks examples of white claims to superior ancestry and civilization. In *A Text Book of the Origin and History, &c. &c. of the Colored People* (1841), James W. C. Pennington felt compelled to ask even the most basic questions—"who and whence are the colored people?" In answering such questions, Pennington, who was black, presented at one point a series of short biographies of native Africans who had established their intellectual abilities beyond all question, so as to prove that the achievement of "the Colored People" could not be marked down to the value of white associations. Certainly many shared Martin Delany's view that "we are not identical with the Anglo-Saxon" and were sympathetic to Delany's argument that "we have . . . inherent traits, attributes, so to speak, and native characteristics, peculiar to our race, whether pure or mixed blood." But any attempt to identify the nature and force of those native characteristics involved one in the absurdities of American racial culture.

In short, African-American life in the nineteenth century (and, of course, beyond) was restricted and otherwise shaped by law. Regardless of where they lived, black Americans faced laws designed to restrict or otherwise define the terms of their geographical and social mobility, voting rights, educational access, occupational opportunity, and even identity. Throughout the first half of the nineteenth century, many Southern states passed laws designed to force free blacks out of the state, and many Northern states passed laws restricting black immigration *into* the state, along with numerous laws excluding black Americans from voting privileges, jury service, militia service, and access to public education and other community support. As increasing numbers of mixed-race people populated the landscape, white Americans pressed further and further into absurdity a legal system often asked to decide who was and who was not to be counted as white, and then defining the field of allowable activities for those determined to fall beyond the pale of whiteness. Such decisions took place in a dominant culture that often seemed obsessed with creating racial stereotypes and ruthless caricatures of blackness. African Americans found themselves variously degraded, ridiculed, and feared on a regular basis in newspaper articles and cartoons, on the blackface minstrel stage, in books, and in public forums. Even the most dismissive of such gestures could present black identity as a threatening presence and black liberty as a frightening concept. These people, variously restricted, unrecognized, or unprotected by law, were regularly characterized as a threateningly lawless mass.

In their attempts to respond to such claims, many African Americans turned their thoughts to Africa, hoping that by clarifying the historical record they could reposition themselves in the present—but those roots made for an uncertain collective tradition. Misconceptions, faulty information, racist stereotypes, historical omissions, and tangled oral traditions combined to complicate any shared sense of a common continental heritage, let alone the complicated and shifting political history of African tribes and nations themselves. Many African Americans worked to provide historical accounts of both Africa and the global African diaspora, most notably in such works as James W. C. Pennington's *Text Book*, published in Connecticut in 1841, and Robert Benjamin Lewis's *Light and Truth; Collected from The Bible and Ancient and Modern History, Containing the Universal History of the Colored and Indian Race, From the Creation of the World to the Present Time*—a book first published in Maine in 1836 and significantly expanded in 1844. Beyond such rare histories, African Americans shared research and information about Africa in every forum available to them, from newspapers to public (and often published) orations, from the schoolroom to the pulpit. But such efforts were often themselves undermined by misinformation, conjectures, and myths about the African influence in global history, and sometimes involved arguments over what historical figures might be identified as black and what historical developments might be traced to African origins. Even basic access to African history was frequently subject to racist politics in the United States. The American Colonization Society (ACS), formed in 1816 and devoted to encouraging black American emigration to Africa, published a number of favorable accounts of African history in the attempt to make emigration attractive, and some African Americans drew from those sources to construct the historical foundations for a community determined to claim their rights to U. S. citizenship. Most notable was David Walker's 1829 manifesto *David Walker's Appeal*.

Beyond the struggle for reliable historical information was an African continent, and a historical field, that resisted any neat conceptual framework. The history of the slave trade, along with efforts to colonize parts of Africa with nations comprised of the formerly enslaved, made Africa the site of significant historical disruptions, and the fractured communities of the United States in many ways found their analogues in such constructed nations as Sierra Leone and Liberia. After freed slaves from England failed to form a settlement in Sierra Leone in 1787, the efforts were revitalized by the Sierra Leone Company, a commercial enterprise sponsored by English anti-slavery advocates. Former slaves from the Americas established the settlement Freetown. After delegalizing the slave trade in 1807, the British government took over the settlement in 1808 for use as a naval base to enforce the new prohibition and as a refuge for those freed from captured slave ships. Liberia, founded in Africa by the ACS in 1821, was settled by freed slaves in 1822 and similarly claimed as part of its mission the attempt to halt illegal slave trading. Originally led by white governors appointed by the ACS, Liberia gained independence in 1847, and while the assimilation of Africans was a goal, the differences between Liberians from the Americas and native Africans was significant. In both cases the community in colonized Africa resembled that in the United States—piecemeal, and searching for a lasting coherence and collective influence. One African-American settler in Sierra Leone, Paul Cuffe, includes at the end of his *Brief Account of the Settlement and Present Situation of the Colony of Sierra Leone* (1812) an address to "my scattered brethren." Another leader from the United States, Alexander Crummell, similarly referred to the community of Liberia in 1861 as "a motley group, composed, without doubt, of persons of almost every tribe in West Africa, from Goree to the Congo. Here are descendants of Jalofs, Fulahs, Mandingoes, Sussus, Timmanees, Veys, Congos, with a large intermixture every where of Anglo-Saxon, Dutch, Irish, French and Spanish blood—a slight mingling of the Malayan, and a dash, every now and then, of American Indian." Later in the century, Crummell would bemoan the disrupted ties between African Americans and Africans, arguing in an 1894 letter published in the *Southern Workman* (the official organ of the Hampton Institute in Virginia and a central forum for black writers and readers) that "the dinning of the 'colonization' cause into the ears of the colored people—the iteration of the idle dogma that Africa is THE HOME of the black race in this land; has served to prejudice the race against the very name of Africa. And this is a double folly:—the folly of

the colonizationists, and the folly of the black man; i.e. to forget family
ties and his duty to his kin over the water."

This context complicates any attempt to refer to a settled or clearly
defined African-American community, culture, or history in the nineteenth century. Without the imposing force of federal and regional legal systems, and corresponding social practices, one might be able to
identify African-American identity and history purely in terms of an-
cestral heritage, inherited folkways, cultural practices, or other cultural
formations, connecting individuals to generally identifiable roots in
Africa, Europe, and elsewhere. But the reality is much more complex.
People of African heritage variously adopted and transformed many of
the cultural practices associated with white, Euro-American identity,
and many participated in and identified themselves with the founda-
tional institutions and events of the United States, including Christianity, military service, and the national mythology of liberty and equality.
That their observance of and service to such institutions and ideals often was restricted, unrecognized, or violated only highlighted for many
blacks their importance. As various studies of African-American religious practices have demonstrated, African religions influenced and
were influenced by religious practices in the United States, precisely
because diverse, established traditions encountered one another in a repressive setting, leading to hybrid practices over time. The restrictions
on African-American civil rights, mobility, enterprise, education, and
identity similarly forced other transformations of cultural roots and
established practices over time. As many black Americans recognized,
the identity most readily available to them as individuals and as a group
was that imposed by the dominant culture—a degraded concept of
blackness or Africanness that spoke more forcefully of white misconceptions and insecurities than of black culture and history.

The challenges for African Americans were only augmented by their
relatively small numbers in the urban centers where collective organization was most feasible. In Boston, for example, blacks made up only 3.1
percent of the city's population in 1830, and their numbers declined over
the years, to 1.3 percent in 1860. In part this resulted from such political
pressures as the Fugitive Slave Law of 1850, which undermined the security of fugitive slaves and their families, along with difficult living conditions and inadequate access to health care, as suggested by the higher

infant morality rate suffered by black communities. While a smaller and more geographically contained community may foster dynamic interactions and collective solidarity, the Boston community was challenged as well by its own diversity—a community made up of many immigrants, from the American South and from foreign regions, communicating in English, Spanish, French, and various African languages and dialects.

Black communities in other major centers were similarly contained and diverse. By 1860 African Americans constituted only 3.9 percent of Philadelphia's population and a significantly smaller percentage of the populations of New York City (1.5 percent), Brooklyn (1.6 percent), and Cincinnati (2.3 percent). Cleveland had fewer than fifteen African Americans in 1830, and just under seventy by 1840. While Columbus, Ohio, saw an increase in its black population by 1850, amounting to 7.1 percent of the city's numbers, by 1860 the figure was only 5.4 percent. Indeed, blacks made up only 1.6 percent of Ohio's population in that year. In a culture that often presented the black presence as a significant threat, African Americans found themselves disadvantaged on all sides, dominated in numbers and limited in their access to political, legal, or economic leverage.

Thus what we generally term African-American history in the nineteenth century often involved efforts to oppose white America's imposition of a black collective identity. Blacks worked to create a collective identity defined not negatively but positively, not from without but from within this community joined by the terms of oppression but linked also by shared cultural practices, community affiliations, and the joys and responsibilities of family, work, and self-governance. Just as individual identity is developed through a blending of heritage and experience, so collective identity involved the challenge of recovering and celebrating a shared heritage, gathering and recording histories, and asserting authority over the possibilities of black experience in the United States. Community development depended greatly on access to a deeper historical understanding of one's identity, a broader understanding of those who might be part of the same community of experience, and appropriate forums for discussing differences and forging alliances. In the process, African Americans turned to social organizations and other associations that compensated for their lack of access to mainstream cultural institutions and organizational affiliations.

That black Americans felt a need to develop their own associations in a society already rich in social, occupational, religious, and political organizations only emphasizes the extent to which they felt both excluded from and threatened by the established social order. However diverse they might be culturally, politically, or ideologically, and however scattered they were geographically, African Americans understood that a unifying collective identity was useful in a nation that grouped them together in everything from law to popular culture. The white historian George Bancroft devoted much of his majestic *History of the United States* to a study of the different destinies of "the three races, the Caucasian, the Ethiopian and the American, [which] were in the presence of one another on our soil." By Bancroft's accounting of history, the American race would become simply "the red man," Caucasians would claim the title of Americans, and Ethiopians, always tied to the slave trade, would eventually return to "the burning plains of Nigritia," there to "toil for the benefits of European civilization." As noted, early efforts toward that destiny were promoted by such organizations as the American Colonization Society, in which all black Americans were identified only in relation to Africa, the continent to which they were expected to return. Such views were promoted as well at the end of the Civil War in such works as the Reverend Hollis Read's *The Negro Problem Solved; or, Africa As She Was, As She Is, and As She Shall Be* (1864).

Many of the white Americans who promoted this view of black American destiny believed themselves to be friends of African Americans, and many black Americans either joined such efforts or formulated emigration schemes of their own, both before and long after the Civil War. But behind all such schemes was a generalized collective identity, associated with a similarly generalized Africa, that didn't even begin to account for the diversity of Africans in the United States. While African Americans struggled to identify themselves, white America had clear notions of what it meant to be black, and imposed these notions on black Americans in virtually every area of life.

This is not to suggest that all of white America opposed black rights and development but rather to underscore the extent to which white Americans struggled to imagine that those who were not white could be equal partners in the Republic. Martin Delany captured the situation well in his 1852 book *The Condition, Elevation, Emigration, and Destiny of the Colored People of the United States.* "The colored people are not yet known," he wrote, "even to their most professed friends among the white Americans." Such professed friends "presumed to *think* for, dictate to, and *know* better what suited colored people, than they knew for themselves," with the result that white Americans knew mainly what white Americans imagined black Americans to be. As Delany and many other African Americans argued in countless orations, newspapers, pamphlets, and books, blacks needed more than anything else the collective will and means to represent themselves—to identify and address their own needs, to define and struggle for their own goals.

Delany was especially clear, in *The Condition* and elsewhere, about the challenges ahead, the difficult path toward black independence and self-reliance. In part the problem was that black Americans lived in a white supremacist culture, which would not easily be persuaded to share power and opportunity, or even the basic rights of citizenship. In part, too, blacks had been conditioned by this culture to accept their situation. As Delany put it, African Americans had experienced "a system of regular submission and servitude, menialism and dependence, until it has become almost a physiological function of our system, an actual condition of our nature." The African-American community, Delany worried, was being shaped and defined by default, by a cultural system that joined the members of the community only through a common experience of oppression. "White men are producers—we are consumers," Delany asserted—and what was being produced and consumed were the means of collective association, of community organization, as well as the material products of those associations.

In effect, then, African Americans faced the challenge of creating the governing institutions needed to transform a scattered collective into an imagined and operative community. Largely excluded, nationally and in most states, from the rights and privileges of citizenship, African Americans created organizational structures and affiliations by which they could at least potentially know themselves as what Delany termed "a nation within a nation." Delany devoted much of *The Condition* to establishing not only African-American rights to the full claims of American citizenship but also the extent to which black Americans constituted a self-sustaining and potentially self-governing community. Ultimately, though, he argued that African-American rights would never be recognized in the United States, and that African-American destiny would follow emigration.

Other writers similarly defined community in part by relocating a sense of collective mission. In his 1859 essay "The Education of the Colored People," for example, the Reverend Amos Gerry Beman of New Haven declared that "The colored race is an element of power in the earth, 'like a city set upon a hill it cannot be hid.' Thanks to our friends— and to our foes—and to the providence of God." Beman's community was the combined work of friends, foes, and providence. Its defining characteristic was its unique position in representing a national contradiction, a glaring gap between professed principles and actual practices. William J. Watkins made largely the same point in his 1853 address "Our Rights as Men," arguing before a Massachusetts state legislative committee on the militia that though black soldiers had fought in the American Revolution, they had not been allowed to join the nation in freedom and citizenship thereafter. Envisioning the community formed by its experience with that fundamental national failure, Watkins built to a forceful question addressed to whites: "Why should *you* be a chosen people more than *we*?"

This book explores the grounds for Watkins's question, and the answers forged through the collective experience of African Americans. Thus while *A Nation Within a Nation* describes African-American organizations, it also explores their role in the development of an African-American identity and community. Over the past few decades, historians have sought to delineate the various ways by which black Americans developed and *performed* a sense of community, through public observances and events, religious practices, publications, and their involvement in anti-slavery efforts and other social reform movements. A great deal of work remains before we will have a satisfying picture of nineteenth-century African-American life in all its diversity, but scholarship has drawn us deeper into African-American churches and denominations, the black periodical press, black linguistic practices, African-American literature, and the enduring "Africanisms" in American culture. This book, instead of assuming the existence of a well-defined African-American community, explores one important way in which group identity was conceptualized and practiced.

❖

While African-American history before the Civil War is by no means limited to cities, urban centers offered free blacks the best opportunities to congregate in formal organizations and associations. The nature and security of those organizations differed from place to place as organizers dealt with local variations of racial restrictions, economic opportunities, community stability, and the financial means to support enduring associations. Cities in the South were a challenging environment for black organizations as African Americans were constantly under the surveillance of pro-slavery governments. Still, important organizations emerged in many Southern cities. In the North, despite the legacy of Northern slavery and ongoing racism, blacks found more favorable opportunities to associate. Certain Northern cities—particularly Philadelphia, Boston, and New York—benefited from dynamic black communities with deep historical roots, and many other Northern cities witnessed the development of vibrant black communities. Indeed, cities provided African Americans with the opportunity to *stage* and *perform* community by way of public celebrations, rituals, and parades.

These performances were especially evident in African-American festivals that celebrated important anniversaries, including January 1, both for Toussaint l'Ouverture's declaration of the independent state of Haiti and for the outlawing of the American Atlantic slave trade in 1808; July 5, for the passage of gradual abolition legislation in 1799 and 1817; and August 1, to commemorate British emancipation in the Caribbean colonies. With the exception of Haitian independence, these were distinctive events on the African-American historical calendar, quite apart from the special observances of white Americans. Through these celebrations, African Americans observed a history still in the making, one that revealed tensions between African-American and white history. If white Euro-Americans could also be proud of such historical achievements, the celebrations were designed in part to remind the dominant culture that this work remained unfinished, that the very principles associated with the ending of the slave trade or with Caribbean emancipation were being violated each day in the United States. One holiday came to embody that tension dramatically: March 5, the date of Crispus Attucks's martyrdom

in the Boston Massacre of 1770—and also later the date of the U.S. Supreme Court's 1857 *Dred Scott* decision, in which the Court declared that
African Americans had no rights that white Americans were bound to
respect. This glaring national contradiction was highlighted during an
African-American festival at Faneuil Hall in Boston (a site itself associated with both the slave trade and the American Revolution) on March 5,
1858. Such events were public demonstrations of the importance of community, of a collective memory that marked an alternate history different
from the national narrative that variously excluded, debased, or otherwise marginalized African Americans.

Such events were also important demonstrations of community *organization*, drawing together not only individuals from various occupations
and social classes but also the groups to which many of those individuals
belonged. African-American associations provided not only the foundation for such events but also a dynamic system of communication and
community outreach. In Detroit, for example, the establishment of two
black churches—the Colored American Baptist Church (1837) and
Bethel Church (1839)—encouraged and developed a number of other
organizations, including a young men's society, a debating society, and
a temperance society, all of which had the benefit of the libraries and
reading rooms housed in the churches. In Philadelphia in 1794, members of the Free African Society formed St. Thomas's African Episcopal Church. In all cities, one organization naturally led to or supported
another, particularly in that many blacks were members of more than
one. They worked in churches, benevolent societies, literary societies,
and anti-slavery organizations, among other associations, to address the
needs of a black community that in many ways was understood in relation to these organizations. It was one thing, after all, for blacks to attend
a church in which they found themselves sitting in segregated sections or
waiting for their turn to participate in communion; it was quite another
for them to observe their religion in a building of their own, through a
religious institution they administered, in services they led.

Such developments were by no means limited to the North. Both free
and enslaved blacks in the South also managed a sometimes surprising
degree of community organization. As suggested by the Address from
the Colored Citizens of Norfolk, delivered at the close of the Civil War,
African Americans in that city had long benefited from organized as-

sociations that enabled church leaders to speak for an established community. Before the war Norfolk was home to a number of benevolent societies, including the Norfolk Lyceum, the Sons of Liberty, the Bible Stars, the Daughters of St. Luke, the Sons of Adam, Zion's Sons, the Humble Sons of God, and the Good Samaritans. Richmond similarly hosted a vibrant black religious community, and the black churches there provided a foundation for a network of "secret societies" that served the community in various ways, from funerals and death benefits to trade organizations to education and social life. Baltimore was more vibrant still, with more than thirty mutual aid societies of 35 to 150 members each in operation by 1835. Among their other organizational efforts, African Americans in Baltimore also established two savings banks by the 1840s, along with the Masonic Order-Friendship Lodge No. 6, the Star in the East Association, and the Daughters of Jerusalem Association. The wide range and interrelated interests of organizations served to promote communication, social affiliations, and collective security.

Important community organizations quickly followed the settlement of blacks in the Midwest and the West as well. African Americans in Indianapolis established the Bethel African Methodist Episcopal (AME) Church in 1836, along with as many as five black Baptist churches between 1831 and 1846, and they formed the city's first black Freemason lodge in 1847—Union Lodge No. 1, formed in association with the black Ohio Grand Lodge. Even in less populated areas, black settlers testified to the importance of organized associations by way of the church. Members of Beech Settlement, an Indiana farming community, founded the Mt. Pleasant Church in 1832—and after associating the church with the AME denomination, Beech Settlement organized the Indiana Conference of the AME church in 1840. As the gold rush helped encourage black migration farther west, African Americans formed small but well-organized (if often contentious) communities there as well. The St. Andrews African Methodist Episcopal Church was organized in Sacramento by the Reverend Bernard Fletcher in 1851, and in 1856 the Reverend John Jamison Moore founded the AME Zion Church of San Francisco, a church that in a matter of a few years boasted a brick building, fifty students, and a well-stocked library. Other churches developed in California during this period, along with fraternal orders throughout the 1850s, and California's black communities formed a Franchise League that met from 1855 to the 1880s in a series of black state conventions. These activities were aided by the establishment of a black press in California—*The Mirror of the Times* (1856), edited by Mifflin W. Gibbs, and the *Pacific Appeal*, founded in 1862 by Philip A. Bell and Peter Anderson.

With such achievements came new problems. The importance of black associational efforts was indicated by the restrictive and sometimes violent response of white Americans to the specter of an organized black community. The early nineteenth century saw a number of anti-black riots, sometimes involving competition over labor opportunities but often a response to any sign of black organization and solidarity. In a series of anti-black riots from 1832 to 1849 in Philadelphia, for example, white mobs attacked the manifest signs of black success, destroying black churches, a Masonic hall, a home for black children, and other centers of African-American activity. In the 1840s a series of Maryland laws highlighted the perceived threat of black organizations and associations. An 1842 statute made it a felony for free blacks to become members of secret societies. This was modified in 1845, when blacks were allowed to form charitable societies in Baltimore provided they could establish that they were of good character, paid a special tax, and received written permission from the mayor. An 1846 act was more insistent, prohibiting the incorporation in Maryland of black lyceums, fraternal lodges, fire companies, and a wide range of literary, philosophical, and charitable societies. An organized, literary, charitable, and physically safe black community apparently was considered a great threat to the social order. This was the legal environment in which blacks were forced to search for and establish common ground. Behind these examples were numerous laws at all governmental levels—local, state, and federal—restricting black mobility, access, representation, and opportunity in virtually every way imaginable. African Americans formed organizations and societies in their efforts to create a workable society within that restrictive environment, only to find those efforts themselves frequently outlawed or otherwise restricted.

Given the challenges they faced and the violence they frequently encountered, it is hardly surprising that black organizations included various militia groups. Samuel Ringgold Ward noted the rise of such groups in his *Autobiography of a Fugitive Negro* (1855), observing that "the young blacks of the Republic are everywhere acquiring a love for martial pastimes. Their independent companies of military are becoming common in many of the large towns." Among such military companies were the Hannibal Guards, formed in Brooklyn in 1848; the New Bedford Independent Blues, formed in Massachusetts in 1855; the Independent Village Guards, formed in New York City in 1855; the Liberty Guard, formed in Boston in 1857; and the Independent Company of Detroit, formed in 1861. By the late 1850s Pittsburgh alone boasted two militia units, and there were at least four units formed in New York City. Some of the militias were largely ceremonial: their units marched with broomsticks. Many, though, were armed with guns and other weapons. Moreover the groups varied in both numbers and force. The Boston Liberty Guard boasted fifty-five men with guns while the Attic Guard of Morris Grove, Long Island, had sixteen men carrying axes. Still, these militias were of great symbolic importance to those who witnessed them.

As the names of some of the militia units reveal, many of these groups looked to African history for their inspiration, and many others announced their independence and devotion to liberty. Other groups revealed a growing sense of black self-determination by honoring prominent African Americans at the head of the struggle—including the Douglass Guards of Reading, Pennsylvania, and the Henry Highland Garnet Guards of Harrisburg, Pennsylvania, both formed in 1859. While the calls of Garnet, Walker, and others were never answered in the form of an organized, national, and militant resistance to slavery and the denial of civil rights, the very sight of these militia companies spoke volumes about black vulnerability and an increasing determination among African Americans to secure their future through organization and collective effort. As Frederick Douglass noted after viewing black military companies on parade in New Bedford, "If a knowledge of the use of arms is desirable in any people, it is desirable in us."

This dynamic process of working with and against existing conditions, and then of addressing the new challenges presented by the dominant culture's legal or even violent response to their efforts, is often missing from accounts of African-American history. Although historians have documented the legal repression of black Americans, a great deal of their history—in books, museums, historical timelines, and Black History Month presentations—focuses more simply on African-American achievements, usually represented by notable individuals.

These narratives are likely to include particularly notorious Supreme Court rulings or other moments of American legal history—the *Dred Scott* decision, the Fugitive Slave Act, *Plessy v. Ferguson*, among others—but they do not begin to capture the complex legal and social circumstances in which African Americans found themselves. They did indeed *find themselves* through their negotiations with this complex legal world that made an invented category, race, the most significant identifier in American social life. Through their collective negotiations with legal, economic, social, theological, and scientific impositions, people of African heritage who were identified as black in the United States founded, forged, and learned to improvise a collective identity that was never a settled fact but was always in the process of becoming.

❖

Historians have accounted for this complex history most thoroughly in their accounts of the anti-slavery movement, for slavery was in many ways the defining framework of African-American life before the Civil War. This is not to say that all blacks opposed slavery or were active or even theoretical abolitionists. Some owned slaves themselves, and some free blacks were either indifferent to or even objected to the efforts of abolitionists, especially after slavery was largely abolished or otherwise dismantled in the North. It would be difficult, though, to identify or even imagine a black American before the Civil War whose life was not deeply influenced by the nation's experience with slavery. Even when it was ended in the Northern states, slavery was a national system, and it required the maintenance of racial ideologies in political, legal, economic, theological, and scientific spheres. Thus anti-slavery sentiment and political action played a central role in most African-American organizations formed over the years. As David Walker put it in a passage in his famous *Appeal*, "The preachers and people of the United States form societies against Free Masonry and Intemperance, and write against Sabbath breaking, Sabbath mails, Infidelity, &c. &c. But the fountain head [slavery and oppression], compared to which, all those other evils are comparatively nothing, and from the bloody and murderous head of which, they receive no trifling support, is hardly noticed by the Americans." Through numerous organizations, black Americans attempted to force the nation to notice this great evil.

These efforts were significantly interracial, often productively so. Still, they often provided new reminders of the deeply racist culture in which African Americans lived and worked. Racial prejudice was a regular presence in anti-slavery circles, and the most influential anti-slavery organizations were formed and led by white men. Some white Americans were anti-slavery in their sympathies but not abolitionist in their politics. They believed slavery to be a moral problem but not necessarily one that men could solve; they looked for the eradication of slavery to arrive in "God's own time." Others insisted that slavery should be abolished, though views on how and when this great end should be accomplished varied widely. The anti-slavery movement, never a singular or politically homogeneous affair, was made up of both groups. For many black Americans, the abolitionist cause encompassed both slavery in the South and racial discrimination in the North. For some white activists, abolitionism referred solely to slavery while equal rights and social equality were separate and possibly more formidable causes.

Prominent white abolitionists sometimes made their underlying racial convictions known—referring to Anglo Saxons as "the superior race," as Theodore Parker once did, or restricting black contributions to anti-slavery events. Frederick Douglass, for one, felt the force of such restrictions both on the anti-slavery lecture circuit (where he reportedly was asked to play only a subordinate role, telling of his abuses but leaving the larger argument to his white colleagues) and when he broke from the white abolitionist William Lloyd Garrison, editor of the *Liberator*, to form his own newspaper, the *North Star*. In 1855 Douglass used his newspaper to record his complaint about the restricted black role in the anti-slavery movement, declaring that "nothing is done . . . to inspire us with the Idea of our Equality with the whites." "We are a poor, pitiful, dependent and servile class of Negroes," Douglass wrote, "*'unable to keep pace'* with the movement, to which we have adverted—not even capable of *'perceiving what are its demands, or understanding the philosophy of its operations!'*" What was missing from the anti-slavery movement, Douglass contended, and what seemed beyond the abilities of "the self-appointed generals of the Anti-Slavery host," was basic: "a *practical recognition of our Equality.*"

To be sure, many white Americans, both male and female, gave their all
to the abolitionist cause, and the interracial friendships they developed
were strong and lasting. Still, like Douglass, many blacks found cause to
note a difference between theory and practice in the movement. Even in
this struggle, African-American identity was less a settled fact than an
ongoing process.

The racial dynamics behind the history of the anti-slavery movement
can be glimpsed even by the names of some of the early organizations
formed by white Americans. In 1775, for example, a group of Philadelphia Quakers organized the Society for the Relief of Free Negroes
Unlawfully Held in Bondage, an organization devoted to the relief of
free blacks who were kidnapped into slavery. Perhaps recognizing that
the organization's name and mission implicitly accepted the validity of
enslavement, that organization was reorganized in 1787 as the Pennsylvania Society for Promoting the Abolition of Slavery, Relief of Free
Negroes Unlawfully Held in Bondage, and for Improving the Condition
of the African Race. This time the organization was devoted in part to
the promotion of like-minded groups, and apparently with some success.
The year 1789 saw the organization of the Maryland Society for Promoting the Abolition of Slavery and for the Relief of Free Negroes and Others Held Unlawfully in Bondage, which was followed in the next year by
the Connecticut Society of the same name. In 1800 the Delaware Society
for Gradual Abolition was reorganized as well, now called the Delaware
Society for Promoting the Abolition of Slavery and the Relief and Pro-
tection of Free Blacks and People of Color Unlawfully Held in Bondage
or Otherwise Oppressed.

The development of these societies, along with their unwieldy titles,
indicates the members' early awareness that the problem of slavery was
neither a simple nor an isolated concern. As black abolitionists would
continue to insist through the years, to oppose slavery without advocating
racial justice and civil rights was to adopt a naïve approach to the problem and its solution.

While tensions over the definition of the anti-slavery cause would
continue, the movement itself became increasingly focused. Most historians agree that anti-slavery efforts reached a turning point around 1830,
when a transition to a more aggressive approach was marked by a series
of events: Walker's publication in 1829 of the *Appeal*; the slave rebel-

lion led by Nat Turner in Southhampton County, Virginia, in 1831; and Garrison's founding of what would become the most influential of the anti-slavery newspapers, the *Liberator*, in 1831. Walker's *Appeal*, which was smuggled into the South, represented a militant insistence on black rights, and soon there was a price on Walker's head. Turner's rebellion led both to debates over the advisability of slavery in the South and to increasingly strict and often violent suppression of religious gatherings and teachings in enslaved communities. Garrison's *Liberator* went beyond calls for the gradual abolition of slavery to a message of immediate abolition delivered in a decidedly insistent and morally righteous tone. "I am in earnest," Garrison announced in the paper's opening editorial. "I will not equivocate—I will not excuse—I will not retreat a single inch—AND I WILL BE HEARD." In and of themselves these events did not cause the shift in the anti-slavery movement, but they reflected a culture increasingly influenced by the religious revivalism of the 1820s, which led to aggressive calls for moral reformation and cultural change, and by increasingly insistent black protest meetings and publications, including pamphlets like Walker's *Appeal* and the first African-American newspaper, *Freedom's Journal*, founded in 1827. Anti-slavery activity became centered in the North, where blacks began to insist on playing a central role in reenvisioning American life and working for social reform. When the first U.S. anti-slavery political party, the Liberty party, was established in Warsaw, New York, in 1839, many believed there was cause for hope that important cultural change had begun, and that the system of slavery might eventually be addressed with conviction and force at the national level.

When Garrison formed the New England Anti-Slavery Society, the organization convened in Boston's African Meeting House, the center of Boston's black political and social activity. At least a quarter of the signatories to the organization's constitution were African Americans, and soon the all-black Massachusetts General Colored Association merged with the integrated Anti-Slavery Society, with some black members rising to leadership roles in the new organization. Similarly the all-black Female Anti-Slavery Society of Salem, formed in Massachusetts in 1832, reorganized in 1834 as the integrated Salem Female Anti-Slavery Society. This new era saw a proliferation of Northern-based anti-slavery societies, including, among many others, those in Cleveland (1833), Philadelphia

(1834), Vermont (1834), and the largest and most influential of these organizations, the American Anti-Slavery Society (1833).

Blacks played prominent roles both on the lecture stage and behind the scenes, often becoming prominent speakers and writers through their association with anti-slavery organizations. In 1838 Charles Lenox Remond became the first black hired by the American Anti-Slavery Society, and in the 1840s the movement was aided by such speakers as Frederick Douglass, William Wells Brown, Henry Bibb, and Samuel Ringgold Ward, among many others, who toured the United States and Europe, promoting the anti-slavery message and earning financial and political support for the movement. Their travels were extensive and exhausting (Douglass and Remond, for example, once visited more than thirty sites in the Midwest over the course of three months in 1843) and were often marked by racism and threats of physical violence.

At the time, public speaking was generally considered a man's domain, and female orators were often regarded with disdain. But women also spoke at both regional and international levels of the movement. In 1854 the Maine Anti-Slavery Society made Frances Ellen Watkins Harper one of the first professional women orators in the United States by hiring her as a public lecturer. Other influential anti-slavery speakers included Sojourner Truth, Sarah Parker Remond, and Barbara Steward.

While these successes in interracial alliances were notable, blacks were never allowed to forget the deep divide between themselves and white Americans. The Pennsylvania Abolition Society, organized in 1784, did not admit its first black member, Robert Purvis, until the 1830s. And while Purvis and two other African Americans participated in the three-day organizational meetings for the founding of the American Anti-Slavery Society in 1833—meetings that included sixty-three delegates from ten states—he and his black colleagues, along with others, were not considered delegates. In 1834 white mobs in Philadelphia physically attacked black individuals, destroyed a number of houses, and burned the New African Hall and Presbyterian Church. Pro-slavery mobs rioted regularly, as in New York City in 1834; Utica, New York, in 1835; Cincinnati in 1836; and elsewhere—indeed, more than one hundred incidents of mob violence were recorded in the 1830s. Many of these acts were aimed at abolitionists generally, black and white. In 1835, for example, Garrison was publicly harassed and paraded through the streets of Boston at the end of a rope. Another white abolitionist, Marius Robinson, was kidnapped and tarred and feathered in 1837, and another, Elijah Lovejoy, was murdered by a mob in Alton, Illinois. But there was no mistaking the racism behind many of these acts of violence, along with a racist subtext in debates over slavery.

In response to such events, and to the merely sentimental abolitionism they frequently encountered in the movement, blacks resolved to address the connected matters of slavery and racial equality on their own terms. Many began to turn to the militant self-determination represented by David Walker's *Appeal*, a turn highlighted by Henry Highland Garnet's publication, in 1848, of *Walker's Appeal, with a Brief Sketch of his Life by Henry Highland Garnet*. In *Garnet's Address to the Slaves of the United States of America*, the black abolitionist joined Walker's *Appeal* to the text of an address he had first presented to the National Convention of Negro Citizens at Buffalo, New York, in August 1843. On that occasion Garnet had called for a militant response by enslaved communities to their condition, just as Walker had earlier admonished the black community for their acceptance of their situation. "Tell them in language which they cannot misunderstand," Garnet advised, "of the exceeding sinfulness of slavery"—and he provided the language for the confrontation: "Let your motto be resistance! *Resistance*! RESISTANCE!" Garnet's address was deemed too violent and too far removed from the Garrisonian school of moral suasion as the appropriate anti-slavery course of action to gain official endorsement from those, including Frederick Douglass, who attended the convention, though it lost that endorsement by the narrowest of votes. In many ways, though, Garnet's words were designed to inspire his audience in Buffalo as much as those slaves in the South. When he proclaimed that it is better to *"die freemen than live to be slaves,"* he was emphasizing the connection between the enslaved of the South and the insecurely free of the North ("nor can we be free while you are enslaved," he noted).

By the time Garnet made his remarks, many in the anti-slavery movement had recognized the need for direct action in addition to the ongoing attempt to move hearts and minds against slavery. In 1835 the prominent black activist David Ruggles collaborated with others to form the New York Committee of Vigilance, an organization devoted to assisting fugitive slaves (Frederick Douglass among them) and to preventing the kidnapping and enslavement of free blacks. Other such organizations followed, including many efforts that have since become associated with the Underground Railroad, a vast if only loosely organized network of regional associations devoted to aiding and encouraging fugitive slaves. By the 1850s such efforts became increasingly prominent because of the Compromise of 1850, by which Congress attempted to resolve the sectional conflict over slavery in the new territories. The Compromise included an updated and strengthened Fugitive Slave Act—which, many Northerners argued, required all American citizens to become slave catchers. The law placed the issue of runaway slaves under federal jurisdiction, allowing federal commissioners to force citizens to aid in the recapture of those slaves who reached the North while also denying fugitive slaves trial by jury or the right to testify on their own behalf. In response, large mobs formed in Boston to protest the reenslavement of Thomas Sims in 1851 and Anthony Burns in 1854, to mention two of the most famous of these cases. In 1851 a determined group of African Americans met a group of slave catchers in Christiana, Pennsylvania, and forced them to retreat; and in that same year a large number of black and white protesters (some estimate the number to be as high as ten thousand) stormed a courtroom in Syracuse, New York, and rescued a fugitive slave, William "Jerry" Henry. 1858 was the year of the famous Oberlin-Wellington (Ohio) rescue, in which Professor Simon M. Bushnell and a group of students (black and white) from Oberlin College, Ohio, came to the aid of a fugitive named John Price.

The South's determination to preserve and protect the system of slavery, however, was great, making these local confrontations seem like a prelude to a larger battle for political and ideological control over the nation's future. The Compromise of 1850 was followed by other measures that added to the violations of African-American rights and civil security. In 1854 Congress approved the Kansas-Nebraska Act, which allowed voting citizens of those territories (and the vote was, of course, restricted) to determine for themselves whether they would enter the Union as a slave or a free state. This act prompted greater violence in the territories and contributed to the formation of the Republican party as an anti-slavery political force. In 1857 the Supreme Court announced its decision in the case of *Dred Scott v. Sanford*, in which Chief Justice Roger B. Taney declared that African Americans had no rights that white Americans were obliged to respect. The political and ideological debates that followed this decision helped further define the already sharp divisions that were leading the nation toward open conflict.

When the white abolitionist John Brown led his group of black and white soldiers in a raid on the federal arsenal at Harpers Ferry, Virginia, in 1859, what had long been an open if localized war became sharply focused. Brown became a martyr to a cause that by this time had a long history of soldiers and martyrs. In that same year the *Anglo-African Magazine*, a black publication in New York, published the reports of an early revolutionary with those of a later one, placing Nat Turner next to John Brown, black militancy next to white, and called for Americans to recognize the inevitable struggle ahead and to decide what role they would play in it.

❖

In many ways, then, not only the system of slavery but the struggles of the anti-slavery movement pressed the issue of African-American self-determination through organization. In his *Appeal*, David Walker warned of the dangers of being "dis-united, as the coloured people are now, in the United States of America." Years later Garnet might well have been speaking to all African Americans when he observed in his address to the slaves, "Your condition does not absolve you from your moral obligation," adding that "the time has come when you must act for yourselves."

In the chapters that follow is at least part of the story of how African Americans acted for themselves before the Civil War. This is by no means a complete story. Because the anti-slavery movement has already received so much scholarly attention, it is not the focus of discussion here, though readers will find that virtually all black organizations involved, to some degree, the struggle against slavery. Instead of entering this history by the usual means, I concentrate on other organizational efforts, including mutual benefit societies, fraternal organizations, churches, state and national conventions, literary and educational societies and schools, and the black press.

It would be difficult to present this history in a neatly chronological fashion, since African Americans in different cities and different regions acted both independently and occasionally in concert with one another, sometimes taking inspiration from past developments to address new regions with slightly different community needs and sometimes dramatically different political and legal environments. Accordingly, the chapters that follow are organized thematically, allowing readers to trace the separate but deeply intertwined histories of black benevolent societies, churches, schools, conventions, publications, and fraternities, and other related attempts to respond to their world.

What we identify as "African American" refers to a complex cultural and historical process, a set of skills joined with an ability to improvise in the face of new but familiar threats and opportunities. African American identity, in other words, does not precede this process or conclude it. Rather, it can best be understood through attention to the process itself, the patterns of a people's negotiation with this process, and the developing affiliations among various individuals and organizations.

2

Mutual Interest, Mutual Benefit, Mutual Relief

ON JANUARY 2, 1809, William Hamilton, a carpenter and respected member of New York City's African-American community, spoke to the New York African Society, an organization then less than a year old. Hamilton noted the significance of the date: it was the first anniversary, one day before, of Congress outlawing the Atlantic slave trade. With that significant reminder of the common history of "Africans and descendants," Hamilton turned to the ongoing work of securing that community. He spoke of the "many and repeated attempts" in New York "to establish societies of various kinds among the people of colour," and he noted that all those attempts had "soon perished or dwindled away to a number so small as scarcely to deserve the name of society." He had greater hopes for the group gathered to hear his remarks, for though the African Society had been in existence only briefly, he noted, "the number of its members exceed by three times the number of any civil institution yet attempted among us." Whether because of better planning or a more mature understanding of the importance of collective endeavor, Hamilton suggested, the tide seemed to be turning for New York City's black community.

Hamilton's vision for this communal effort ranged from the grandiose to the mundane. On the one hand, he emphasized that while individuals in isolation were vulnerable to the demands of a harsh world, anything was possible through organized effort. "Man in the abstract," he observed, "is subject to almost every inconvenience that can be named, his hand is feeble, his sight short, his movements slow; but united with his fellow man he is strong, he is vigorous, he turns the channel of mighty rivers, throws down huge mountains, removes thick forests, builds great cities, pushes on the great machine of trade." Certainly this was a message anyone might wish to hear—but while all things might be possible, Hamilton was deeply aware of the more immediate challenges African-American communities faced: "to improve the mind, soften the couch of the sick, to administer an elixir to the afflicted, to befriend the widow, and become the orphan's guardian." Hamilton's vision, in other words, depended on the process of history, by which attention to immediate needs would create the foundation for greater ambitions and future achievements. He envisioned the African Society as "a wide spreading dome that shall stand the admiration and praise of succeeding generations." And on the front of that dome would be a motto that could serve for virtually all African-American associated efforts: "MUTUAL INTEREST, MUTUAL BENEFIT AND MUTUAL RELIEF." From the commonplace to the lofty, from immediate needs to future ambitions, the range of African-American hopes for the organizations they formed all rested on their devotion to this motto.

One could say, though, that Hamilton had the motto backward, for these organizations developed as immediate needs (mutual relief) led to solid rewards (mutual benefits), which helped to promote a sense of common cause and community (mutual interest). Of course, from their beginnings black associational efforts encompassed a variety of activities and goals and benefited from a great deal of cross-fertilization. Hamilton, for example, presented his 1809 address after the members of the African Society "moved in procession from the African School Room to the Church." Most organizations were involved in educational or religious activities even when defined by other concerns. But in a nation that touted its devotion to liberty while relying on the system of slavery, and in state and local cultures that denied to those of African heritage everything from voting rights to educational opportunities, African Americans recognized that grand ideals and future ambitions were deeply rooted in and dependent on present conditions. When New York City's African Dorcas Association (1828) provided clothes to children of the African Free Schools in the hope of increasing attendance there, it did so with a strong recognition of the connection between fundamental needs and gradual uplift, between present conditions and future ideals. The history of African-American organizations follows a similar process—what one might call the means of securing the community so it could be defined in terms other than the degrading characterizations of the white supremacist culture.

❖

One indication of the forces driving the organization of African-American communities was the fact that white Americans perceived them to be either a threat or an unwanted presence even in death. Before the Civil War (and in many cases, long after), most cemeteries were racially segregated. Even when cemeteries allowed for African-American burials, the grounds were divided into segregated sections. The Public Burying Ground in Lynchburg, Virginia, for example, included "colored" sections, and many cemeteries were divided by social class, citizenship status, and religion. The organization of black communities was thus inspired in part by the need to attend to a community's lost family members and loved ones. In 1786, for example, blacks in Philadelphia petitioned for a burial space for community members. In New York City the Abyssinian Benevolent Daughters of Esther Association owned a cemetery in which members had assigned plots and in which husbands and children could be buried for a modest fee. In Cincinnati the United Colored American Association was organized in 1844, in part to buy land to provide for a black cemetery. Segregated burials led to the founding of societies in the South as well—for example in Richmond, where the Burying Ground Society of the Free People of Color established the Phoenix Burial Ground in 1815, followed in 1840 by the Union Burial Ground (later the Union Mechanics Burial Ground).

As with other restrictions they encountered, African Americans took the segregation of death as an opportunity to assemble and even celebrate their community. Particularly in enslaved communities, funerals offered rare opportunities to gather beyond the supervision of whites, and the gatherings were often elaborate events, variously involving religious ceremonies, grand processions, music or drumming, and festive or official dress (the latter when the dead were members of fraternal organizations, for example). Reports of funerals in Charleston, South Carolina, note both their frequency and the numbers they attracted—sometimes hundreds of African Americans in the procession. So important were such events that many white Americans viewed them as a threat to the public order. In the 1720s the Common Council in New York City restricted both the time (before sunset) and the number of mourners allowed for black funerals. In 1831, following Nat Turner's rebellion in Southampton County, Virginia, the state's General Assembly prohibited African Americans from conducting their funerals without white supervision— a law not always observed in practice, as some whites either didn't care or didn't think it right to impose themselves on such events. Connecting restrictions and liberty, death and rebellion, and the dead to the living, African-American burials, and the societies created to make them possible, were important developments in black communities.

Transforming a restrictive environment into an occasion for a collective enterprise by attending to basic needs is the story as well behind the earliest and most important of African-American organizations, the mutual aid societies that inspired so much hope in William Hamilton's 1809 address. The Perseverance Benevolent and Mutual Aid Association was formed in New Orleans, Louisiana, in 1783 as an organization devoted to the collective good and to promoting the formation of African-American social clubs in the city. In Philadelphia the Free African Society was organized by black leaders in 1787, and the Friendly Society of St. Thomas's African Church was formed in the following decade. The Brooklyn African Tompkins Association was founded in 1845, and in 1849 African Americans in Dayton, Ohio, formed a mutual aid society when black residents of the city were denied the benefits for which they paid municipal taxes. Some mutual aid societies, as Hamilton noted in his address, were short-lived, but many lasted long enough to inspire a great many other organizations. For example, New York's African Society for Mutual Relief, at which Hamilton spoke, lasted beyond the Civil War, and other societies benefited from connections—in the form of institutional support and shared membership—with other societies and associations or with churches.

At their most basic level these societies operated as health and life insurance associations. While Philadelphia's African Insurance Company, a stock company founded in 1810 with $5,000 in capital, is generally acknowledged to be the first black-owned and -operated insurance company in the United States, mutual aid societies served much the same purpose, though with a membership more broadly committed to the three tenets of Hamilton's vision for the New York African Society: mutual interest, mutual benefit, and mutual relief. Typically, on being admitted to the society, new members would pay a small fee—twenty-five cents for Boston's African Society, one dollar for the Friendly Society of St. Thomas's African Church. Thereafter members would be required to contribute regular payments, often about twenty-five cents a month. Constitutions of the societies regulated both the management and distribution of the funds. Members received assistance during sickness, and the societies provided help for the widows and orphans of deceased members. Most societies were also devoted to promoting moral standards among their members, and some made it clear in their constitutions that appropriate character was a basic requirement of membership. Boston's African Society, for example, included in its constitution a warning "that any Member bringing on himself any sickness or disorder by intemperance, shall not be considered as entitled to any benefits or assistance from the Society." For other societies the caution was implicit, communicated through the religious observances that frequently were a part of the society's meetings. William Hamilton's address to the New York African Society, for example, took place in a church, was preceded by "a Solemn Address to Almighty God, by Mr. James Varick, Chaplain" and a hymn; and the talk was followed by two more hymns, a collection, and a "Solemn Prayer."

Such observances speak to the broader sense of mission characteristic of the great majority of mutual aid societies. One of the first of these organizations was the African Union Society, formed in 1780 by free blacks in Newport, Rhode Island. While the African Union Society included funds for those in need as well as for the widows and children of deceased members, the society was directed more broadly to the many challenges of black self-determination. It encouraged industry and temperance, emphasized the importance of legal marriage for couples, and promoted real estate investment. It also hosted weekly religious services. In all these efforts the society attempted to address the pressures of black life in a white supremacist culture—pressures that were behind the African Union Society's primary mission, the advocacy of black emigration to Africa. In 1787 that central mission prompted vigorous but ill-fated efforts to establish a settlement in Africa, which led to various alliances and contacts, including an appeal to the white British abolitionist

Granville Sharp, who was then involved in efforts to settle British blacks in Sierra Leone. The Newport group joined with other African Americans in New England in these efforts but ran into numerous complications, some involving their determination to avoid white dominance in these efforts and to achieve self-rule once in Africa.

As the Newport group connected with African Americans in Boston, and then as both groups connected with interested representatives of the community in Providence, the movement encouraged a regional appreciation of collaborative effort. In hindsight, however, this developing collective identity revealed weaknesses as well as strengths—in the group's relation to both Africans and white Americans. The group looked to unite with Africans, but its members tended to assume that they were superior to native Africans in their experience with Euro-American civilization and Christianity. And while the group announced a collective desire to distance themselves from whites, they did so in a way that suggests how invested they were in that civilization. Hoping to distinguish themselves in the face of degrading assumptions and stereotypes, the group announced their belief that "the More remote we are situated from the white people the more we will be respected." This utterance indicated their understanding of the fundamental connection between their status and white America; but it also revealed how their self-respect depended on the opinions of others.

Despite this early enthusiasm for emigration, the challenge of *locating* the African-American community grew to become a matter of considerable dispute and a source of ongoing tension within the community. When prominent white Americans formed the American Colonization Society in 1816, dedicated to colonizing free blacks from the United States in western Africa, divisions within the black community became more pressing. Some prominent blacks supported the movement despite the demonization of blacks so thinly veiled by the ACS's stated mission, but the great majority of African Americans came to oppose colonization efforts directed by white America. Indeed, considerable resistance to the ACS became a significant organizing principle of early African-American political activism. But many prominent blacks developed their own plans for emigration to an imagined safe harbor of black nationality. Emigration to Haiti was advocated by some but just as vigorously opposed by others, and other plans were advocated or embraced by such men as Martin Delany and Henry Highland Garnet, who insisted their plans were separate from any white-sponsored movement. Preparations for a grand emigration to Canada had inspired the formation of the first national convention of black Americans, but Canadian communities remained in the shadow of U.S. efforts, and the experience of those who settled there revealed that the struggle for survival and against racism would not stop once blacks crossed the northern border. In the decade before the Civil War, even many who had resisted talk of colonization began to look to Haiti and elsewhere for a more welcoming environment. Behind all the debates attending colonization or emigration schemes were the pressing realities of African-American life in a culture in which many believed that equal rights, social equality, and shared political governance were ideals that would never be applied across racial lines.

The efforts of the ACS and even of black-initiated emigration plans, in other words, helped define the developing African American community, in part by highlighting the need for organization. As Garnet put it when declaring his opposition to "those who, either from good or evil motives, plead for the utopian plan of the Colonization of a whole race to the shores of Africa," the project of colonization was in some ways redundant, for, he argued, "we are now colonized." While the African Union Society found hope in relocating to another continent, other organizations faced the challenge of relocating African Americans where they already lived—that is, addressing the colonization inherent in their situation in the United States.

In an address to the Afric-American Female Intelligence Society of Boston in 1832, the black activist Maria Stewart complained that "we this day are considered as one of the most degraded races upon the face of the earth." Certainly she was not alone in observing this characterization of black Americans, but her explanation of this condition was significant. "And why is it, my friends," she asked, "that we are despised above all the nations upon the earth? Is it merely because our skins are tinged with a sable hue? No, nor will I ever believe that it is. What then is it; Oh, it is because that we and our fathers have dealt treacherously one with another, and because many of us now possess that envious and malicious disposition, that we had rather die than see each other rise an inch above a beggar." Stewart understood the extent to which white America regularly effected an intellectual, psychological, and spiritual colonization of

African Americans, and she understood as well that one of the consequences of that condition was disunity. While various black associations
recognized the need to attend to economic hardship, then, they recognized as well the need to promote unity, to advocate the cause of mutual
interest and mutual benefit in addressing the necessities of mutual relief.

Mutual aid societies promoted unity by way of both substance and cer-
emony. In addition to providing for the needs of families debilitated by
sickness or death, some societies included in their charters the possibility
of using surplus funds to purchase land. The New York African Society, for example, purchased a lot in 1820 that included a boardinghouse,
whose rents covered the costs of the mortgage. Behind this property the
society built a meeting house, available for rental to other organizations.
Eventually the society purchased other rental properties, adding to the
funds available to its members.

The African Society was also committed to the ceremonial promotion
of community. In addition to participating in the commemorations of
January 1, July 5, August 1, and other important dates on the African-
American calendar, members celebrated the anniversaries of the society
itself in processions through New York City streets and parks, complete
with banners, a grand marshal, and military displays, followed by an oration and dinner. In 1809 the Wilberforce Philanthropic Association of
New York City proudly recorded the procession for an event that featured an oration by Joseph Sidney to commemorate the abolition of the
Atlantic slave trade:

> The Wilberforce Philanthropic Association, assembled at Liberty
> Hall, together with the Musical and Maritime Associations, agreeably
> to the orders of the committee of arrangement, appointed by the gen-
> eral meeting of the people of colour; and marched in procession, up
> Leonard Street, down Broadway, to the Lyceum in Warrent Street, in
> the following order, viz.: The Grand Marshal; two Africans, escorted
> by the deputy Marshals; the Committee of Arrangement, the Chair-
> man and Secretary, the Orator and Reader, the Wilberforce band of
> Music, with the Association, the Maritime and Musical Associations,
> decorated with their badges, and accompanied with their appropriate
> banners. The novelty of the procession attracted the notice of an im-
> mense concourse of citizens, and presented a spectacle both grand and
> interesting. It was the Jubilee of Liberty; the triumph of Philanthropy.

This summary, one might say, was nearly as important as the spectac-
ular procession itself, for it identified a high degree of organization both
within and among African-American societies. Appropriate badges and
banners all presented a unified front to interested spectators, and all in
service not only to the cause of liberty but also to the triumph of philanthropy. By way of such public displays, the black community announced
not only its presence but also its organization.

Those who belonged to mutual aid and other societies understood
that unity could be fleeting, easily disturbed in a culture in which black
Americans were segregated, exploited, caricatured, and frequently pitted
against one another. Expectations of proper decorum in the societies were
accordingly strict. The Friendly Society of St. Thomas's African Church,
for example, included a provision in its constitution that "if any two
members shall be so imprudent as to wrangle during the time of meeting,
they shall both be dismissed from the Society, and shall not be suffered to
meet again until satisfaction is made." While the causes of such disputes
could be many, society members understood that among those causes
were the divisions created by color prejudice and by the consequences
of the racial ideologies that defined American culture. The same racial
prejudice that oiled the national machine often made African-American
unity a slippery business, and those who participated in societies knew in-
timately how easy it might be to slip into divisive behavior. In an address
delivered to the Garrison Independent Society, an association of young
men from ten to twenty years of age, the sixteen-year-old speaker spoke
for the importance of "the preservation of unity among us" and warned,
"let not the accursed demon prejudice hover about us." "Prejudice," he
observed, "is the cause of slavery, and its attendant evils; and which,
united with malice, is the cause of disunion in societies." The speaker
noted the high stakes involved in this unity. "The colored people," he
observed, "have been told repeatedly, that, by being united, and helping
one another, they will, ere long, be enabled to witness the downfall of the
Colonization system, and the triumph of equal rights."

In the context of nineteenth-century American culture, such goals
were not far removed from William Hamilton's belief that, through collaborative effort, men could shift the course of rivers, demolish mountains, remove forests, and build great cities. Most societies attested,
similarly, to their hope of great achievements. In various ways they hoped

to contribute, in effect, to Hamilton's vision of "a wide spreading dome that shall stand the admiration and praise of succeeding generations." But they worried about possible cracks in that dome.

❖❖❖

There were reasons to be concerned, for African-American organizations reflected tensions from within as well as without, and frequently they reinforced the community divisions they might be assumed to overcome. Each group had its conditions for membership—sometimes exclusionary—and most societies represented prevailing assumptions and prejudices about social class, religious affiliation, and gender. The names of many of these societies speak of a determined resistance to prevailing prejudices, emphasizing a common, proud identity in their use of the title "African," for example, to combat the imposed commonality involved in the white Euro-American degradation and philosophical dismissal of all things African. Thus Philadelphia's Free African Society emphasized their common heritage upon their establishment in 1787, proudly presenting themselves as "the free *Africans* and their descendants, of the City of Philadelphia." Among the society's founders was Richard Allen, one of Philadelphia's most prominent black leaders and later one of the central founders of the African Methodist Episcopal church. Originally the society gathered in Allen's house, but as it grew it moved to larger quarters, and in 1789 the society began to meet at the Quaker African School House. When the Quaker influence began to assert itself over the society's proceedings (including the practice of fifteen minutes of silence at the beginning of meetings), Allen led a number of men out of the house and out of the organization. He then attempted to assemble members of the society in an effort to turn it back to what were, for him, more acceptable religious practices. The encompassing "African" dome, in short, had many cracks.

Many societies reflected socioeconomic differences in the black community. The subject of social class among antebellum African Americans is rather complex, since what may appear to be clear class divisions can include a variety of finer distinctions. The great majority of African Americans found themselves confined to black ghettos in the major cities—"Nigger Hill" and "New Guinea" in Boston, "Little Africa" in

Cincinnati, and the integrated but impoverished Five Points area of New York City. African-American workers were frequently excluded from skilled positions, and economic and professional restrictions on blacks were supported by law, social prejudice, and sometimes violence—particularly at those times when they were perceived to undermine white workers' struggles for better wages and working conditions. Some blacks, for example, substituted for striking white longshoremen during a New York City strike for better wages in 1855, though they were denied this work when the strike ended.

Blacks were not alone in trying to work against prejudice for employment opportunities. Over time they found themselves competing against waves of European immigrants vying for both employment and acceptance in the broader community. Prejudice against the Irish, considered by many white Americans to be a separate and inferior race, was substantial, but increasingly the Irish were accepted at least as peripheral members of the white nation. Some blacks overcame the odds to become ministers, professional lecturers, or newspaper publishers, and others established successful entrepreneurial careers as caterers, restaurateurs, and owners of other small businesses. Some blacks achieved great wealth and influence, in the North and even in the South, home (in Louisiana) to the largest number of wealthy black entrepreneurs before the Civil War. By and large, though, for most blacks upward mobility—from unskilled to skilled labor, for example—was both difficult and rare, and downward mobility all too possible. In such a context it was only natural that blacks would draw fine distinctions within similar occupational classes.

While some societies were devoted to specific professions, most had no written requirements for membership. There were exceptions, of course, particularly concerning gender but also involving social status. The Free African Society's organizational name, for example, highlights not only the common bond of heritage but also the tie of nominal freedom in a culture that associated race with slavery. In the Brown Fellowship Society, formed in Charleston, South Carolina, in 1790, membership was restricted not only to those who were free but also to those who were light-skinned. Religious affiliation was an important determinant of membership in some societies, for many were either directly associated with a church, like the Friendly Society of St. Thomas's African Church, or enjoyed an informal relationship—the use of a church for a meeting

place, for example. But while distinctions among African-American societies was sometimes deliberate, one suspects that most of them simply
reflected social affiliations and cultural process. The constitution of Boston's African Society, for example, included no restrictions on membership beyond excluding those "who shall commit any injustice or outrage
against the laws of their country," and the document accounted for different educational levels of potential members—requiring, for example,
that new members must read the constitution "or cause the same to be
read to him." Prospective members, however, had to "be presented by
three of the Members," after which the applicant must be "approved of"
by the other members. In short, membership in most societies followed
the process of acquaintance, familiarity, and affiliation that comes naturally through the nature and location of one's employment, residence,
and religious observance.

The most common division in mutual aid societies was based on
gender, for most were either implicitly or explicitly restricted to male
membership. There were exceptions—for example, New York City's
African Marine Fund, which explicitly referred to "both male and female members" in its constitution, and which allowed women to hold
office—but women were largely left to form separate groups while
playing supporting roles in the men's organizations. Given that these
societies were devoted to addressing the effects of social injustice and
the lack of representation, one might expect a different story, particularly since women were so often at the center of the most pressing
cause, the anti-slavery movement. While strict gender boundaries characterized antebellum American society, most historians agree that the
anti-slavery crusade served as an important foundation for the developing women's movement. Women were active, if sometimes in the back-
ground, in virtually every area of anti-slavery efforts, from fund-raising
to political activism, and many of the most influential anti-slavery publications were written by women. There were, of course, tensions—and
when the American Anti-Slavery Society, led by William Lloyd Garrison, included women's rights in its mission and women in its leadership, some men who were disturbed by this (and by what they viewed
as the organization's extreme denunciations of pro-slavery churches)
withdrew to form the short-lived American and Foreign Anti-Slavery
Society. But given the intimate connections between the anti-slavery

movement and black activism, one might expect greater challenges to the assumption of male leadership and membership in other organizations. For a variety of reasons—including religion, social convention, and perhaps even inherited African practices, as some scholars have suggested—most societies were segregated by gender.

This hardly stopped African-American women from organizing or from contributing to organizations dominated by men. At the 1837 Anti-Slavery Convention of American Women, the first of its kind, among the groups represented were the Rising Daughters of Abyssinia, the Colored Ladies Literary Society of New York, and the Female Anti-Slavery Societies of Philadelphia and Boston. The vice president at that convention, Grace Douglass, was a black activist from Philadelphia. But while women made inroads to representation and leadership through the anti-slavery movement, they often turned to their own associations to address both the cause of women and the more general struggle for social justice.

African-American women organized both in response to restrictions by men and in their own efforts to address the needs of the community. The African Benevolent Society of Newport, Rhode Island, for example, allowed both men and women in its membership but restricted voting rights and leadership to men. In response, in 1809 women formed the African Female Benevolent Society. In Philadelphia the African Benevolent Society was complemented by the Female African Benevolent Society, formed in 1821. And while women were both members and officers of New York City's Abyssinian Benevolent Daughters of Esther Association (1839), men were appointed as "guardians" for the organization.

Women's societies proliferated in the early decades of the nineteenth century, including Philadelphia's Female Bond Benevolent Society of Bethel (1817) and Female Beneficial Philanthropic Society of Zoar (1827), the United Daughters of Bethlehem City and County of Philadelphia (1835), or Cleveland's Colored Ladies Benevolent Sewing Society (1852), formed in response to the Fugitive Slave Law of 1850 and devoted to the abolition of slavery and the promotion of temperance. Often the mission of these societies reflected the contributions considered appropriate for women. Women also played supporting roles in churches—as in, for example, New York City's Female Mite Society (1830), devoted to providing for the needs of ministers, or Philadelphia's Female Methodist Assistant Society (1827). Women were especially involved in caregiving as well, playing central roles in forming New York's Colored Orphan Asylum (1833) and the Society for the Relief of Worthy Aged, Indigent Colored Persons (1845).

Regardless of the conditions of their formation, most of the women's societies sought to act in concert with the organizations led by black men and with white men and women. The all-black Women's Association organized in Philadelphia in 1849 included members who maintained their membership with the racially mixed Philadelphia Anti-Slavery Society. The Women's Association involved men in its work and was addressed, at its organizational meeting, by the black activist Martin Delany, who provided the organization with its constitution. In a demonstration of such cooperation, the African-American mutual aid societies published a notice to the public in the *National Gazette and Literary Register* in 1831, announcing their common sense of mission and reporting "for the satisfaction of the public, . . . a statement of their expenses for charitable purposes during the last year." Of those organizations that opened their records for this notice (several did not provide this information), sixteen were listed as "male societies" and twenty-seven as female. The male groups had paid out $2,202.71 in 1830–1831; the female societies had paid out $3,616.58. Clearly Philadelphia's women were both active and effective, and the city's various associations perceived the need both to promote an image of unity and to affirm their moral responsibility and civic duty.

Some organizations restricted their membership in order to meet the needs of occupational and professional groups, or to address the racial politics of employment and city services. These groups, like the mutual aid societies generally, were responses to a harsh racial environment that made African-American life tenuous. At times these efforts, like those of many black organizations, exposed the very conditions that prompted them. For example, a group of blacks frustrated by growing racial tensions in Philadelphia early in the nineteenth century, which threatened the security of African-American homes and businesses, in 1818 announced plans to form its own fire department, the African Fire Association. The response from the white community was so sharp that several prominent members of Philadelphia's black community urged the group to reconsider its plans, and the African Fire Association accordingly never progressed beyond the planning stages.

African-American workers in various occupations and community endeavors could similarly expect to be met with repressive measures, including legal restrictions and violence. Promoting and protecting occupational groups was thus a priority for mutual aid societies, and one more way in which they reflected cultural patterns of affiliation while still working toward a broader group identity. In Philadelphia the Coachman's Benevolent Society was formed in 1825, and both the Humane Mechanics and the African Porter's Benevolent Society organized in 1828. The Baltimore Caulker's Association brought together black shipyard workers in 1838, and in New York City the next year William Powell founded the Colored Sailor's Home, funded in part by the American Seamen's Friend Society. The Colored Sailor's Home was the first to provide stopover lodging for black men who worked on commercial ships.

While most of these organizations were designed to serve the needs of African Americans in certain occupations, many were also devoted to improving the condition of and raising the ethical and educational standards for black working-class men and women. Specifically for this purpose, an ambitious organization was launched in 1850, the American League of Colored Laborers, which elected the prominent black minister Samuel Ringgold Ward as its president and Lewis Woodson and Frederick Douglass as vice presidents. In addition to these well-known activists, the group included some of the black community's most successful businessmen, ministers, and educators, but the historical record suggests that the League did not last long beyond its first organizational meeting.

❖

Although the American League of Colored Laborers, like many other organizations, was short-lived, its formation was revealing both in its leadership and in its message. Many antebellum organizations were devoted to uplift—a cause that often revealed deep divisions between the developing black middle class and the working class, between African Americans who claimed leadership and representative status and those who confronted daily the harshest conditions of black life in the workplace and in racially and economically segregated neighborhoods. Some initiatives undertaken by white Americans became patronizing, if sincere, efforts to promote education and moral behavior among what was often viewed as an inferior and threatening class. In Cincinnati, for example, white female philanthropists formed in 1817 the Female Association for the Benefit of Africans in an effort to encourage religious and secular study.

Blacks too recognized the pressures and temptations of life under degrading, repressive conditions, and their sense of mission in responding to the ongoing crisis of black working-class life was sometimes startlingly direct, as suggested by the title of the Society for Suppressing Vice and Immorality, formed by black leaders in Philadelphia in 1809. Many blacks were also active in the national temperance movement, the organized efforts to discourage the use of alcohol that would become increasingly influential over the course of the century. The minister and former slave James W. C. Pennington, for example, was a leading force in the organization of the Brooklyn Temperance Society in 1830; in Frankfurt, Kentucky, African Americans formed a temperance society in 1832; and Boston's New England Temperance Society of People of Color was founded in 1835. The problems addressed by such organizations were not limited to the black working class, for organizers understood that African Americans at all economic levels suffered the effects of economic depression, disease, and labor competition, and were often excluded from or marginalized by the larger society's efforts to address these problems.

Beyond the temptations of drink or vice, African Americans looked to address the condition of a people excluded from educational opportunities and conditioned to think of themselves as inferior. Virtually all mutual aid societies included education and moral reform as part of their mission, and, as noted, most societies made proper moral character a fundamental requirement of membership. In an address at New York's AME Church in 1813, George Lawrence expressed his perhaps overly optimistic belief that "this government founded on the principles of liberty and equality, and declaring them to be the free gift of God, if not ignorant of their declaration, must enforce it." Aware that not all in the United States, especially those in the Southern states, might agree with this proposition, Lawrence advised that "as the continual droppings of water has a tendency to wear away the hardest and most flinty substance, so likewise shall we, abounding in good works, and causing our examples to shine forth as the sun at noonday, melt their callous hearts, and render sinewless the arm of oppression." The process that Lawrence envisioned depended on the work of African-American societies. "My brethren," he announced, "you who are enrolled and proudly march under the banners of Mutual Relief, and Wilberforce Societies, consider your important standings as incorporated bodies, and walk worthy of the name you bear, cling closely to the paths of virtue and morality, cherish the plants of peace and temperance."

With the societies, in short, came not only ethical standards but also representative status—a public display of virtue capable of answering racist assumptions. "It has been said by your enemies," Lawrence added, "that your minds were not calculated to receive a sufficient store of knowledge to fit you for beneficial or social societies; but your incorporation drowned that assertion in contempt; and now let shame cover their heads, and blushes crimson their countenances." In many ways Lawrence's speech was a celebration of the success of African-American societies and of the power of unity within the black community, but he closed with an admonition to guard against disunion and to recognize "the arm of oppression" and the fragile hope upon which all societies were founded.

The need for societies devoted to uplift were meant to counter not only oppression but also its generational effects—the many ways that African Americans had been prepared to collaborate in the perpetuation of their condition. Many societies were formed in response to the habits of black Americans. Owen T. B. Nickens, a Cincinnati whitewasher and teacher, established the city's Moral Reform Society in 1839 to work against the examples of intemperance, licentiousness, gambling, Sabbath breaking, and blasphemy that he witnessed around him. In Boston, leaders like David Walker worried about even more fundamental threats to the security and unity of the African-American community, both from within and without. In an 1828 address to one of the most important of these organizations, the Massachusetts General Colored Association, founded sometime between 1826 and 1828 in an attempt to serve blacks throughout the North, Walker observed that "had our opponents had their way, the very notion of such an institution might have been obliterated from our minds" by "those who delight in our degradation." Observing that of 2.5 million "colored people in these United States," roughly a fifth could claim to be "about two

thirds of the way free," Walker understood very well the challenge
such organizations faced. "That the major part of us are ignorant and
poor," he observed, "I am at this time unprepared to deny."

Walker addressed both the possibilities of organized efforts and the
inevitable result that some African Americans would ask "what good associations and societies are going to do for us." For Walker, the black
community was in danger of being defined by an ongoing process of degradation and acceptance, a "hereditary degradation" that would leave the
children of those in Walker's audience in a state "inferior to that which
our fathers, under their comparative disadvantages and privations, left
on us." Or as Martin Delany put it in 1852, "The degradation of the slave
parent has been entailed upon the child, induced by the subtle policy of
the oppressor, in regular succession handed down from father to son—
a system of regular submission and servitude, menialism and dependence, until it has become almost a physiological function of our system,
an actual condition of our nature." This degradation, both Walker and
Delany warned, ran deep. Walker provided examples, among them the
gangs of African Americans who would kidnap and sell into slavery fellow members of the black community.

Philanthropic societies were devoted not only to the work of virtue,
then, but also to the need to make others aware of the unified African-
American presence in that work. In numerous orations, blacks spoke
of the record that societies would leave for future generations and the
foundations prepared for future achievements. Those involved in these
societies understood that they must necessarily be devoted not only to immediate needs but also to future possibilities. As important as their work
was the story of what they were doing, the alternative history they were
creating. Many societies were devoted as much to the telling of that story
as to other aspects of their collective mission. In a piece published in the
Liberator in 1832, Maria Stewart worried about a culture, both white and
black, that discouraged African Americans from publicizing their ambitions and abilities. "Many bright and intelligent ones are in the midst of
us," she wrote, "but because they are not calculated to display a classical
education, they hide their talents behind a napkin." Perhaps addressing
disunion, class differences, and jealousies within the African-American
community as well as commenting on the division between blacks and
whites, Stewart declared, "I should rejoice to behold my friends or foes

far exceed my feeble efforts. I should be happy to discern among them patterns worthy of imitation, and become proud to acknowledge them as my superiors." Establishing patterns worthy of imitation was virtually the mission statement of every benevolent society formed by African Americans, and Stewart gave voice to many in her sense of what success for these societies might entail. "O, how I long for the time to come," she wrote, "when I shall behold our young men anxious to inform their minds on moral and political subjects—ambitious to become distinguished men of talents—view them standing pillars in the church, qualifying themselves to preach the everlasting gospel of Our Lord Jesus Christ—becoming useful and active members in society, and the future hopes of our declining years." Although her vision was confined to young men, it was a good example of what many African-American societies promoted. It was designed in part to provide young blacks with a different sense of what they might be "calculated to display" in their private and public lives.

While such visions constituted an alternative story in a white supremacist society, in many ways African-American organizations were devoted to an extremely familiar story. Whether to prove their worth in the face of racist detractors or to give voice to interests and ambitions for which they might otherwise have no outlet, African Americans turned to societies to promote understandings of education, civilization, and character quite similar to those claimed by white Americans. Pressing the case for a decidedly patriarchal culture, Stewart reflected the basically conservative message behind many progressive and even radical black organizations: a vision of a world in which men were prepared to be pillars of society. Elsewhere Stewart argued that blacks needed to follow the example of white America—that is, to demonstrate self-respect, self-determination, and, when necessary, bold action. Similarly, in a eulogy on the white British abolitionist William Wilberforce in 1833, William Whipper echoed many African-American leaders in his sense of the need to demonstrate to white Euro-Americans the character and determination of the black community. "If we should fail to render ourselves worthy of so powerful an advocate," Whipper argued, "we shall retard the influence of those virtues. If we fail to walk in the paths of elevation, marked out for us by the laws of our country and the achievements of philanthropy, we shall not only destroy the prospects of those who come after us, but will weaken the cause of those who come forward for our support." The names of many societies named for white abolitionists—the Wilberforce Philanthropic Association, the Benezet Philanthropic Society, the Juvenile Garrison Independent Society, or the Rising Sons and Daughters of Lucretia Mott, among many others—indicate that African Americans envisioned an interracial alliance, an ideal society represented by the efforts of a select group of white abolitionists, philanthropists, and social reformers.

Nonetheless blacks well understood that while white America promoted ethical character and moral virtue, the challenge ahead was not simply one of imitating those pursuits. Many activists pointed out that blacks faced fundamentally different obstacles than those faced by the white middle or upper classes. As Maria Stewart observed in 1832, "few white persons of either sex, who are calculated for any thing else, are willing to spend their lives and bury their talents in performing mean, servile labor." And Stewart spoke of the "noble souls" of many African Americans who aspired "after high and honorable acquirements" and yet were "confined by the chains of ignorance and poverty to lives of continual drudgery and toil." "Continual hard labor," Stewart observed, "deadens the energies of the soul, and benumbs the faculties of the mind. . . . Many of the most worthy and interesting among us" were "doomed to spend our lives in gentlemen's kitchens," a state of affairs that naturally caused many to "lose their ambition, and become worthless." Under such conditions, talk of lifting the race by imitating the privileged class of white America had little appeal or practical value.

Addressing this same concern, M. H. Freeman observed in the pages of the *Anglo-African Magazine* in 1859, "We are too apt to take the precepts that are taught to the ruling race in this country and apply them to ourselves without considering that different traits in our character, either natural or acquired by our different circumstances, require an entirely different treatment." Freeman argued that "the energetic, scheming, grasping, Anglo-Saxon with his eager desire for wealth" needed to "be constantly reminded of the vanity of riches, and the transitory nature of worldly wealth." But for African Americans to work toward the virtues espoused by middle-class white America, a different approach was in order, for the causes of degradation within the black community were different from those in the white middle class. Freeman's message of uplift and respectability, accordingly, concentrated on the bottom line: "We need directly the contrary teachings, and I approve the good sense, if not the good taste of the praying brother who among other blessings, besought the Lord 'to give us a little more money.' Wealth is power, and he who possesses it will command a degree, at least, of respect."

Not content to wait for an answer to that prayer, African-American societies included among their services to their communities a strong sense of the links between employment opportunity, financial independence, and character. Throughout the life of antebellum organizations, a consistent theme is that the power of labor would provide the best response to the degradation of the black Americans. It was considered the best strategy for effecting systemic change and for challenging prejudice. Black leaders lamented the condition of servitude that many of their brethren accepted as their only means of a livelihood. While such lamentations sometimes led to heated debates, revealing class divisions within the organized black community, few disputed the need to attend to economic matters in dealing with issues of collective character and self-determination. As Martin Delany put it in 1852, what African Americans needed most was "a knowledge of the wealth of nations; or how to make money." "White men," he argued, "are producers—we are consumers. They build houses, and we rent them. They raise produce, and we consume it. They manufacture clothes and wares, and we garnish ourselves with them." Delany's point was echoed the following year at the Colored National Convention in Rochester, New York. Its official proceedings declared that "as a whole, we constitute, to a very large extent, a body of consumers and non-producers." African Americans needed to pay attention to the workings of the economic system if they were to have any hope of fundamentally altering their collective condition. "We live in society among men," Delany emphasized, "conducted by men, governed by rules and regulations. However arbitrary, there are certain policies that regulate all well organized institutions and corporate bodies." African-American organizations, he suggested, could not afford to rely on philosophical ideals to the exclusion of close attention to the arbitrary rules of other corporate bodies. "These are the means by which God intended man to succeed," he said, and this explained "the white man's success with all of his wickedness, over the head of the colored man, with all of his religion." To struggle against this wickedness, one must adopt God's intended means.

Many societies were devoted to doing just that. In Philadelphia the American Society of Free People of Colour, founded in 1830, encouraged African Americans to pursue "mechanical and agricultural arts." In New York City the Phoenix Society, founded in 1833, encouraged young men and women to attend school while also providing job training. The Philadelphia Association for the Mental and Moral Improvement of People of Colour (1838), while advocating immigration to Canada in hopes of a more favorable environment for collective industry, also encouraged blacks to pursue agriculture and education. The Sons of Enterprise in Cincinnati, founded in 1852, promoted temperance and other virtues but also worked to assist African Americans in economic endeavors, including the purchase of real estate. The National Council of Coloured People, formed in 1853, worked to encourage vocational training. Indeed, many societies worked to help blacks find work, to provide a network of support for that work, and to offer a foundation whereby African Americans could move from unskilled menial labor to a wider field of employment possibilities. Thus, they believed, they would help create a community of producers as well as consumers, men and women who understood that among them they held the skills and talents needed for an independent and powerful community. In succeeding chapters we will revisit this theme, for African Americans understood that beneath the immediate sting of racist rhetoric and social exclusion was an economic system that protected and maintained a white supremacist culture—in the obvious form of slavery in the South or in the more indirect form of degraded and vulnerable labor in the North. Apart from abstract ideology, blacks would need to master the concrete mechanisms of this system by which their character, their possibilities, and their rights were so forcefully defined and restricted.

They understood the terms of this struggle, which accounts for the full range of African-American societies. When the white Unitarian minister and moderate abolitionist James Freeman Clarke argued in 1859 that "colored people ought to make money," he was in many ways simply echoing the opinions of Martin Delany and others in the African-American community. But Clarke, continuing, revealed the prejudice that marked the limitations of this strategy. "A colored man who makes a thousand dollars," he argued, "does more to put down prejudice, than if he made a thousand moderately good speeches against prejudice, or wrote a thousand pretty fair articles against it. No race in this country will be despised which makes money. If we had in Boston or New York ten orangoutangs worth a million dollars each, they would visit in the best society, we should leave our cards at their doors, and give them snug little dinner-parties." No doubt Clarke was right, but those African Americans who insisted on something more than recognition as the equivalent of wealthy orangutans understood the level of prejudice involved in Clarke's vision of social acceptance.

Frederick Douglass captured the situation well in his lecture at the inauguration of the Douglass Institute in Baltimore, Maryland, in 1865, where he argued that "when prejudice cannot deny the black man's ability, it denies his race, and claims him as a white man. It affirms that if he is not exactly white, he ought to be. If not what he ought to be in this particular, he owes whatever intelligence he possesses to the white race by contract or association." Like Douglass, African Americans understood that white recognition and acceptance would go only so far. In that same speech Douglass asked, "Now, what are those elemental and original powers of civilization about which men speak and write so earnestly, and which white men claim for themselves and deny to the Negro? I answer that they are simply consciousness of wants and ability to gratify them. Here the whole machinery of civilization, whether moral, intellectual or physical, is set in motion." Those who promoted black uplift understood very well that there were many reasons why many blacks might struggle to achieve even "consciousness of wants." In any event, such consciousness, once attained, would face a "machinery of civilization" geared toward obstructing or denying the "ability to gratify" such wants.

The purpose of African-American mutual aid and benevolent societies, then, was in part reactive and in part pro-active. On the one hand, blacks needed to respond to the effects of restricted employment, extensive poverty, obstructed education, social segregation, and economic vulnerability, all of them usually without the representation that one might expect to come with taxation. On the other hand, blacks needed to create the means by which the "consciousness of wants" that guided the great mass of their people might be reformed, developed, and refined so as to set in motion the moral, intellectual, and physical "machinery of civilization." Mutual benefit and benevolent societies were in many ways the means by which African Americans approached the full scale of this work, starting with the most immediate "wants" and working toward long-term needs and ambitions. These societies helped offer not only basic security but also collective solidarity, both in the public processions they staged and in the private virtues they encouraged. In their progression from the African Union Society (1780) to the National Council of Coloured People (1853), they negotiated with the dual demands of a pan-African and a national identity, an African heritage and a rising manifestation of the African diaspora unique to the United States. They provided the foundation for an African-American community to be both conceptualized and developed. But for the mutual benefit and benevolent societies to be successful—to promote the cause of mutual interest, mutual benefit, and mutual relief—they needed the help of a great many other organizational efforts, the most important of which was the church.

3

"Plain and Simple Gospel"

THE STORY of African-American religion might begin at various points, but let's open with the story of one black family trying to attend church. James and Sarah Easton, both from Massachusetts, were the parents of seven children, born between 1786 and 1799. James was a highly respected ironworker who produced iron for and supervised various construction sites in Boston, including the Tremont Theater. Known as a man of integrity, he had served as a fortifications engineer under George Washington in the American Revolution, after which he had eventually settled near Boston, where he was a prominent business leader in and beyond the black community. He was also a highly determined man, particularly when it came to what he viewed as the ideals and the promise of the American Revolution. So when his church constructed a "Negro porch" to separate black congregants from white—something frequently done at the time—the Easton family continued to sit on the main floor until they were forced out. Later the family purchased a pew in a Baptist church, which some white members members of the church shortly coated with tar. The following Sunday the Easton family arrived at church carrying their own chairs, and they refused to move even when they were prevented from setting them up. Still, they returned on subsequent Sundays until finally they were banished from the congregation.

In many ways, what is often referred to as the "Black Church"—a major center of African-American religious, political, economic, and social activity—can trace its origins to such racist practices. While they might have been more adamant than most, the Easton family's experience was fairly common, and many blacks finally decided that if white Christians were going to segregate the observance of religious faith, black Christians would have to create institutions of their own in which faith could enjoy

free observance. In 1787 the African-American congregants of Philadelphia's St. George Methodist Church encountered a situation similar to
that of the Eastons at their church—the construction of a special gallery
for black worshipers. During the preceding year, prayer meetings for
African-American Methodists had been organized by Richard Allen, a
former slave who had become a licensed Methodist preacher. Along with
other black church leaders, Allen had advocated the building of a house
of worship for this group, but both the church and the separate prayer
meetings were strongly opposed by the white clergy. When African-
American congregants were asked to accept the segregated gallery, however, they left the sanctuary and began to organize on their own. By 1794
some in the group, now associated with the Church of England, formed
the St. Thomas African Episcopal Church, with Allen's colleague, Absalom Jones, as its pastor.

Many black Christians, though, favored the Methodist denomination,
and the search for free religious observance thus led to the development
not only of a black church but of an African-American denomination. Richard Allen, among those drawn to Methodism for its "plain
and simple gospel," purchased a blacksmith shop and developed it into
a church, the Bethel Church, which was dedicated that same year by
white Methodist bishop Francis Asbury. Unlike St. Thomas, the Bethel
Church was for some years served by white clergymen appointed by the
Methodist conference, though Asbury ordained Allen a deacon in 1799,
the first black person at that rank. During this same period, African-
Americans Methodists in Baltimore had similarly organized, forming
a prayer group in 1786. Later, when asked to accept segregated seats in
a special gallery, along with the requirement that they would receive
communion only after white members of the church had been served,
they established the Colored Methodist Society. After some years of
continued tensions with white Methodist leaders, in 1816 sixteen representatives of black Methodists met in Philadelphia's Bethel Church,
where they created the African Methodist Episcopal Church, an organization that was granted independent existence by the Supreme Court
of Pennsylvania. Daniel Coker of Baltimore was elected bishop of this
new denomination, but when he declined the honor, Richard Allen
was made the church's first bishop. The AME church would go on to
become one of the most influential organizations in African-American

history and culture, a guiding institution in black political life, and an important publishing center.

Throughout the United States, black churches developed wherever African Americans gathered. Often these churches were responses to the racism found in white churches—that is, churches that announced themselves as white not only in their leadership but also in their attempt to control African Americans' experience of worship. In other cases, black churches developed simply out of the fact of racial segregation and the need for black communities to gather together for religious observances. Increasingly, the development of black churches and denominations provided a haven for those who encountered treatment similar to that received by the Easton family or the congregants of the St. George Methodist Church. Frederick Douglass, for example, relates in his second autobiography, *My Bondage and My Freedom* (1855), the story of his own religious quests after he escaped from slavery. "Among my first concerns on reaching New Bedford," he states, "was to become united with the church, for I had never given up, in reality, my religious faith." Having been associated with the Methodist church during his enslavement, Douglass attended its place of worship in New Bedford, only to discover that the church practiced racial segregation even for "the sacrament of the Lord's Supper, that most sacred and most solemn of all the ordinances of the Christian church." First the white congregants were served, and only afterward did the pastor invite the black congregants to the altar, assuring them that "God is no respecter of persons." "The colored members— poor, slavish souls—went forward," Douglass reported; "I went *out*, and have never been in that church since, although I honestly went there with a view to joining that body." Douglass turned instead to New Bedford's African Methodist Episcopal Zion Church, but this only was the beginning of an ongoing religious struggle under the restricted "freedom" he had achieved. As his comments about the other black members of the Methodist church suggest, his was part of a larger, collective journey that cannot be reduced to a singular story of the "Black Church."

❖

The story of African-American Christianity is varied in its origins and complex in its regional and denominational details. The early periods of enslavement brought Africans to the Americas by way of the soul-scorching Middle Passage. People came from many different cultures and represented a variety of religious beliefs and practices. These varied religious traditions would eventually become intertwined with the forms of Christianity encountered in the Americas, but this was a process that took place over generations and differed across locales. To envision this process, one might imagine many streams being channeled into a relatively narrow outlet, with the resultingly turbulent, mixed, and often powerful currents representing the many elements of African-American Christianity—a generally identifiable body of water but one fed by numerous sources and charged by numerous and different points of pressure.

In the United States, African-American Christianity was influenced by the different environments in which it developed. Religious beliefs and practices in enslaved communities, for example, were shaped both by white surveillance and control (especially after such religious-inspired insurrections as that of Nat Turner in 1831) and by the influx of newly enslaved populations from the African continent before (and to some extent after) the abolition of the transatlantic slave trade in 1808. Religious practices in nominally free communities that developed after the abolition of slavery in the Northern states were different, though they were nonetheless influenced by white racism. Most historians agree that African Americans did not turn to American Christianity in significant numbers until they were drawn by the evangelical efforts of the First Great Awakening in the first half of the eighteenth century. Later in the century, black Christian communities began to be a presence in American churches. And toward the end of the eighteenth century, separate black churches, and then black denominations, began to develop. The varied currents of African-American religious beliefs were very much a presence, even under the seemingly smooth surfaces of common beliefs of the religious organizations.

Although conditions for black religious organization were naturally more favorable in the free communities of the North, the Midwest, and the West, the story of African-American churches begins in the South. Historians generally agree that the work of a group of enslaved black men led to the formation of the first independent black church, on the Galphin Plantation in South Carolina. This church, founded in Silver Bluff,

South Carolina, in 1773, was led originally by David George, a man who had been converted by George Liele, the first licensed black preacher in Georgia. Liele established a black church at Yama Craw, outside of Savannah, Georgia, and was involved in the Silver Bluff church as well, part of his preaching among several plantation congregations. The Reverend Jesse Peter, pastor of the Silver Bluff church from 1788 to 1793, led many in its congregation to the First African Baptist Church of Augusta, Georgia, a church officially organized by David Tinsley, a white pastor, in 1793. These preachers and others who followed laid the groundwork for the development of an Afro-Baptist faith in the South, a series of independent but interconnected churches which featured a blending of West African and Euro-American Baptist beliefs and practices. Roughly a dozen African-American Baptist congregations were established in the South before 1800, whereas independent black Baptist churches in the North were not established until the early nineteenth century.

Efforts to establish black churches in the South were of course complicated. Consider, for example, the experience of Andrew Bryan, enslaved by William Bryan on the Brampton Plantation in Savannah, Georgia. Andrew Bryan was baptized by Liele before Liele left the area with British troops at the close of the American Revolution. Andrew felt called to be a minister in 1788, at which time he was examined and found acceptable. After his ordination he baptized close to fifty of his fellow slaves, and a church was organized that long functioned under various names: the Ethiopian Church of Jesus Christ at Savannah, the colored Baptist Church, the First African Baptist Church—and, later, the First Bryan Church. In many ways this is a classic example of the development of black churches, from inspiration to collective mission to institution. But this church, like others, met with resistance—in the form of an appeal to a grand jury by white area residents, presenting "as a grievance Negroes in different parts of this country being permitted to assemble in large bodies under pretence [sic] of religion," and protesting "William Bryan, Esquire for permitting Negroes to assemble, in large bodies, at the plantation called Brampton, within this county, in violation of the patrol law." Eventually the black congregation was allowed to continue their worship, but not before Andrew Bryan and other leaders of the church were publicly whipped.

In part because of their experiences with racism in the church, African Americans drawn to the Baptist faith established their own churches wherever black communities developed. Some of these churches were both prominently located and influential in black public life—beginning with the first African-American Baptist congregation in the North, the Joy Street Church in Boston, established in 1805 under the leadership of Thomas Paul, one of the most influential black leaders of his day. Many others quickly followed, including the Abyssinian Baptist Church in New York City (1808) and churches in Philadelphia (1808); Trenton, New Jersey (1812); Albany, New York (1821); and Detroit (1837), among many others. As African Americans found opportunities to move west in hope of more sparsely settled lands where they could pursue lives relatively free of Southern slavery and the deeply institutionalized racism of the North, Baptist churches were soon established in turn. Illinois, for example, saw the foundation of a black Baptist church in Wood River in 1818 and the establishment of the Colored Baptist Association in 1839, an organization that split a decade later, with the southern Illinois churches forming the Mount Olive Association. St. Louis's First African Baptist Church, established in 1822, was the city's first all-black church, and by 1825 the church had its first official minister, John Berry Meachum, a former slave. At the Beech Settlement in Indiana, a black farming community, a Baptist church was organized in the 1830s, though it didn't last very long, and another, the Six Mile Church, was formed there in 1852. In Indianapolis the Second Baptist Church was formed in 1846, and a Baptist church was established in Virginia City, Nevada, by 1863.

In the South, Baptist churches ranged from the informal and rural to the imposing and urban—from such churches as the Little Mine Road Baptist Church of Spotsylvania County, Virginia, formed in 1849 and originally gathered in a tent, or the African Baptist Church of Lexington, Kentucky (1810), led by Peter Duerett, a slave and preacher known as "Old Captain," to such institutions as the African Baptist Church of Lynchburg, Virginia, formed in the mid-1840s, or the First Baptist Church (1830) and the Bank Street Baptist Church (1840) of Norfolk, Virginia.

Churches such as these did not simply acknowledge the existence of a black community in need of a common place of worship; early black churches *created* communities that earlier had been defined largely by a common condition of degradation. Although blacks brought religious traditions from West Africa—either experienced directly or inherited from earlier generations—to their understanding and experience of Christianity in colonial America and the United States, they did not seek to form their own churches because of doctrinal differences with white-led churches in which they participated. Rather, they formed their own churches either in acknowledgment of their sequestered position—enslaved on a plantation, for example—or, more frequently, because of racist practices in their churches. Once formed, however, black churches, rural or urban, repositioned black communities by encouraging a network of connections and a self-defined community—that is, a community that could understand itself not by common degradation but by a common spiritual quest. As churches developed, they served as important homes for the African-American congregations they served, often including land, a building, responsibilities of governance, and a common social mission. In Portland, Maine, six men wrote a letter of protest in 1826 concerning the segregation of African-American congregants in special pews and sections of the church, a letter published in the *Eastern Argus*. That action led in 1828 to the formation of the Abyssinian Religious Society, which built a meeting house. Responding to the conditions outlined in that public letter, the black parishioners of Portland's Second Congregational Church formed their own church, the Fourth Congregational Church, in 1835, which merged with the Abyssinian Religious Society in 1842 to form the Abyssinian Congregation Church and Society. The Abyssianian meeting house became, in turn, not only a place of worship but also a center of political activism and social reform, hosting abolition and temperance meetings, the Female Benevolent Society, the Portland Union Anti-Slavery Society, black conventions, a school, and various public events. Did a black community exist in Portland before the formation of the Abyssinian Religious Society? Certainly. Did that community change, develop, and redefine itself as a result of the ARS? Absolutely.

Such developments in African-American community organization were further encouraged by the growth of the African Methodist Episcopal church, in part because it followed the Methodist reliance on an episcopal system of governance, with bishops providing the highest level of leadership and elected delegates meeting at a conference each year. The AME's origins lay in Philadelphia's Bethel Methodist Church (later Mother Bethel African Methodist Episcopal Church), dedicated in 1794, which had an enormous influence on the course of nineteenth-century African-American history. In 1816 representatives of the Philadelphia church, led by Richard Allen, met with other black Methodists from Philadelphia, New Jersey, and Baltimore and formed the AME church. In a few short years the denomination included congregations as far away as Washington, D.C., and Pittsburgh, with new churches being founded as blacks moved west. In Indiana, for example, the Bethel African Methodist Episcopal Church was formed in 1836; by the late 1830s the congregation of the Mt. Pleasant Church in Indiana's Beech Settlement converted to the AME faith; and the Indiana Conference of the AME church was organized at Beech Settlement in the fall of 1840. By 1854 the first AME church in California, St. Cyrian AME Church, was established in San Francisco, and about that time an AME church was formed in Grass Valley Township, Nevada County, California. By 1863 there was an AME church in Virginia City, Nevada. In 1890 the black scholar William S. Scarborough, reflecting on the improbability of African-American progress through the nineteenth century—"progress more marked than that of any other people in the same length of time and under the same circumstances"—noted the importance of the AME church. "Surely the history and growth of African Methodism in these United States," he remarked, "are an evidence not only of progress, but of permanence as well. From a small seed—infinitesimally small as it were—has grown a magnificent tree, as wonderful as it is magnificent. In every State and Territory, wherever the negro is found, African Methodism is known." Indeed, the AME church provided the framework as well as the means for understanding and experiencing community, not simply locally but throughout the states and territories of the United States.

As this vast development of churches and denominational conferences indicates, the AME church promoted a national African-American community in part by addressing one of the major restrictions on black life in the nineteenth century, mobility. Of course, free blacks could and did move to various parts of the Americas—but the resettlement of individuals and families is one thing while transplanting communities is quite another. Black mobility was made possible in part by the AME church's missionary efforts that utilized itinerant preachers. Consider, for example, one of the most influential of these traveling preachers, William Paul Quinn. Quinn had been a spectator at the 1816 Philadelphia meeting when the AME Conference was organized, and he was one of the first seven AME itinerant preachers appointed by the church. Over time he held various church positions, including head of the Pittsburgh Circuit, though eventually conflicts with Allen led to his excommunication from the church. After Allen's death in 1831, however, Quinn petitioned to be readmitted, and after his return to the AME organization in 1833 he was assigned missionary duties in the Midwest and West. In 1835 he was named general missionary to the West. Over the course of his career, he traveled as far west as California and as far south as Louisiana. He worked in free and slave states, in urban and rural areas, in settled and relatively unsettled regions, establishing congregations and churches and representing, in his travels and in his ministry, an active and mobile network of black spiritual and social concerns.

By way of an organizational framework with men like Quinn, the AME church gathered African Americans otherwise separated geographically and caught in the contingencies of regional or local laws and conditions. It made possible not simply a sense of community but the active connections of a nationally organized society. Through association with AME regional conferences and with the denominational organization at large, blacks discovered themselves across space and time, active participants in an organization that could claim for itself a history unique to the African-American experience.

The African Methodist Episcopal Zion church was also influential, but on a smaller scale. When the New York Conference of the Methodist Church voted to recognize the rights of African Americans to have their own church meetings, black congregants in New York City's John Street Methodist Episcopal Church rented a hall to form their own congregation, chartered in 1801 as the African Methodist Episcopal Church of the City of New York, known also as Zion Church. At first the congregation was led by a white pastor, William Stillwell, but gradually a new configuration of the church emerged. When white Methodist clergy in New York sought greater control over church properties in 1820, both Stillwell and the congregation resisted, and in 1821 representatives from various churches in New York, Connecticut, and Pennsylvania met to form an independent body, with James Varick, a black church leader, chosen as its first bishop in 1822. In 1848 the general conference of this new body voted to add "Zion" to its name, both to honor its founding church and to distinguish itself from the AME church founded in Philadelphia.

Although the AME Zion church developed more slowly than AME, its influence was nonetheless powerful, and it included among its early congregants such prominent African Americans as Frederick Douglass, Sojourner Truth, and Harriet Tubman. Like the AME church, the AME Zion church provided a framework for community mobility through the efforts of such men as John Jamison Moore, once pastor of the Big Wesley AME Zion Church in Philadelphia, who moved to California in 1852, founding in that same year the first black church in San Francisco.

While most of early African-American religious history involved Protestant denominations, particularly Baptist and Methodist, Catholic churches too were part of the landscape. Catholics often suffered from suspicion or outright discrimination in the overwhelmingly Protestant United States, and many of the most significant developments in black Catholicism occurred in the late nineteenth century. Although three black men were ordained as Catholic priests before the Civil War— James Augustine Healy (1854), Alexander Sherwood Healy (1864), and Patrick Francis Healy (1864)—these three brothers were light enough to pass as white, and generally they did so. The first unmistakably black priest, Augustus Tolton, was ordained after the war, in 1886, and the first African-American Catholic Congress was held in Washington, D.C., in 1889. Still, the Catholic church was a presence for some African Americans before the war. In Boston, for example, at the end of the eighteenth century, immigrants, probably with French-Caribbean connections, formed the city's increasingly significant black Catholic population. Some of its members joined in the development of black churches in the following decades.

Especially noteworthy is the first Catholic order for black American women, the Oblate Sisters of Providence, founded in Baltimore in 1829. Two Haitian women living in Baltimore, Elizabeth Lange and Marie Balas, had started a school in 1818 for free black girls. It was held in their home until 1828, when James Joubert, a French-born Catholic priest, offered the backing of his religious order, the Sulpicians, leading to the founding of the St. Frances Academy. The second-oldest Catholic order for women of color was founded by Henriette Delille, a free woman of African and European descent born in New Orleans. The Sisters of the Holy Family, the result of Delille's efforts, was established in 1842, with the mother house located in New Orleans. While not nearly as influential as other African-American religious organizations, black Catholics too worked to establish the foundations upon which new community structures might be built.

❖

As the governing contingencies of the Catholic church suggest, African-American religious organizations were sometimes less than independent and were often challenged by the governing racial order in the United States. In the South, black denominations were almost always overseen by whites, and even in the North, Midwest, and West churches were constantly constrained by the pressures of a white supremacist culture—in matters of church governance or the special needs of a black ministry for communities sometimes devastated by poverty, harsh working and residential conditions, and limited access to educational opportunity. Internal divisions also complicated the mission of various churches, for it is a rather tall order to establish and run a church, let alone a denomination. Moreover these churches struggled with the tensions of an enabling radicalism, which helped justify separate religious organizations in response to white racism and what some viewed as a sustaining conservatism—the patriarchal order of the Christian doctrine of the time. Even after establishing such important frameworks for promoting community, in other words, African-American churches and denominations had to negotiate the dynamics of the community as it developed.

The most pressing challenge to black Christians was of course racism. In terms of black religious organization, however, this generalized racism is better understood specifically as white surveillance and control. Black congregations in the South, for example, were required by custom and sometimes by law to include a white observer, and many Southern black churches were led by a white pastor. One of the earliest black Baptist congregations, founded on the plantation of William Byrd III in 1758 at Lunenburg (now Mecklenburg), Virginia, was organized by two white preachers, Phillip Mulkey and William Murphy. The African Baptist Church in Lexington, Kentucky, on the other hand, was led by a black preacher, Peter Duerett, until the white town trustees assigned another black preacher, London Ferrill, to the pastorship. In this case white authority made itself known even in the transition from one black preacher to another—and as a result the followers of the displaced pastor, Duerett, split off and formed the Pleasant Green Baptist Church. As noted earlier, the development of independent churches and denominations in the North came as a result of white racist practices in the North's interracial churches, revealing at both the church and the denominational level that white authority was as insistent in the North as it was in Lexington, Kentucky.

Beyond the surveillance of individual churches and congregations, white religious and cultural figures regularly asserted their assumed authority over black moral and religious life. Such assertions could come in any number of forms—for example, in the denominational conference meetings that led to the transition from New York's black Zion church, led by a white pastor, to the formation of the African Methodist Episcopal Zion denomination. In that case the dispute had to do primarily with denominational claims over property owned by individual churches, but white authorities made other claims as well.

A striking example of this broader form of white surveillance is David Christy's 1863 book *Pulpit Politics; or, Ecclesiastical Legislation on Slavery, in its Disturbing Influences on the American Union.* Christy is best known for his 1855 book *Cotton Is King,* in which he presented slavery as a firmly entrenched problem which could not be limited to or blamed on the South. Southerners quickly applied his argument to the defense of slavery. Christy demonstrated that it was virtually impossible for Northerners with money not to be in some ways the beneficiaries of slavery. The economic system that depended heavily upon slavery, Christy noted, reached far beyond the South, and many in the North who attacked slavery still profited by it, if only indirectly. Ultimately Christy argued against anti-slavery efforts and promoted, in this and other publications, what he viewed as slavery's benefits: it brought blacks into Christian civilization while defining the moral mission for whites.

In *Pulpit Politics,* Christy attempted to make anti-slavery efforts the enemy not only of slaveholders or the national union but of Christianity itself. He promised to "place before the people all that is known on the subject of slavery, in its bearings on the moral progress of the African race. By this means it is believed that the public will be able to judge, with greater accuracy, how far the action of the Churches may have been in accordance, strictly, with the legitimate duties of the Gospel ministry; or how far it may have partaken of a fanatical character, calculated unnecessarily to disturb the peace of the Church, and endanger the safety of the Union."

Interestingly, Christy took Northern churches to task for driving so many black congregants out of the church, and he praised the development of black churches and denominations, specifically the AME and the AME Zion churches. Ultimately, though, Christy clearly opposed anti-slavery activity in the churches and supported the assertion of white authority over black moral life. "We find such evidences of religious progress among the colored people," he states, "as to afford ample reasons for believing that their moral elevation is practicable; but practicable, not by their neglect, as hitherto prevailing, but only by their careful training under the control of enlightened teachers who will subject them to proper moral restraints." Christy's message was but an amplified version of the operating assumption in many white communities about the threat of blackness, the need to assert white authority, and a condescending (even when favorable) view of independent black religious organizations.

For many African Americans, Christians like Christy seemed more the rule than the exception. The presumption of white moral superiority, joined with an agenda to control the black population, had led to a serious weakness in what some blacks referred to as "American Christianity." This perspective on the racial presence in American religion was ably represented in a fictional series, "Afric-American Picture Gallery," written by William J. Wilson, a popular author who wrote regularly for two of the most influential black newspapers of the time, *Frederick Douglass' Paper* and the *Weekly Anglo-African*. In this series, published serially in the *Anglo-African Magazine* in 1859, Wilson wrote under the pen name "Ethiop" and drew his readers to a pair of pictures—the first identified as the interior of "a negro church" in a plantation setting in the South. The second, Wilson explained, "entitled *After Preaching*, represents the congregation standing about outside the church in groups around the faithful leaders, who, being men carefully selected by the white piety of the sunny South, are of course, all of the Uncle Tom school." (Wilson here referred to the portrait of submissive black Christianity promoted in Harriet Beecher Stowe's influential novel *Uncle Tom's Cabin* as well as in the various stage versions that proliferated after the novel's publication.) "In the back-ground," Wilson added, "may also be seen a few young, determined-looking faces, on which are expressed disbelief in, and detestation of, the whole affair." "These faces," Wilson continued, "in contrast with the others of the congregation, give a most striking effect to the picture. They are the unruly, the skeptical, the worthless of the block—the wicked ones, who would rather run the risk than be bound up in the religious love so feelingly and so faithfully proclaimed to them—the religious love of the land."

Out of this skeptical class, we are told, "comes our Nat Turners" as well as "our Margaret Garners" and "our Douglasses"—that is, people associated with slave rebellion, individual resistance, and black activism. The portrait of piety and of religious contentment and peace gives way, through Ethiop's description, to a portrait that "may be studied with profit by any Southern Preacher, master or monster who will take the trouble to visit the Afric-American Picture Gallery."

Racial tensions were a presence even in seemingly progressive churches in the North, and perhaps one of the most striking testimonies in this regard is that of Samuel Ringgold Ward. Ward's parents guided their family through their escape from slavery in 1820, settling first in New Jersey and later in New York City. In New York, Ward attended the African Free School, then clerked in the law offices of prominent black abolitionists. He later taught school in New Jersey and New York, and in 1839 became a licensed preacher by the authority of the New York Congregational Association. His subsequent career as a minister included his service as pastor to an all-white congregation in South Butler, a village in Wayne County, New York.

Ward was not alone in being a black pastor to a white congregation. In 1785 Lemuel Haynes was ordained by the Association of Ministers in Litchfield County, Connecticut. Beginning in 1788 he served as minister to a white congregation in Rutland, Vermont, for more than thirty years. Still, such arrangements were unusual—and Ward credited his congregation for its Christian transcendence over the usual racial prejudice, noting that "the mere accident of the colour of the preacher was to them a matter of small consideration." But Ward understood the special challenges he faced in leading a church in which the "congregation were all white persons save my own family." "If I should acquit myself creditably as a preacher," Ward observed in his 1855 *Autobiography of A Fugitive Negro*, "the anti-slavery cause would thereby be encouraged. Should

I fail in this, that sacred cause would be loaded with reproach." Race, in other words, was an urgent presence even in churches where it otherwise seemed a negligible factor.

Ward had no illusions about the realities of American racial culture—or about the complicity of American Christianity in promoting and sustaining that culture. Indeed, for Ward, the condition of blacks throughout the United States, enslaved or nominally free, was fundamental to his understanding of the moral challenges faced by any black Christian. In his autobiography, while reflecting on his service to an all-white congregation, Ward noted the temptations presented by a deeply racist culture:

> Being deprived of the right of voting upon terms of equality with whites—being denied the ordinary courtesies of decent society, to say nothing of what is claimed for every man, especially every freeborn American citizen—I very well know, from a deep and painful experience, that the black people were goaded into a constant temptation to hate their white fellow-citizens. I know, too, how natural such hatred is in such circumstances: and all I know of the exhibition of vindictiveness and revenge by the whites against *their* injurers—and the most perfect justice of the Negro regarding the white man according to daily treatment received from him—caused me to see this temptation to be all the stronger: and convinced me also, that the white had no personal claim to anything else than the most cordial hatred of the black.

Ward did not see this treatment of black Americans as distinct from the practice of American Christianity. Indeed, he declared, "the oppression and the maltreatment of the hapless descendant of Africa is not merely an ugly excrescence upon American *religion*" but rather "a cardinal principle, a *sin qoa non*, a cherished defended keystone, a corner-stone, of American faith." So definitive was this maxim that Ward believed that in talking about American Christianity the word "*religion* . . . should be substituted for Christianity; for while a religion may be from man, and a religion from such an origin may be capable of *hating*, Christianity is always from God, and, like him, is love."

A devastating presence in American religion, race influenced in turn any understanding of what should follow from one's religion—the expression of Christian charity and fellow concern. Ward once observed that "Those who have done us injury think it a virtue to express sympathy with us—a sort of arms'-length, cold-blooded sympathy; while neither of those would, on any account, consent to do towards us the commonest justice. What the Negro needs is, what belongs to him—what has been ruthlessly torn from him—and what is, by consent of a despotic democracy and a Christless religion, withholden from him, guiltily, perseveringly. When he shall have that restored, he can acquire *pity* enough, and all the sympathy he needs, cheap wares as they are; but to ask for them instead of his rights was never my calling." How could one talk seriously of the power of Christian faith when that power was insufficient even to inspire active efforts to secure the rights of African Americans, of fellow Christians? More to the point, how could one follow David Christy and talk of the need for the "moral elevation" of African Americans when the bar of moral standards had been set so low? Ward, for one, would not degrade himself "by arguing the equality of the Negro with the white," particularly given his belief that "to say the Negro is equal morally to the white man, is to say but very little."

Ward's concerns covered the whole of American culture, but the core of his attention naturally involved the system of slavery, easily the most influential presence in American religion during the first half of the nineteenth century. Many churches grappled with slavery, sometimes with admirable if deeply mixed results. The minister and several congregants at the Black Creek Baptist Church in Virginia, for example, manumitted their slaves, and in a November 1786 meeting they ruled that slavery was "unrighteous." This is not an isolated example, but even in such cases church members looked only so far to follow the implications of their decisions, rarely carrying their righteous zeal to other churches or even enforcing it in their own. It was rarer still that such views on slavery led to corresponding views on racial equality.

As anti-slavery organizations like the American Anti-Slavery Society, led by William Lloyd Garrison, denounced Christians and churches associated with the system of slavery, and as growing numbers of blacks participated in Christian churches, the philosophical, political, and doctrinal tensions within many churches and denominations developed into deep divisions. Representative of the views of many white Christians was David Christy's charge that "the agitation in favor of emancipation has been uncalled for, and not necessary to the discharge of any Christian duty toward the colored people; and . . . Christian ministers, therefore, have been inexcusable in agitating the subject of slavery, so as to distract and divide the Churches, and lead to the ruin of the country." Such perspectives helped lead to splits among various religious denominations—the Presbyterians in 1837, the Methodists in 1844, and the Baptists in 1845. Disagreements over the morality of slavery, and over the role of churches in addressing such questions, mapped out what would become a markedly different religious landscape in the United States, one in which entire churches and denominations were defined in part by their views on or participation in the enslavement of a population that included a great many Christians.

Christy believed that abolitionist ministers and other anti-slavery Christians were disrupting the order of American Christianity, and others clearly agreed—long before Christy's book was published. Heated debates over the scriptural grounds for slavery were common in the nineteenth century and appeared in such books as George Bourne's *A Condensed Anti-Slavery Bible Argument; By a Citizen of Virginia*, published in 1845, and Thornton Stringfellow's *Scriptural and Statistical Views in Favor of Slavery*, published in 1856. African-American writers contributed to the debates as well, and often in forceful ways. Daniel Coker's *A Dialogue Between a Virginian and an African Minister*, published in 1810, presented a fictional dialogue about slavery between a black minister and a white Virginian. The Virginian referred to his own minister's justification of slavery, and the black minister challenged that understanding of the Bible. Finally the Virginian conceded not only that slavery was wrong but also that he had been misled about the Bible. In his 1829 *Appeal*, David Walker was more direct: "Can any thing be a greater mockery of religion than the way in which it is conducted by Americans? It appears as though they are bent only on daring God Almighty to do his best—they chain and handcuff us and our children and drive us around the country like brutes, and go into the house of the God of justice to return him thanks for having aided them in their infernal cruelties inflicted upon us." Debates over the biblical grounds of slavery were voluminous, and they continued to be published and played out in sermons, essays, pamphlets, and books, from Samuel Sewall's *The Selling of Joseph: A Memorial* (1700) to Christy's *Pulpit Politics* in 1862, and beyond.

As African Americans organized, they naturally took aim at both the system of slavery and "American Christianity." Particularly revealing in this regard is the statement that emerged from the 1843 National

Convention of Colored Citizens, held in Buffalo, New York, where those in attendance debated and voted on four resolutions concerning American churches. Beginning with an affirmation of the delegates' belief "in the true Church of Christ," which "will stand while time endures," the first resolution declared that any true church "will evince its spirit by its opposition to all sins, and especially to the sin of slavery, which is a compound of all others." "The great mass of American sects, falsely called churches," this resolution continued, "which apologize for slavery and prejudice, or practice slaveholding, are in truth no churches, but Synagogues of Satan." The second of the resolutions emphasized this last point, identifying "slaveholding and prejudice sustaining ministers and churches (falsely so called)" as "the greatest enemies to Christ and to civil and religious liberty in the world." The resolutions that followed called upon "the colored people in the free States" to resist these churches, which would make them "guilty of enslaving themselves and others."

Such views were echoed in slave narratives, perhaps the most powerful publications in the anti-slavery cause. The corruption of religion was often their primary subject. In the appendix to the *Narrative of the Life of Frederick Douglass, an American Slave* (1845), Douglass returned to his potentially disturbing commentary on religion throughout the narrative proper. "I find," he observed, "since reading over the foregoing Narrative that I have, in several instances, spoken in such a tone and manner, respecting religion, as may possibly lead those unacquainted with my religious views to suppose me an opponent of all religion." To correct possible misunderstandings, Douglass wrote, "What I have said respecting and against religion, I mean strictly to apply to the *slaveholding religion* of this land, and with no possible reference to Christianity proper; for, between the Christianity of this land, and the Christianity of Christ, I recognize the widest possible difference—so wide, that to receive the one as good, pure, and holy, is of necessity to reject the other as bad, corrupt, and wicked." Douglass clarified his position further by emphasizing that he was referring not only to the practice of Christianity in the South but to "the Christianity of America," "north and south."

Douglass's observations would be echoed in many other narratives over time. Henry Bibb, for example, in *The Life and Adventures of Henry Bibb, An American Slave* (1850), confessed, "I find in several places where I have spoken out the deep feelings of my soul, in trying to describe the horrid treatment which I have so often received at the hands of slaveholding professors of religion, that I might possibly make a wrong impression on the minds of some northern freemen, who are unacquainted theoretically or practically with the customs and treatment of American slaveholders to their slaves." Bibb then presented a detailed defense of his presentation of slavery, focusing on the slaveholders' professions of Christian belief. Finally he asked, "Is this Christianity? Is it honest or right? Is it doing as we would be done by? Is it in accordance with the principles of humanity or justice?" Answering his own questions, Bibb wrote, "I believe slaveholding to be a sin against God and man under all circumstances."

Similarly Henry "Box" Brown noted at the end of his 1851 *Narrative of the Life of Henry Box Brown*, "I have no apology whatever to make for what I have said, in regard to the pretended christianity under which I was trained, while a slave." Like Bibb, Brown presented a brief justification of his criticism of "pretended christianity," noting finally, "I pray that God may give them light to see the error of their ways, and if they know that they are doing wrongly, that he may give them grace to renovate their hearts!" Following this statement with a listing of laws regulating slavery, Brown indicated just how much was being done wrongly, and how much must be involved in the attempt "to renovate their hearts."

Such views naturally highlighted the importance of African-American churches and denominations—formed because of the failures of American Christianity, and therefore institutions from which one might expect a more thoughtful approach to racial justice and Christian determination. To some extent this is what these churches provided, but there were important disputes even in black churches and denominations. Consider again Frederick Douglass's experience with churches in New Bedford after his escape from slavery. As noted, he left the first church he attended when he found that black congregants were not allowed to take communion with white congregants. He then turned to New Bedford's African Methodist Episcopal Zion Church, by 1839 earning a license to work as a local preacher. Many years later he reflected on this time of his life, noting in 1894, "My connection with the little church continued long after I was in the antislavery field. I look back to the days I spent in little Zion, New Bedford, in the several capacities of sexton, steward, class leader, clerk, and local preacher, as among the happiest days of my life."

But Douglass did not stay with this church, either. When he first sought out a church community in New Bedford, as he observed in *My Bondage and My Freedom*, he had not fully appreciated the oppressive power of the church—that is to say, those institutions through which Christianity was observed in the United States were also invested in the social, economic, and political order of the nation. "I was not then aware," he writes, "of the powerful influence of that religious body in favor of the enslavement of my race, nor did I see how the northern churches could be responsible for the conduct of southern churches; neither did I fully understand how it could be my duty to remain separate from the church, because bad men were connected with it." Soon Douglass was forced to recognize that he could not find refuge from the corruptions of slavery even in the AMEZ church, forcing him to the same conclusion about his religious responsibilities, though in softer tones: "I could not see it to be my duty to remain with that body, when I found that it consented to the same spirit which held my brethren in chains."

Douglass's complaints against the church have to do with the pressures of creating a nationwide denominational presence, a religious institution rather than simply a congregation joined by a common faith. Although the AME and the AMEZ denominations were centers of a great deal of anti-slavery activity (to this day the AMEZ church identifies itself as the "Freedom Church"), Douglass's struggles are nonetheless revealing. At the 1856 AME general convention, a proposed regulation barring slave-holders from membership was defeated, in part out of concern that such a regulation would hamper Southern missionary efforts. After the Civil War, Douglass found himself in a dispute with the church when he expressed his appreciation for the efforts of those who had led the movement that, he asserted, led to the abolition of slavery.

Douglass's fellow journalist and race leader Martin Delany shared his colleague's skepticism about the efficacy of even African-American approaches to religion. Delany well understood that many blacks received religious guidance through a highly faulty white lens. "In religion," he once wrote, "because they are both *translators* and *commentators*, we must believe nothing, however absurd, but what our oppressors tell us." Accordingly he argued for a motivated black approach to religion. "You must make your religion subserve your interests," he advised his black readers, "as your oppressors do theirs! ... They use the Scriptures to make you submit, by preaching to you the texts of 'obedience to your masters' and 'standing still to see the salvation,' and we must now begin to understand the Bible so as to make it of interest to us." But Delany worried that such advice would fall on deaf ears, for though he clearly seemed proud when he observed that "the colored races are highly susceptible of religion," he also lamented that "they carry it too far." It led them to rely upon unfounded hope, and "consequently, they usually stand still."

Some divisions in African-American churches resulted from the tensions inevitable in communities devoted to uplift, anti-racist reform, and institutional development. As the AME church developed, for example, divisions arose between church leaders and the laity, or between educated and uneducated members. Richard Allen believed that African Americans were naturally drawn to Methodism for its "plain and simple gospel," an attraction that in some parts of the community became an anti-intellectual mode of faith and worship. Commenting on such developments, Frances E. W. Harper, in her novel *Iola Leroy* (1892), had two African-American characters talk of religion, one an educated man and one a folk preacher. When the first, Robert Johnson, suggests that the preacher, known as Uncle Daniel, should study theology, Daniel responds, "I'se been a preachin' dese thirty years, an' you come yere a tellin' me 'bout studying yore ologies. I larn'd my 'ology at de foot ob de cross. You bin dar?" Harper, one of the most accomplished and dedicated black reformers of the nineteenth century, here captured what had been an ongoing quarrel within—but not limited to—the AME church.

These disputes had an audience: a white community all too ready to replicate early white surveillance in Southern churches by commenting on the so-called spectacle of black religion. Consider, for example, John Jasper, probably the most famous black preacher of the nineteenth century. Jasper was born a slave in 1812 in Fluvana County, Virginia. He became a legendary Baptist preacher in his region and eventually a national celebrity for the fiery sermons he delivered in his Richmond church. Jasper was known for speaking his preachings in what then was associated with plantation dialect. His most famous sermon, often reprinted in dialect form, was "The Sun Do Move," in which he argued that the Bible establishes that the sun is not stationary but rather revolves around the earth. Jasper delivered this sermon more than 250 times, including once before the Virginia General Assembly, which recessed for the occasion. Jasper's sermons were often attended by white congregants as well as black, though reportedly many went to see him purely for entertainment. Even one of his closest white associates, the clergyman William Eldridge Hatcher, first attended one of Jasper's sermons out of curiosity, accompanied by a friend with "a strong leaning towards ridicule." Hatcher's description of that sermon is revealing:

> Shades of our Anglo-Saxon fathers! Did mortal lips ever gush with such torrents of horrible English! Hardly a word came out clothed in its right mind. And gestures! He circled around the pulpit with his ankle in his hand; and laughed and sang and shouted and acted about a dozen characters within the space of three minutes. Meanwhile, in spite of these things, he was pouring out a gospel sermon, red hot, full of love, full of invective, full of tenderness, full of bitterness, full of tears, full of every passion that ever flamed in the human breast. He was a theatre within himself, with the stage crowded with actors. He was a battle-field;--himself the general, the staff, the officers, the common soldiery, the thundering artillery and the rattling musketry. He was the preacher; likewise the church and the choir and the deacons and the congregation.

While one might encounter any number of white evangelical preachers at the time who might also fit this description, black preachers were inevitably seen through the lens of a dominant culture given to parody and caricature. Blackface minstrel shows, the most popular and influential entertainment form of the nineteenth century, regularly included "black" characters who would speak in an affected manner, betraying their ignorance by stumbling over large words and legal or philosophical concepts. While many white Americans may have been moved to new religious depths by Jasper's sermons, many others clearly saw them as the church equivalent of a minstrel show.

The great majority of those involved in African-American churches were satisfied to let white misunderstandings stand. Many more found deep spiritual and cultural roots in the simple gospel of Afro-Christian modes of worship. Yet some in the churches, particularly among their leadership, found the "foot of the cross" spontaneity of folk preaching to be at odds with the church's educational and theological mission as congregations grew. Daniel Payne, for example, began his religious training at the Lutheran Theological Seminary in Gettysburg, Pennsylvania.

Licensed to preach in 1837 and ordained in 1839, he first affiliated with the Franckean Evangelical Lutheran Synod. He encountered the AME church in 1840 when he started a school for African Americans. Soon he joined AME, in part because of the restricted authority allowed black pastors in the Lutheran church. Payne became an AME bishop in 1850, but even before that he sometimes found himself at odds with others in the church, in part because he believed in a formal service led by educated ministers. Although the General Conference accepted his recommendations for a standardized course of study for AME ministers in 1844, Payne often met with resistance in his efforts to promote formal study and worship practices. Interestingly, among those who praised his efforts was David Christy in *Pulpit Politics*. Exploring a particular battle in which Payne was involved, about the governance of the church, Christy drew a revealing conclusion. "The applicability of the Bishop's argument to the abolition interpretation of the Constitution of the United States," Christy claimed, "will be at once apparent. Had his strong common sense, as applied to a question respecting constitutional church polity, been exercised in relation to the National Constitution, we should never have had the troubles that are now upon us." If Jasper's sermons could be viewed as minstrel entertainment, in short, so too could Payne's promotion of education and organizational discipline be recast as an argument against the abolition of slavery and for a white supremacist interpretation of the gospel mission of American Christianity.

Beyond such class divisions—both observed and manipulated by white spectators—were even more fundamental divisions about gender. Of course gender divisions were fundamental throughout American culture, but it was some time before male church leaders connected the restrictions they encountered in white-led churches to the experience of women in their own churches. One of the best-known instances of a black woman who felt called to preach is that of Jarena Lee, who in 1809 met with Richard Allen "to tell him that I felt it my duty to preach the gospel." Allen responded that the church's *Discipline*—the guiding book of church policy and regulations—did not allow for women to be preachers. Some time later, however, when Lee stood up during a service to speak after a male preacher seemed unable to continue his sermon, Allen expressed his belief that she had been "called to that work, as any of the preachers present." Still, women would receive official sanction to serve as licensed preachers or ordained deacons in either the AME or the Colored Methodist church only in the late nineteenth century, and they would receive full authority as ordained ministers and deacons only in the mid-twentieth century. The AMEZ church allowed for the ordination of women at the end of the nineteenth century, when the way was led by two women, Julia A. J. Foote, who was ordained as a deacon in 1894 and an itinerant elder in 1900, and Mary J. Small, who was ordained as a deacon in 1895 and an elder in 1898. Before the Civil War, women asserted their authority in the church through such gender-specific organizations as the Daughters of Noah of Bethel Church, founded in Philadelphia in 1822. Thus among the results of African-American organization, in the church as elsewhere, were additional groups that responded to the opportunities created by the developing community.

❖❖

Embracing high and low worship styles and various denominations and independent churches; covering a number of states, regions, and cities; pressed from without by a racist culture and defined from within by a range of responses to that culture; and containing a number of internal conflicts over everything from education to class to the role of women in church leadership, what is commonly called the "Black Church" was hardly a singular enterprise. But the racial oppression that gave occasion, form, and purpose to the organization of black churches still justifies that label. Just as we can say that the African-American "community" of the nineteenth century was characterized by great regional, socioeconomic, and ideological diversity, so it makes some sense to think about how the diversity of black religious beliefs and institutions formed the foundation of an equally diverse African-American religious tradition. With such generalizations, though, comes the danger of falling into overly neat assumptions about African-American communities, beliefs, and history. What connected blacks in the nineteenth century was a culture that insisted on grouping all people of African heritage together—and that insistence was a defining characteristic and even a common bond among a great many otherwise different individuals and communities. While the identities of individual churches and religious institutions were distinct, African-American churches were largely alike in facing the challenges presented by a nation that relied on a system of slavery and an ideology of white supremacy, which made itself felt in the racist practices that shaped black lives in virtually every area of cultural and social life. Meeting those challenges defined the mission of most African-American churches.

How could Christianity be used to justify the system of slavery, including the many abuses committed by those who claimed absolute power over others—abuses that ranged from physical violence and torture to the separation of families and the sexual violation of women? Many pro-slavery advocates used biblical arguments to defend the "peculiar institution," but they were less persuasive in accounting for the actual treatment of slaves. Many opponents of slavery used equally strong biblical arguments, especially in denouncing the abuses it encouraged and protected. For many African Americans, both lines of argument were woefully inadequate, for they failed to address the oppression of blacks in the so-called free states.

At base, black churches were attempts to provide a venue for addressing this larger challenge. Many blacks viewed the problem in theological as well as political terms, addressing the oppression not only of African Americans but of Christianity itself. In a late-eighteenth-century poem that celebrated her enthusiastic acceptance of the religion she gained through enslavement, Phillis Wheatley addressed prejudice among white Christians: "Some view our sable race with scornful eye, / 'Their color is a diabolic die.'" But she drew from her newfound faith a chastening warning to her white Christian readers: "Remember, *Christians*, *Negroes*, black as *Cain*, / May be refin'd, and join th' angelic train." A few decades later David Walker was more direct about the implications of this perspective in his *Appeal*. "It is my solemn belief," he wrote, "that if ever the world becomes Christianized, (which must certainly take place before long) it will be through the means, under God of the *Blacks*, who are now held in wretchedness, and degradation, by the white *Christians* of the world."

As Wheatley's and Walker's comments suggest, many African Americans considered their role in the Christian church to be a special mission. Indeed, if many black Christians of the early nineteenth century were asked the question frequently raised about their beliefs—"How can you adopt the religion of your oppressors?"—one can imagine that many would echo Walker and respond, "We didn't. We became Christians instead." One of the most influential black clergy of the time, the

Presbyterian pastor J. W. C. Pennington, once argued, "The past history of the descendants of Africa is now appealing to her sons and daughters in the four quarters of the globe, to be up and doing for God, for Christ, for the race, for pure religion, for humanity, for civilization, and for righteousness and truth." In an essay entitled "The Great Conflict Requires Great Faith," published in the *Anglo-African Magazine* in 1859, Pennington expanded on these views. "Influences," he wrote, "are constantly bearing upon us strongly calculated to affect us unfavorably towards the institutions of religion. Those institutions, professedly for the benefit of all classes of the family of man, are perverted to the vile uses of oppression." This institutional crisis, Pennington suggested, was also a theological crisis, for "the Bible, the Holy Book of the Great God, is misinterpreted by the ministers; and the church freely opens her bosom to the oppressor, but at the same time closes it against the oppressed; and outlaws God's poor from the shelter which His own hand has built for them in the earth." This perversion of Christianity constituted the major challenge of an Afro-Christian approach to faith and practice. "We are called upon," Pennington wrote, "to discriminate between the professions and practices of men, and that piety towards God, which is solemnly binding upon all men as subjects of His moral government." Or as Daniel Payne put it in 1839, "American Slavery brutalizes man—destroys his moral agency, and subverts the moral government of God."

In linking institutional life with questions of biblical interpretation, and then placing both within the context of governance, both human and divine, Pennington captured what is sometimes taken to be the theological core of nineteenth-century African-American Christianity, the foundation of what has since become known as liberation theology. In effect, liberation theology calls for attention to social order and disorder in determining the proper reading and application of the Bible. God is identified with the condition of the oppressed and specifically with the historical experience of oppression and the struggle for liberation.

Liberation theology, which has many forms, was formally defined by African-American and Latin American theologians in the 1970s. Over time black theology and various modes of liberation theology have developed in relation to one another, formed coalitions, and produced a significant and increasingly influential approach to religious practice and social change. In the nineteenth century, early versions of this approach were defined by slavery and by exclusion and the repression of rights and opportunity in the North and other so-called free states and regions. As Pennington put it, "God has not forgotten how to use His right hand for the deliverance of the poor and oppressed."

M. H. Freeman, principal of Avery College in Allegheny City, Pennsylvania, captured well the theoretical promise of this approach to belief and education in an essay published in the same year and in the same magazine that published Pennington's views. "Teach your child to look upon slavery and prejudice, in the light of reason and revolution, and you at once strip this boasted land and its landed institutions of its grandeur and its glory, and reveal at a glance its true character. Its flaunted freedom and equality, a stupid failure—its high sounding republicanism, a pitiful oligarchy of men-stealers and women-whippers, its religion a shameless inconsistency, and an arrant hypocrisy, lifting its hand red with a brother's blood to Heaven, and mouthing its impious prayers in the face of the great Jehovah, while it tramples on God's image, and traffics in the souls of men."

From their beginnings, then, the great majority of African-American churches and denominations were devoted not only to religious reform but to broad-scale social change. "It is not assuming too much to say," Pennington argued, "that the issues involved in our cause are by far the greatest that now occupy the attention of God or man. They are issues that must be met, or God is dishonored and man is disgraced; they are issues that involve the integrity of God's moral government, and man's best happiness." By attending to what they understood as God's moral government, black clergy found the grounds for attending to the world being created by a culture of racial inequality. Pennington asked, "Shall the glory of one race of men stand reared upon the shame of another? Shall the monuments, towers and palaces of one race stand upon the bones and muscles of another, and these boasted volumes of political economy, literature and theology too, stand written in the life's blood of the weak?" These questions concerned not merely past trials but the understanding being prepared for future generations. In the world the very monuments of past achievements might encourage or even perpetuate deep injustice.

The church's mission, accordingly, was to provide a haven for the development of an alternative culture, one that would provide generations of children with more productive ways of viewing their world, and thus more productive ways of viewing their own possibilities in the world. As the Congregational minister Amos Gerry Beman observed in 1859, "Around us we see thousands being thus fitted every year for the stations which they are to occupy in society. We can look over the history of this country, and see the immense power of the pulpit, the influence which it exerts in the education of the people—not in religion only, but in all that makes the people what they are. It is filled with teachers educated for their positions, able to be instructors and guides; but thousands, nay, millions of the colored race are without proper instruction." African-American churches, for all their diversity, were devoted to addressing this important void. They would prepare better stations for blacks to occupy, and would prepare blacks to occupy them.

Certainly one sign of the success of black churches in this regard is the fact that their achievements—the institutions they created, fostered, or otherwise supported—comprise a central presence in so many areas of African-American life. It is impossible to talk of early efforts in education, literary culture, political organization, mutual benefit associations, or the press without talking of black churches and denominations. Many of the most important educational institutions, publishing forums, and social networks of the nineteenth century were grounded in African-American churches. As an example: St. Louis's first all-black church, the First African Baptist Church, founded in 1822, became home to a Sabbath school, a temperance society, and a school. Typically, black churches throughout the nation served as centers of stability, an organizing network of community, enabling the development of a great many other institutions and initiatives. Some churches also became centers of democratic activity, allowing members who were denied voting privileges in the larger society to vote on a broad range of concerns, to elect leaders, to exercise control over an institution they could claim as their own. And while Frederick Douglass and others found cause to criticize the official stance of some churches toward the anti-slavery movement, the congregations of many black churches were centrally involved in efforts to aid fugitive slaves in their attempts to escape to freedom.

Indeed, one sign of the success of African-American churches is the extent to which they were attacked by white mobs or repressed by white authorities. In 1825 white youths threw cayenne pepper and salt into the wood-burning stove of Richard Allen's church in Philadelphia, and as choking parishioners tried to make their way out of the church, two were trampled to death and several others were injured in the confusion. In the decade that followed, many other black churches became targets of racist attacks, for the success of black churches made them symbols as well as centers of African-American achievement, collective independence, and self-determination. Churches were attacked in the New York City anti-abolitionist riots of 1834, and in 1842 in Philadelphia the Second African American Presbyterian Church was looted and burned. Such violence was a regular presence in African-American life during this period. The black response addressed both the source and effects of racism, both the institutionalization of white supremacist ideology in education, law, economics, and governance, and the many individuals damaged or restricted by those institutions, the many in need of a stable and self-determining community. This too would become part of the church's mission, especially through other organizations that churches helped establish.

4

"The United Wisdom of the World"

ALTHOUGH THE EARLY DEVELOPMENT of black fraternal organizations is one of the most important stories in African-American history, it is also among the most contested. It is nearly impossible to tell the story in simple or absolute terms. Of course, African-American history is plagued by the politics of historical recording—an archive of documents that more often than not reflect the views and priorities of the dominant culture. Too often the record reveals a general disregard of those cultural centers most closely connected with black collective endeavors. Historical scholarship, in turn, reveals a general neglect by mainstream historians of the black experience as a central part of American history. Part of the problem has been that much of African-American history—most notably the experience of slavery—has been recorded in ways that make it difficult to recover the perspectives, and therefore the authority, of African Americans themselves.

Records of the system of slavery were kept by the slaveowners, and many years passed before historians learned to use sources that described black experience from their own perspective. Part of the problem, too, has been that documents pertaining to many centers of African-American activity—including most of the organizations and associations explored in this book—have been segregated from the mainstream historical record. They have been recovered and maintained primarily by individuals such as Robert Mara Adger of Philadelphia or Arthur Alfonso Schomburg of New York, among others—collectors of books, pamphlets, images, and other documents. While early-nineteenth-century blacks left behind them a rich historical record, the great majority of scholars (with important exceptions) didn't attend to it until roughly the mid-twentieth century.

Recovering the history of African-American fraternal organizations involves many of these problems and more, though in many ways this story parallels the development of the African Methodist Episcopal church. That is, fraternal organizations acquired their own history over time, in response to community needs, along with an identity unique to that history. Black Freemasons, for example, and other fraternal organizations shared some qualities but also made their own way. As with the AME church, black Americans sought membership in larger fraternal bodies—and when that proved to be an obstructed path, they sought official sanction to organize their own groups as part of the larger entities. Over time the black or Prince Hall Freemasons became an organization unto themselves, with their own history and their own institutional characteristics, while still sharing a family resemblance and institutional ties to other asonic bodies. And, like the AME church, the black Freemasons became an important center for historical records and for African-American historical agency.

Although mainstream fraternal organizations were devoted to concepts of universal brotherhood, they were also private organizations, selective in their membership and jealous of their authority over their own history. Almost from the beginning, the legitimacy of black fraternal organizations—their claim to an association with the Euro-American fraternal orders—was challenged. This was especially the case for black Freemasons. In the first half of the nineteenth century, African Americans attempted to establish their claims to institutional legitimacy through various means, including a forceful argument presented by Martin Delany in his pamphlet *The Origins and Objects of Ancient Freemasonry; its Introduction into the United States, and Legitimacy Among Colored Men*, published in Pittsburgh in 1853. The disputes have remained largely unresolved. The early twentieth century saw legal battles over the authority of black fraternal organizations to claim the name of and association with broader fraternal orders, and the arguments over the legitimacy of the Prince Hall Freemasons have continued almost to the present. Henry Wilson Coil and John MacDuffie Sherman, representatives of mainstream Freemasonry, claimed to settle the matter when in 1982 they published *A Documentary Account of Prince Hall and Other Black Fraternal Orders*, in which they dismissed, through careful readings of documentary evidence and fraternal jurisprudence, most of the arguments made in favor of the claims of Prince Hall. In 2003, however, the Prince Hall Mason David L. Gray offered an equally compelling reading of the evidence—including a section outlining facts and myths central to these disputes—in *Inside Prince Hall*. In many other publications through the years, the same documents and historical events are identified, reprinted, and examined.

From their beginnings, African-American fraternal organizations provided forums for community dialogue, political organization, economic development, social activism, and collective self-definition. Before the Civil War many black leaders, including a great many men central to the development of black churches, found their platform and experienced their initiation into leadership positions through black fraternal organizations. Like black churches, fraternal organizations spread across the country, providing not only local forums but institutional ties, a means for communicating common interests, developing a common ideology, and nurturing institutional ties capable of drawing together an otherwise scattered people—a "community" otherwise dispersed over a broad geographical and sociopolitical range. But as these were *fraternal* organizations, these connections, like those provided by most churches, also encouraged a patriarchal framework for an understanding of this developing community. Moreover, as with churches, the movement toward fraternal organizations—aided by the racism that excluded African Americans from most mainstream orders and by the questions of legitimacy that undermined the authority of black fraternities—encouraged the proliferation of invented fraternal orders and a fragmentation of the community that was theoretically devoted to "universal brotherhood." The story of African-American participation in fraternal organizations is thus one of documentary confusion, racial disputes, and complex tensions.

❖

To some extent the history of black fraternal organizations overlaps with that of mutual benefit societies and other associations, but the fraternal organizations are nonetheless quite distinct. Other black organizations involved exclusive, often all-male membership, sometimes leading to sister associations for women. And other black organizations were either associated with or modeled after white organizations, sharing similar philosophical ideals—in some cases, similarities that led to interracial cooperation, and, in others, likenesses that promoted a common ideal of society and justice, as long as one didn't look too closely at the fine print. Yet fraternal orders were distinctive in that they were private organizations veiled in mystery and devoted to a potentially global brotherhood. In many cases they also promoted religious tolerance, often calling for belief in a nonsectarian concept of a single diety. And they offered members access to significant cultural power since the membership often included some of the most influential men in government, economics, and religion. In the United States, for example, prominent members of the Masons included George Washington, Benjamin Franklin, John Hancock, and Paul Revere. Given such ideals, access, and influential members, black Americans were naturally interested in joining the ranks of fraternal organizations. Here, one might think, was an organization that, despite its exclusivity in practice, was philosophically opposed to all the distinctions—ancestry, race, religion—that defined and obstructed African-American life at every turn.

The story of black fraternal organizations begins during the Revolutionary War, with its idealistic attitudes toward liberty. At the center of the narrative is Prince Hall, the details of whose life are often contested. Many of Hall's biographers have identified him as originating from Barbados, the son of a white father and a mixed-race mother. He immigrated to Boston sometime before 1760 and became a preacher in a Cambridge, Massachusetts, church. Probably the truth is that Hall was born into slavery and received his manumission from William and Susannah Hall. William was a leather dresser, a trade that Hall himself adopted in freedom, and by 1800 Hall was a property owner, evidently with financial comfort and a security somewhat rare among African Americans of the time.

In 1775 Hall and fourteen other men requested and were granted (for a fee) admission into an Irish regimental Freemason lodge. This association with British Freemasons marks the beginning of what would become known first as African Lodge No. 459, then later African Lodge No. 1, and then, later still, the Prince Hall Grand Lodge of Free and Accepted Masons. In 1797 Hall granted a request from African Americans in both Philadelphia and Providence, Rhode Island, for warrants to establish associated lodges, and thus began the spread of black Freemasonry in the United States.

What makes this story complicated is also what makes fraternal orders such a distinctive part of international, American, and African-American history—they both promote and protect their veil of mystery and secrecy, and are therefore governed by guarded rituals and elaborate restrictions on membership and affiliation. To establish a lodge, a group ordinarily needed a warrant from a governing body, and one of the central questions about Prince Hall Masonry is its legitimacy. Hall established the African Lodge after the Irish regiment moved on, though establishing a lodge without a warrant was not unusual in such circumstances since it enabled Masons to continue meeting. Hall later claimed he had been given a permit from the Provincial Grand Master of Massachusetts to "walk on St John's Day and Bury our dead in the form which we now enjoy." Some scholars within the Masonic order have since debated whether a *permit* may be considered equivalent to the *dispensation* needed for the group to act as a lodge. But Hall recognized the importance of an official warrant, and in 1784 he wrote to a member of the Lodge of Brotherly Love in London, requesting a warrant for the African Lodge. It was granted that year by the Grand Lodge of England, thus establishing African Lodge No. 459 as a legitimate part of the Masonic brotherhood. The warrant, however, did not reach Hall until some years later, and the African Grand Lodge was finally established in 1791. But did the British lodge have this authority over U.S. lodges in the wake of the American Revolution? And did this authority extend to the subsequent development of the black Masonic organization as new lodges were established under Prince Hall's authority?

Despite the ideals of brotherhood so central to fraternal organizations, there is little question that U.S. groups have been marked by racism and that black associations developed in large part due to racist exclusions. In the early twentieth century the tensions between black and white fraternal orders erupted into a series of lawsuits over the right to claim affiliations. In the infancy of black fraternal orders, tensions were more fundamental. Some defenders of the white orders, for example, have noted that black Americans were excluded from white fraternal organizations because of a Masonic "charge" of 1723 which specified that "persons admitted members of a Lodge must be good and true men, *Free-born*, and of mature and discreet age." By such appeals to the governing laws of the organizations, joined with the belief that such laws were distinct from any question of racism in the era of slavery, some white Masonic authorities explained the exclusions that led to the formation of Prince Hall Masonry. In that challenging environment, an influential African-American organization developed.

Hall sanctioned the formation of lodges in Philadelphia and Providence in 1797, but he did so without having received authority from Grand Lodge of England to act as a provincial grand master. Indeed, the relationship between the African Lodge and the British Grand Lodge itself shifted over the years. In 1808 delegates from lodges in Boston, Philadelphia, and Providence decided that their organization would be known as Prince Hall Masons, and by 1815 three grand lodges representing this organization had been established. Meanwhile the Grand Lodge of England purged its rolls in 1813, striking virtually all American grand lodges and thus further complicating the question of black Mason legitimacy. Finally in 1827 the Prince Hall Masons declared their independence in a statement published in the *Boston Advertiser*, announcing that they were "free and independent of any lodge but that of our own."

With independence came new divisions. After some lodges in Pennsylvania withdrew from the African Grand Lodge to establish the Hiram Grand Lodge of Pennsylvania, John T. Hilton, former grand master of Prince Hall Masonry, called a convention in 1847 to form a National Grand Lodge to restore unity among black Freemasons. This organization, the National Grand Lodge of Free and Accepted Ancient York Rite Masons, offered only temporary respite, followed by years of newly organized divisions. Some of the grand lodges involved in the formation of this national organization withdrew their support soon after and reformed under other names. Black Freemasons attempted to achieve official recognition from the United Grand Lodge of England, presenting appeals in the late 1840s that such recognition was "a matter of life or death with us." In 1871, addressing such appeals, the English grand secretary explained the Grand Lodge's position to another British Mason, noting that "We have had many applications from 'Colored Grand Lodges' in America for recognition and exchange of Representatives. As, however, it is a rule of our Grand Lodge never to ecognize more than

One Grand Lodge in the same Country (Berlin excepted) and as we are on terms of amity with the Grand Lodges of almost all the States, it is manifestly impossible, setting aside every other consideration, that we could recognize the Colored Grand Lodges."

By such legal reasoning the racial prejudice at the center of this history was quietly placed in the background, and the legitimacy of Prince Hall and other black Freemasons would continue to be contested—established by some Masonic historians and denied by others, and variously recognized and revoked by grand lodges in the United States. Both in spite of and because of such pressures, black Freemasonry developed broadly. By 1825, for example, black Masons in Washington, D.C., had established Lodge #7, and in 1848 three district lodges formed a grand lodge. By the time that grand lodge was formed, Prince Hall Masonic lodges were established in most of the Northern states and had extended overseas into Liberia.

The story of the other major black fraternal society before the Civil War, the Grand United Order of Odd Fellows, is easier to relate. At the center of this narrative is Peter Ogden, a black man who served as a steward on the ship *Patrick Henry*, and a literary club, the Philomathean Institute of New York City, which included the influential printmakers Patrick H. Reason and James Fields. The members of the Philomathean petitioned to become a lodge of the Odd Fellows, but they were refused—so they turned to Ogden, whose travels had taken him to Liverpool, England, where he had joined the Grand United Order of the Odd Fellows. Odgen took the group's request to England and on March 1, 1843, obtained a charter. Fields became the first grand master of the lodge, and Ogden was honored as past grand master. Reason, who was also an influential Mason, served as grand master and permanent secretary of the black Odd Fellows in the 1850s.

Although the black Odd Fellows have not had the same struggle as the Prince Hall Freemasons in establishing their origins or legitimacy, they too have faced significant challenges over the years, including legal scrutiny in the early twentieth century. A scholar of the Grand United Order of Odd Fellows in America, writing in 1902, looked back to Peter Ogden's initiative, suggested that Ogden "thought it folly, a waste of time, if not self-respect, to stand, hat in hand, at the foot-stool of a class of men who, professing benevolence and fraternity, were most narrow and contracted, a class of men who judged another, not by principle and character, but by the shape of the nose, the curl of the hair, and the hue of the skin." This statement speaks volumes about the racial tensions behind the organizations claiming fraternity and mutual support as their guiding ideals.

For many years the Odd Fellows and Freemasons dominated African-American fraternal activities, though many smaller and sometimes short-lived fraternal associations were formed before the Civil War. Baltimore, for example, saw the establishment of two groups in the 1850s, the Grand United Order of Nazarites in 1854 and the Grand United Order of Galilean Fishermen in 1856. Small and distinctively local organizations appeared in other cities. Many African Americans found their fraternal experience in organizations devoted to temperance and sobriety, frequent concerns in the nineteenth-century United States that were often echoed in black communities. The most influential of the temperance societies were interracial—though, as we shall see, these organizations too were disrupted by racial tensions. The Independent Order of Good Samaritans and Daughters of Samaria, for example, was originally an all-white temperance society, but it eventually became a predominantly black society after white members defected upon the admission of African Americans into its ranks. More inspiring was the Independent Order of Good Templars, a white fraternal organization devoted to temperance, which was open to both women and African Americans—and by the late nineteenth century boasted a large black membership.

Still, the most influential of these organizations remained, before the Civil War, the Odd Fellows and the Freemasons. Like African-American religious denominations, these organizations spread across the country, working in tandem with churches (since there was significant overlap in the membership of fraternal organizations and churches) to encourage and support an understanding of a national African-American community. In 1847 the Odd Fellows granted dispensation to establish lodges in Philadelphia and Harrisburg in Pennsylvania, and in Wilmington, Delaware. In 1848 dispensation was granted for lodges in Baltimore and Bermuda, and later years saw lodges spring up from York, Pennsylvania, to Toronto, Canada, from Cleveland to Buffalo. In 1847 Prince Hall Masonry arrived in Ohio, extended from two lodges in Pennsylvania. After they were joined by a third lodge the next

year, the three lodges combined in 1849 to construct the first Prince
Hall grand lodge west of the Allegheny Mountains. This growth south
and west continued over the years, establishing black fraternal organizations second only to black churches as social, political, and economic
centers of African-American communities.

The attraction of fraternal organizations lay in their offer of a fundamentally different orientation to the social order than was generally
available to African Americans. At the most basic level, fraternal organizations were community networks with access to opportunity and power.
As in benevolent societies and churches, men could collaborate in business and politics, extending their reach by connecting with economic and
social partners. Like benevolent societies too, fraternal organizations allowed members and communities to present a unified face to the broader
public. The regalia of the society identified a common bond among
members, with an internal discipline that countered the stereotypes and
caricatures that dominated the mainstream press and minstrel stage.
Those bonds were strengthened by the private rituals so central to fraternal
organizations—they were the means by which men measured their
achievements and progress in relation to one another and to an established
tradition of advancement. Indeed, the fraternal organizations' unique
marriage of secrecy and public display provided blacks with important
ways to negotiate their way through a world in which their privacy was
often violated and their access to public space often restricted. Through
fraternal rituals and celebrations, black men (and women, in sister organizations) relocated themselves both culturally and historically, identifying
themselves with an international tradition of brotherhood and observances and an important historical tradition. Against the pressure of a
world seemingly determined to reduce the meaning of their lives to the
absurdities of racial ideology and law, they created, participated in, and
inhabited (both in the lodges and in their public displays and acknowledg-
ments of brotherhood) a world of meaning that was both wholly under
their control and connected to a broader, transatlantic community.

For all their many successes, African-American fraternal societies could
never escape the racist grounds on which, of necessity, they had been

built. There was a jarring irony in the fact that Odd Fellows or Freemasons could claim a universal brotherhood steeped in historical and legendary tradition, unified by common beliefs and shared rituals, devoted to individual development, mutual benefit, and common advancement, and yet suffer such complete separation because of racial ideology. Black and white Masonic and Odd Fellow lodges that operated in the same cities had less communication and social intercourse among them than did black American and white British lodges. The white abolitionist Parker Pillsbury made this point in an article published originally in the Pittsburgh *Visitor* and reprinted in Frederick Douglass's newspaper the *North Star* in December 1850. Pillsbury was responding in part to those who wished to keep the anti-slavery movement and the women's movement separate, and especially to those who believed that racial concerns should play no role in the women's movement. Noting that most white Americans thought only of other whites when referring to "the public," Pillsbury turned to fraternal societies for his example. "Free Masons," he wrote, "must be white—both face and apron. Odd Fellows, too, must be constitutionally light of skin; and even the Sons of Temperance, and Daughters likewise, must be bleached to the popular complexional standard, or they are beyond the reach of salvation." Pillsbury advocated a different understanding of the public, but he well understood that even many social reform efforts failed to address the heart of those aspects of society most in need of reform: a racist division that denied the recognitions of brotherhood and sisterhood to many even while proclaiming devotion to those ideals.

Pillsbury was not alone in his criticism of white fraternal societies, though much of that criticism had come years before his comments. While the Freemasons had included in their membership some important Founding Fathers, the organization suffered a challenging public climate in the early decades of the nineteenth century. Many Americans worried about a secret society with its own sense of history and quasi-religious rituals, which might undermine democracy and Christianity. Those concerns came to a point during a public controversy over the disappearance of William Morgan in 1825. Morgan, who had attended a Freemason lodge in Batavia, New York, had threatened to reveal Masonic secrets. His disappearance was taken as evidence that those secrets and the existence of the Freemasons themselves were indeed threatening.

The controversy over Morgan's mysterious fate elevated such fears into a national Anti-Masonic movement that rocked national politics and dominated newspaper headlines. Although by mid-century the Freemasons began to restore their organization and membership, strong traces of the controversy and distrust persisted, as suggested by Pillsbury's choice of fraternal organizations as a negative example of democratic sensibilities. Closer to the initial controversy, David Walker (who was himself a Mason) included Anti-Masonic sentiment among the reform movements that he claimed looked to symptoms while ignoring the central disease of the American social order: "The preachers and people of the United States form societies against Free Masonry and Intemperance, and write against Sabbath breaking, Sabbath mails, Infidelity, &c. &c. But the fountain head [slavery and oppression], compared to which, all those other evils are comparatively nothing, and from the bloody and murderous head of which, they receive no trifling support, is hardly noticed by the Americans." Thus black fraternal organizations were founded on a controversy within a controversy, excluded from both the democratic social order and what many perceived as a threat to that order.

Regardless of these controversies, many African Americans remained convinced of the importance of fraternal societies. Black Freemasons especially worked to maintain a stable organization while arguing for recognition of their legitimacy within the larger fraternal order. The central public defense of this position came in the form of Martin Delany's pamphlet *The Origin and Objects of Ancient Freemasonry*. Delany argued that "the beautiful fabric of Masonry" had been established "to convince man of the importance of his own being and impress him with a proper sense of his duty to his Creator," an achievement that would also provide each man "with a sense of his duty and obligations to society and the laws intended for his government." Delany grounded this universal ideal in African history, arguing that Africans "were the authors of this mysterious and beautiful Order"—indeed, asserting that "it is a settled and acknowledged fact, conceded by all *intelligent* writers and speakers, that to Africa is the world indebted for its knowledge of the mysteries of Ancient Freemasonry. Had Moses or the Israelites never lived in Africa, the mysteries of the wise men of the East never would have been handed down to us."

Understanding the racial significance of the provision that only free-born men be admitted as Freemasons, Delany countered that this requirement was designed to account for those who forfeited their liberty either by crime or "by voluntary servitude for a stipulated sum or reward." In short, African Americans, including those who had been or were enslaved involuntarily, had every right to membership as long as they had not sacrificed that right through crime.

Delany looked back to the historical roots of Freemasonry to place contemporary debates in a different context, one in which African history would play a central role, but he also considered the current situation of the United States. In part he argued that white Freemasons had strayed from their organization's history and founding ideals, but he also accused white American Masons of inconsistency even among themselves, and in perhaps unexpected ways. "A fact worthy of remark," he wrote, "is that there is no comparison between the feelings manifested toward colored, by Northern and Southern Masons. Northern Masons, notwithstanding Masonry knows no man by descent, origin, or color, seldom visit colored Masonic Lodges; and when they do, it is frequently done by *stealth*! While, to the contrary, Southern Masons recognize and fellowship colored men, as such, whenever they meet them as Masons. The writer has more than once sat in Lodge in the city of C— with some of the first gentlemen of Kentucky, where there have been present Col. A. a distinguished lawyer, Esquire L. one of the first Aldermen of the place, and Judge M. President of the Judges' Bench. This is a matter of no unfrequent occurrence, and many of our members have done the same." This significant division of practice, Delany suggested, indicated even greater differences over adherence to principle—that is, to an organization that theoretically "knows no man by descent, origin, or color." In effect, Delany suggested that the legitimacy of black Masons was recognized by at least some white Masons, and that accordingly the fidelity, if not the legitimacy, of other white Masons was subject to question.

But tensions within the Masons occurred among the black lodges as well as between black and white members, and Delany was careful to address this situation. Divisions among black Masons had led to a special effort in 1847 to reunify black Freemasonry. As Delany put it rather hopefully, at this meeting "the differences and wounds which long existed were all settled and healed, a complete union formed, and a National Grand Lodge, established, by the choice and election, in due Masonic form, of Past Master, John T. Hilton, of Boston, Mass." Delany was correct about the central event, though somewhat disingenuous about the lasting consequences. In fact, some lodges soon withdrew from this new dispensation of order—but Delany advanced the brighter side of that development in order to account for lingering divisions. Identifying the 1847 agreement as "the most important period in the history of colored Masons in the United States," he emphasized the importance of unity among black Masons. "Had I the power to do so," he exclaimed, "I would raise my voice in tones of thunder, but with the pathetic affections of a brother, and thrill the cord of every true Masonic heart throughout the country and the world, especially of colored men, in exhortations to stability and to Union. Without it, satisfied am I that all our efforts, whether as men or Masons, must fail—utterly fail. 'A house divided against itself, cannot stand'—the weak divided among themselves in the midst of the mighty, are thrice vanquished—conquered without a blow from the strong; the sturdy hand of the ruthless may shatter in pieces our column guidance, and leave the Virgin of Sympathy to weep through all coming time." While it is unclear whether the Virgin of Sympathy ever had cause to weep, black Masons continued to struggle with internal divisions, and black fraternal orders generally offered only partial unity.

Not all African Americans, however, were convinced of the value of fraternal societies in any event. Some saw them as rather expensive and elaborate distractions from the real work that faced blacks in a period of slavery and racial oppression—invitations to self-satisfying displays and social events marked by ostentatious regalia, parades, and dinners that did little to promote political, economic, and social justice. Representative of such views was the author of a letter published in the *North Star* in July 1849. The anonymous author, who identified himself only as an "Observer," asked the question central to African Americans who were determined not to compromise their claims to full recognition and rights as citizens: "Of what advantage is the Church, State or any human Society or Institution to me, if I must purchase them at the price of chains, slavery and proscription?" For this writer, the rights of membership and displays of public unity available through fraternal societies were part of this compromised liberty, standing in stark contrast to more overt political action. He viewed the public liberties of the fraternal orders in sharp contrast to the limitations that African Americans experienced in almost every other public forum and unified demonstration. "Tell me I may walk in an Odd Fellow Society," he wrote, "and mob me for walking in a Temperance procession. Permit me to pass in a Free Mason procession, and club and stone me to death for being in an Anti-Slavery procession. Go when, where and with whom we please as servants or slaves—but denied place above or beneath ground—scarcely breathing air, or drinking water as gentlemen." Fraternal societies, for this observer and others, amounted to another level of segregation, one marked by a hint of complicity in the oppressive order, a voluntary submission to those public spaces, processions, and forms of unity acceptable to white America.

Observer argued for a moratorium on such activities, suggesting that some displays of African-American unity did more to restrict than to advance the cause of black security, civil rights, and liberty. As he put it, "Let the quiet of the church, the stability of ordinary societies among us, the accumulation of dollars and cents, the anniversaries of Odd Fellow societies, the display of Free Masons, the levees of Sons and Daughters of Temperance, the suppers of Good Samaritans and Fancy Balls and parties, be made subordinate for the time being, to the great and true idea of our moral, social, political and religious recognition." Others agreed. While fraternal organizations provided for community displays and the rituals of mutual elevation, many worried that the realities of the black condition in the midst of a white supremacist culture were lost in the spectacle. Delany could argue that "none but him who *voluntarily* compromised his liberty was recognized as a slave" by early Masons, but the fact remained that many American Masons were slaveholders and that many more were part of the white cultural order that denied admission to blacks. Against the ideals of fraternal organizations were hard realities that needed to be addressed before any black could decide to associate with any organization. Observer's presentation of this argument was again representative: "To make me a sectarian, Odd Fellow, Good Samaritan, Son of Temperance, or Free Mason, before you make me a man and a citizen, is to mock my heart, and insult my head; liberty first, names, societies and conventionalism afterwards." What many African Americans took as a source of pride, others took to be empty mockery, an insult to thinking people who were denied the rights and privileges of citizenship.

Henry Highland Garnet agreed, though his preference was to reform the fraternal associations rather than suspend them. In an 1848 speech to

the Female Benevolent Society of Troy, New York, Garnet bemoaned
the wasteful spending that he believed characterized many African-
American organizations. "Societies," he asserted, "called benevolent, frequently squander more money for the purchase of banners and badges,
and in feasting, than they use in acts of charity. What are the regalia and
other trappings worth, if they signify nothing but sham and parade?"
Garnet was prepared with examples, noting that "in 1846, $5000 were
paid by the oppressed Colored people at the Temperance Celebration
held in Poughkeepsie, N.Y., and yet we do not adequately support a
single Newspaper in the United States." Particularly galling to the well-
educated Garnet was the fact that funds spent for regalia and other trappings could instead be devoted to black education. Speaking of that same
group of temperance supporters, Garnet noted that a celebratory meeting
cost "not less than $10,000; and yet we do not find *a hundred* of our young
men and women in our high-schools and colleges." Among the Odd Fellows, Garnet saw similar extravagance and misdirected funds. "The gorgeous pageant of the Odd Fellows in October 1847," he observed, "drew
from the pockets of the people, at a very moderate calculation, the sum
of $8000, while many of their offspring who ought to be drinking at the
fountain of learning, are mourning by the turbid and cold waters of servile employments." And although he was a Mason himself, Garnet was
particularly critical of his fellow Masons, observing that "The FREE AND
ACCEPTED MASONS can boast nothing over other fraternities in regard to
unnecessary expenditures. The Masons have led off in this course of
wastefulness, and a majority of the other institutions are but children of
the great ORIGINAL, and they resemble their parent more or less." Garnet did not, however, view such organizations as inherently wasteful
or unnecessary distractions from more direct and purposeful political
action—"Let no one say that I seek the destruction of these Institutions,"
he was careful to add—but he did believe that the organizations needed
to remove "the unfruitful branches of the trees, that it may be ascertained
whether their trunks are capable of bearing good fruit."

   Garnet included both men and women in his appeal for education,
quietly highlighting that the most obvious way in which fraternal organizations ignored or obscured broader questions about rights was, of
course, in the fact that they were fraternal—that is, all male societies.
While the Masons and the Odd Fellows developed sister organizations

and involved women in some of their public activities, the fact is that women were excluded from membership. One might think that such a complaint imposes today's standards on the world of the past, but the inclusion of women in organizations was a subject of frequent debate at the time. Members of Garrison's anti-slavery movement, for example, met with considerable resistance when they insisted, both at home and abroad, that women should be recognized as equal members of the organization, with the right to serve as public speakers, and that women's rights should be part of the movement for social justice. In religion, such pioneers as Jarena Lee argued for women's authority to preach under the auspices of the church. In the political realm, Sojourner Truth, while singular in style and in the force of her arguments, spoke for many when she wove women's rights, religious reform, and anti-slavery zeal into the fabric of her orations. It is not surprising, then, that some activists criticized fraternal organizations because they excluded women from membership or relegated women to supporting roles.

One such reproof appeared as an editorial comment accompanying an article published in the *North Star* in July 1848. The occasion was the presentation by a group of women of a banner to the 21 Division of the United Colored American Association, itself a fraternal organization, in Cincinnati. In the editorial note the author, perhaps Frederick Douglass himself, observed, "We see that some of the young ladies took part in the proceedings, whose efforts have been highly spoken of. And why not? It is only necessary to give woman an equal opportunity, and she will prove herself an equal to man in all things." Ignoring the fact that this recognition took place in a fraternal gathering, and that the laudatory speeches exchanged by the men and women there spoke in the conventional language of gender, with the women clearly positioned outside the association's activities, the editorial used this event to criticize other fraternal organizations. "Why do the Sons of Temperance, Odd Fellows, Masons, and other secret societies, solicit woman's aid in the furtherance of their objects," the editorial asked, "and yet deny them the privileges of their institutions?" Familiar with the usual responses to this question, the editorial added, "We know it is argued by some, at least the Masonic, that their order cannot be changed. Can as much be said of the others, especially the 'Sons,' who are of recent origin? Be this as it may, we advocate equal rights, without regard to sex or color, and shall therefore do our duty in this, by reminding others of the importance of doing that which is right, especially in all coming time." A week after this statement appeared, Douglass, commenting on the famous 1848 Women's Rights Convention at Seneca Falls, observed, "Many who have at last made the discovery that the Negroes have some rights as well as other members of the human family, have yet to be convinced that women are entitled to any." For many, this comment applied equally well to some black men as to many in white America, making the fraternal organizations rather too much a replica of the organizations from which they sought recognition and legitimacy.

Just as the peculiar nature of fraternal organizations—their association with other histories, private rituals, and singular claims to universal brotherhood—provided black men with the means to leverage a different position in the social order, to be both insiders and outsiders in white-dominated traditions, so did the exclusion of women from these organizations offer women an opportunity to make a case as both insiders and outsiders. Such opportunities are nowhere more evident than in "An Address Delivered at the African Masonic Hall" by the activist (and friend of David Walker) Maria Stewart in February 1833. Stewart used the location of her public speech, and the fraternal order and patriarchal authority it represented, to her advantage, calling men to task for their shortcomings in arguing for African-American rights. "I would ask," she said early in her remarks, "is it blindness of mind, or stupidity of soul, or the want of education that has caused our men who are 60 or 70 years of age, never to let their voices be heard, nor their hands be raised in behalf of their color?" Lest her message within this Masonic Hall be lost, Stewart turned to the central symbol of Freemasonry, King Solomon's temple. Two decades later, Martin Delany would present Solomon's temple as an attempt to combine "the united wisdom of the world" into "a more practical and systematic principle, and stereotyping it with physical science, by rearing the stupendous and magnificent temple at Jerusalem." "In this period," Delany wrote in 1853, "the mysteries assumed the name of Masonry, induced from the building of the temple: and at this time, also, commenced the universality of the Order, arising from the going forth of the builders into all parts of the world. This then, was the *establishment of Masonry*." In 1833 Stewart looked to this same symbol and turned it to other purposes. "Like King Solomon," she declared to the gathered crowd, "who put neither nail nor hammer to the temple, yet received the praise; so also have the white Americans gained themselves a name, like the names of the great men that are in the earth, while in reality we have been their principal foundation and support." Black fraternal organizations, Stewart suggested, were involved in an age-old problem, the subjugation of labor, and black Masons were ironically providing the masonry supporting the edifice of white cultural authority and power.

❖❖

Although many blacks were critical of fraternal organizations, and although these groups struggled with internal and external pressures and tensions, still their value to African-American communities cannot be denied. Against Stewart's view of submissive black Masons was an earlier assessment, echoed through the years, of the fundamentally different worldview made possible through Freemasonry. In 1789 the Reverend John Marrant presented a sermon before African Lodge 459 that is generally regarded as the first published speech by a black American. Marrant was an early colleague of Prince Hall, and the two men represent the significant ties between the development of African-American authority in religion and civil society, in churches and fraternal organizations. Promoting the view that through their fraternal associations black men had access to "all other titles we have a just right as Masons to claim—namely, honorable, free and accepted," Marrant looked to the legendary roots of Freemasonry to envision a global movement. Referring to the building of Solomon's temple, Marrant included both masons and "men who carried burdens" among those who "were partitioned into certain Lodges, although they were of different nations and different colors, yet were they in perfect harmony among themselves, and seemingly cemented in brotherly love and friendship." When their work on the temple was completed, "they departed onto their several homes, and carried with them the high taste of architecture to the different parts of the world." That tradition of a spreading knowledge was, for Marrant and others, central to the value of Freemasonry, a process that led from the organization's roots in Africa to the struggles of African Americans centuries later.

For black Americans, that tradition provided both opportunity and authority to compare themselves with white Americans on culturally and socially equal grounds—as fellow Odd Fellows or Masons. They could do this regardless of whether white Americans acknowledged that fellowship, a failure that would simply add weight to the scales of the comparison. Prince Hall, for example, built this comparison into his 1797 "Charge," in which he reminded his fellow Masons of their duty to "give the right hand of affection and fellowship to whom it justly belongs, let their colour and complexion be what it will, let their nation be what it may, for they are your brethren, and it is your indispensable duty so to do." By such acts black Masons would live up to their professed ideals, their duties as Masons, and they would also press the point of mutual recognition. Should that recognition be denied by white Masons, Hall observed, "we & the world know what to think of them be they ever so grand: for we know this was Solomon's creed, Solomon's creed did I say, it is the decree of the Almighty, and all Masons have learnt it: tis plain market language, and plain and true facts need no apologies."

From Solomon's creed to the decree of the Almighty, African Americans could find in fraternal organizations high callings dressed in plain market language. For Hall and others, far from being an anti-democratic organization, as the Anti-Masonic movement would later claim, Masonry and other fraternal organizations offered, through their rituals, a democratizing structure by which to measure social interactions that otherwise were veiled by the racist smoke and mirrors of American cultural practices. Masonry, one might say, was for African Americans an exclusive society that exposed the terms of exclusivity in the broader culture.

For this reason some black leaders saw great democratic promise in fraternal organizations, especially because they offered instructional forums particularly suited to the needs of a community largely denied the advantages of formal education. In his 1797 "a Charge," Prince Hall reminded his fellow Masons that, regardless of the conditions of their lives, they were capable of independent thought and judgment. "Although you are deprived of the means of education," he told them, "yet you are not deprived of the means of meditation, by which I mean thinking, hearing and weighing matters, men, and things in your own mind, and making that judgment of them as you think reasonable to satisfy your minds and give an answer to those who may ask you a question." If this was a responsibility to be met by all Masons—disciplined and ethical thought—then Freemasonry provided the tools by which men of any educational level could meet it. As Hall put it in 1792, "If thus, we by the grace of God, live up to this our Profession; we may cheerfully go the rounds of the compass of this life, having lived according to the plumb line of uprightness, the square of justice, the level of truth and sincerity." Hall's rhetoric refers to Masonic symbolism, the tools by which even illiterate men could read and follow the guidelines that would lead to advancement and success. Years later Martin Delany reiterated this point, observing that in ancient days "man adhered but little, and cared less, for that in which he could never be fully instructed, nor be made to understand, in consequence of his deficiency in a thorough literary education—this being the exclusive privilege of those in affluent circumstances." The challenge, then, was to formulate a system of moral and intellectual instruction accessible to all, and this, Delany argued, Masonry provided: "All these imperfections have been remedied, in the practical workings of the comprehensive system of Free and Accepted Masonry, as handed down to us from the archives at Jerusalem. All men, of every country, clime, color and con- dition, (when morally worthy,) are acceptable to the portals of Masonic jurisprudence." In a community in need of both the hope and the tools required for individual and collective uplift, many blacks believed that the rituals and ideals of fraternal organizations offered valuable answers.

Thus it is not surprising that a great many African-American com- munity leaders have been members of fraternal organizations, often finding in them a platform and a network for rising to national recogni- tion. This was true before the Civil War as well. Among the prominent blacks who were Masons were Richard Allen, minister and founder of the AME church, and his colleagues Absolom Jones and John Marrant; the activist David Walker; the editor of one of the first African-Ameri- can newspapers, Samuel Cornish; men who rose to considerable wealth and influence, including Paul Cuffe and James Forten; the most promi- nent black actor of the day, Ira Aldridge; the inventor Lewis Latimer; and such important abolitionists, writers, and political leaders as Wil- liam Wells Brown, Martin Delany, Henry Highland Garnet, Alexander Crummell, Booker T. Washington, and W. E. B. DuBois. For these men and for many others, black Freemasonry provided networks of commu- nication and cooperation as well as opportunities to interact with distant communities, develop and exert influence, and rise to levels of promi- nence within and beyond the black community. For some, like Delany,

Masonry also offered a mode of thought and the rhetorical tools needed to challenge settled thought and negotiate unsettling challenges.

While some blacks worried that fraternal processions and celebrations amounted to a waste of funds, empty display, and political distraction, they nonetheless recognized the potential suggested by such displays. In an article titled "The Odd Fellows' Celebration," published in *Frederick Douglass' Paper* in September 1856, James McCune Smith highlighted that potential. Smith recognized that there were larger political battles to be fought, but he suggested that the fraternal celebration offered a symbolic demonstration of the troops that could be gathered for those greater struggles. "There were some six hundred men in the line," he wrote; "they marched four abreast, the officers with swords in their hands, all decked, rank and file in gorgeous regalia, with their magnificent standards floating in the breeze, and three splendid bands discoursing eloquent music; they looked, in all respects, like an '*army with banners*.'" The sight "set the imagination to work, inquiring how far South such an army might march, if well drilled and well marched, and how such an army would increase and its members become officers."

Smith was not alone in such flights of fancy. His vision of a swelling force was shared by the white abolitionist John Brown, who believed that his 1859 raid at Harpers Ferry would spark the formation of a great army joined in open rebellion against slaveholding forces. It was not a far reach to look at a fraternal procession and imagine a community coming together in disciplined resistance to an oppressive nation.

While Smith knew he was engaging largely in wishful thinking, for others his dream suggested the specter of a disciplined black resistance and became something like a haunting nightmare. Certainly this was the case for a writer who submitted a letter to the *National Journal* shortly after Nat Turner's rebellion in Southampton, Virginia, in 1831, a letter later reprinted in the *Liberator* under the title "Free Masonry Among the Blacks" roughly a month after Turner was tried and executed. Advocating the abolishment of Freemasonry, the writer worried about "the spirit of revolt which has been manifested in the Southern States among the slaves," a spirit that "has filled me with horror." For this writer, fraternal processions were by no means a distraction from black political action but rather an indication of a gathering force. "It is a fact well known," he reported, "that in various parts of the Union, free blacks hold their lodges, and make as fantastic a parade and show, as any of the lodges of the white masons. I am told that they are in fact as perfect in their Masonic formalities—as solemn in their oaths and obligations, as the white Masons. If there was to be devised a scheme for organizing and preparing the Southern blacks for insurrection, none that I can conceive of, is so admirably calculated for the purpose as Free Masonry introduced among free negroes. They of all others are most forward in promoting the spirit of revolt among slaves."

This writer saw in black Masons a determination to organize and an anti-slavery zeal that threatened the white social order. And he believed that this threat was no longer theoretical: "That a plan has been maturing for many years by the better informed free blacks at the north, most of whom are Free Masons, for the final liberation of the slaves of the south, I firmly believe; and I as firmly believe that those plans have been made in the dark recesses of the African Lodges. The various means by which they may prepare the minds of the southern slaves, and train them to a confederated band of insurgents, are there started, discussed, and when ripe, are carried into practice." The writer envisioned a highly organized network of communication and planning, one promoted in part by preaching ("one of the means by which they operate," the writer claimed). This network was made possible by "the systematic secrecy which pervades the masonic order," a secrecy that "enables them to practice the deepest deception." At a time when some believed there might be a connection between the publication of *David Walker's Appeal* (which was smuggled into the South) and events like Nat Turner's rebellion, this writer saw an underground network operating through fraternal organizations. "By such means," he asserted, "the free blacks of the north hold a direct communication with the slaves of the south; and it is from them, more than from any other cause, that I attribute the late melancholy occurrences in Southampton and other places."

African Americans understood such flights of imagination, and there was no doubt some truth to this writer's fears, for certainly Southern black churches and other groups provided centers for organized resistance, often helping fugitive slaves escape in secrecy. Even beyond such organization, though, many blacks understood the value of using the specter of a secret organization to their purposes. Thus in many ways the legend of the Underground Railroad was as important as its actual

operation, challenging the slaveholding powers with the possibility of a
secret and organized resistance, undermining their confidence about the
security and stability of the slavery system.

Martin Delany built on such strategies in his serialized novel *Blake:
or the Huts of America; A Tale of the Mississippi Valley, The Southern
United States, and Cuba* (1859–1862). Delany told the story of "the formidable understanding among the slaves throughout the United States
and Cuba" who combined in "a deep laid secret organization" whose key
secrets were never revealed. And the free-born AME minister and Freemason Moses Dickson encouraged reports that he had founded a secret
society among the slaves called the Knights of Liberty, a hidden army
of thousands waiting for the order to revolt. Dickson would later form
two fraternal organizations, the Knights and Daughters of Tabor and
the Heroines of Jericho, for which he created the rituals. Such organizations were often complexly involved in African-American struggles for
political leverage, and the peculiar nature of fraternal societies—the public displays wrapped in private mysteries—often played important roles
in those struggles.

One example of how blacks understood the advantages of the veil
of secrecy and ritual is provided again by Delany, who frequently used
the rhetoric and rituals of Freemasonry in his writing. In her celebratory biography of Delany, Frances A. Rollin quotes (from conversations)
Delany's story of his attempt to see Abraham Lincoln. Told that such an
interview would be impossible, Delany answered with assurance:

> the mansion of every government has outer and inner doors, the outer
> defended by guards; the security of the inner is usually a secret, except
> to the inmates of the council-chamber. Across this inner lies a ponder-
> ous beam, of the finest quality, highly polished, designed only for the
> finest cabinet-work; it can neither be stepped over nor passed around,
> and none can enter except this is moved away; and he that enters is the
> only one to remove it at the time, which is the required passport for
> his admission. I can pass the outer door, through the guards, and I am
> persuaded that I can move this polished beam of cabinet-work, and I
> will do it.

Once Delany succeeds in meeting with Lincoln, he switches to that
other field of action equally enshrouded with mystery and myth, the Underground Railroad. Delany advises Lincoln on the desirability "of the

full realization of arming the blacks of the South, and the ability of the blacks of the North to defeat it by complicity with those at the South, through the medium of the *Underground Railroad*—a measure known only to themselves." If this is the proposal Delany presented to Lincoln, it was, to put it mildly, extravagant in its claims but revealing in its strategy.

An important African-American publication directly indebted to Freemasons was Robert Benjamin Lewis's ambitious history *Light and Truth; Collected From the Bible and Ancient and Modern History, Containing the Universal History of the Colored and the Indian Race, From the Creation of the World to the Present Time*. The book was first copyrighted in 1836 and published in Portland, Maine, by Daniel Clement Colesworthy, a white printer and writer associated with black causes and individuals. A significantly expanded edition appeared in 1844 by a "committee of Coloured Gentlemen" that included Thomas Dalton, once grand master of Prince Hall Grand Lodge. Made possible by Masons, *Light and Truth* is also influenced by Masonic modes of understanding and instruction. In a chapter on "The Arts and Sciences," for example, Lewis follows a lengthy section on Egyptian architecture, without transition, with one on "The Explanation of the Five Virtues." The five virtues Lewis identifies—Truth, Justice, Temperance, Prudence, and Fortitude—are central to Freemasonry. Years later, in his *Official History of Freemasonry* (1903), a fellow black Mason, William H. Grimshaw, would refer to the same qualities. For Lewis, such cardinal virtues were guiding principles for historical understanding and the means by which African Americans could locate themselves historically and politically.

Freemasonry and other fraternal associations offered Lewis, Delany, and many other blacks a tradition of historical interpretation that, as they believed, extended back to the Egyptian mysteries. It also offered a framework for understanding the relations among community, historical consciousness, and individual character. In 1834 William Whipper, advocating for the temperance cause, argued that "If our hostility to slavery arises, as it justly should, from its deleterious and demoralizing effects on the human family, ought not our hatred to intemperance be founded on the same principles?" Whipper observed that human weakness was a universal condition, the one realm of life in which one would encounter no distinction of wealth, race, or gender. "It is found in the palace," Whipper observed, and "it exists in the forum; it mingles with society; its abode is by the fireside; it is felt in the sanctuary; it despises the prejudices of caste; it seeks its victims alike among the learned and ignorant, the poor and the rich; it confines itself neither to the geographical lines of state or territory, of nation or continent, but disdaining all local attachments, it claims for its domain the map of the universe." Against the force of a culture that magnified every individual black failure as a characteristic quality of the race, Whipper quietly reminded his audience that what distinguished African Americans was their relatively unprotected state, the many restrictions on independent action and choice that marked their lives.

These same restrictions, though, highlighted the importance of working to reform society, a responsibility for all but one that held particular urgency for African Americans. "Is not every man of color in these United States morally, politically and religiously bound to support the temperance reform, as advocated in our country?" Whipper asked. Could his argument prove persuasive, could African Americans rise to this challenge, Whipper imagined the force the black community might wield: "I believe that if the three hundred thousand free colored people possessed such a character, the moral force and influence it would send forth would disperse slavery from our land. Yes, it would reverse the present order of things; it would reorganize public opinion, dissolve the calumnies of our enemies, and remove all the prejudices against our complexion."

Fraternal societies, whether devoted to temperance or to a ritualized preservation of a tradition of abstract ideals and practical methods, represented for many the hope of a combined moral force and influence, the means toward a fundamental reconstitution of society.

5

"The Collected Wisdom of Our People"

IN THE DEVELOPMENT of mutual benefit societies, churches, and fraternal organizations, African Americans looked to build permanent foundations capable of both supporting and encouraging a sense of community. Equally important to their progress were the black state and national conventions that ordinarily took place just a few days each year. These conventions enabled blacks to take stock of their situation and plan for the future. The gatherings customarily involved men, for male delegates were slow to recognize the need for women to play formal roles as delegates. Female contributions often appeared as marginal items in the formal publications connected to the conventions. Still, the meetings allowed African Americans to recognize and define themselves as members of a self-governing community, to promote the uplift of the race both in speeches published to the world and in practical measures adopted through the conventions' resolutions, and to redefine what it meant to be black and how stereotypes of black character and potential promoted in the white press might be overturned.

The national convention movement extended from 1830 to 1864, and similar enterprises followed the Civil War. As with so many aspects of African-American organizational history, the convention movement had its origins in both positive and negative developments of the time. On the one hand, it was designed to respond to the social and political challenges facing the black community, and in this way the conventions affirmed the persistence of the racist culture with which blacks had to contend. The first convention, which met at Bethel Church in Philadelphia in September 1830, grew from the suggestion of Hezekiah Grice of Baltimore as a means to discuss emigration to Canada—a response to oppressive laws and an environment of violence against African Americans in

Ohio and elsewhere. But the conventions were also a sign of the *success* of black efforts to organize.

Of the state and national conventions that followed from that first event, one might say that they were gatherings not only of men and women but also of organizations, as representatives of churches, fraternal bodies, anti-slavery organizations, and various local and regional societies and associations came together to address the needs of a national community of black Americans. From the beginning the conventions looked beyond their immediate purpose and extended their range to include educational efforts in the United States; approaches to establishing the black community as a commercially secure and independent entity; responses to the ongoing work of the American Colonization Society; commentary on the degradation of religion and on American governing ideals; arguments in support of the recognition of black citizenship; and debates within the black community over the proper course of action in the anti-slavery cause.

To represent the diverse interests and organizational affiliations of African Americans capable of attending the conventions, organizers established the broadest possible terms for determining delegates wherever concentrated populations of black Americans could be found. For an 1841 state convention in Pennsylvania, for example, a call for delegates was "sent to every county and large town in the state," with no established process for choosing those local representatives. Organizers of the national convention in Rochester, New York, in 1853 announced in the pages of the *National Era*, "All colored churches, literary and other societies, are invited to send at least one, and not more than three delegates to the Convention." Organizers obviously hoped to build on associational efforts already under way, and numbers were clearly more important than balanced representation. In a report published in the *North Star* in 1847, the African-American activist and historian William C. Nell reported that sixty-seven delegates had been sent to that year's national convention in Troy, New York, including forty-four from New York, fifteen from Massachusetts, two from Connecticut, and one each from Pennsylvania, New Jersey, New Hampshire, Vermont, Kentucky, and Michigan. The Rochester convention fared somewhat better, with reportedly "more than one hundred delegates . . . present, representing towns, cities, and societies in several States."

Following these published calls, local groups were free to decide how to select delegates, a process that favored those in positions of authority and that relied on both formal and informal networks of communication. For example, Frederick Douglass's paper, the *North Star*, announced a meeting of Rochester's "colored citizens, male and female," in 1848 "for the purpose of choosing delegates to the Cleveland Convention." For a planned state convention in Albany, New York, in 1840, the *Colored American* reported on a "meeting of the colored people at Oswego village" held in the office of T. E. Grant—probably Tudor E. Grant, a local barber and community leader. The group responded to the convention's call with high formality, in the form of a resolution:

> Whereas, the stone of caste and color covering the well from whence flows the streams of liberty, as in common with other men, and feeling that we are deprived of those rights which can only make us men, or a people; And whereas, this stone can only be removed by the ballot box, therefore, Resolved, that we feel this call one of the greatest movements that has ever been made for our elevation. Whereas, the elective franchise has been denied us on account of our color, and we feel it one of the greatest privileges that we can be denied of, Resolved, Therefore, that it is one of the great spokes in the wheel of the carriage for the elevation of a depressed people, for raising them in the scale of importance and of reflecting credit upon their character. Resolved, That it is obligatory upon a people who are just wakening from the death shade of a long night of ignorance and oppression, to shake off the putrid garments of their degradation, and move for a great effort for our natural and imprescriptible rights.

According to the paper's report, "the meeting resulted in choosing T. E. Grant as a delegate of the said Convention."

Black Chicagoans, preparing for the national convention in Cleveland, Ohio, in 1848, similarly responded with some degree of formality, choosing two delegates during a meeting at a Baptist church and authorizing one of them, John Jones, to act "as a committee of one to go to Alton, Illinois to speak before the State Association of Colored People and impress upon them the necessity of sending delegates to the National Convention of Cleveland."

The flexibility allowed in the selection of delegates was clear in the reports of the conventions. For the 1847 convention at Troy, a group described in the press only as the "constituency" at Northampton, Massachusetts, was singled out by William C. Nell in his report on the convention for its approach to choosing and establishing the authority of its delegate. The group, Nell reported, "being impressed with the importance of abolishing all complexional distinction, and thus influencing the Convention by a picture demonstration, recorded their names in full upon his credentials, two-thirds of whom, were white citizens, which fact was received by the Convention with hearty applause, suggesting an expression of the hope from several members, that future gatherings will be characterized by delegates in good numbers of white and colored persons, prompted by a common feeling against slavery and prejudice." In a somewhat different attempt to represent the interests of African Americans, leaders in New York City, preparing for the national convention at Troy, held a public meeting at a church to extend the number of delegates they hoped to send to the convention, choosing eighteen "additional delegates" who were charged "to act in conjunction and in harmony with those previously appointed." The new delegates were chosen to represent "the bone and sinew of the people of this great city: the seamen, workingmen, and mechanics."

The loose structure of the convention movement was perhaps inevitable, given that these meetings were as much attempts to create state and national networks as to convene representatives from networks already established. In many ways this looseness helped the growth of the convention movement, as when black Chicagoans met in the American Methodist Church in 1853 to select a committee to address, in the form of resolutions, the "forlorn condition of the colored citizens of Illinois." One of the resulting resolutions was to hold a state convention in the city.

For some, though, this informal process for establishing conventions and for choosing delegates to attend them threatened to undermine the effectiveness of state and national gatherings. In a letter to *Frederick Douglass' Paper* in June 1851, for example, a writer from Brooklyn complained about "a call for a 'State Convention'" published in that paper and others, and "signed by some half dozen citizens of Albany." The writer wrote not to "question the necessity for a united effort, through a Convention of our people," but rather to comment on the process by which that unified effort had been organized. "It should be deliberated upon previously," the writer argued, "the various measures discussed, delegates appointed and instructed, the measures and mind of leading individuals made known—The inquiry is, Has this been done? Have the plans been arranged? Have measures been discussed? Have delegates been appointed and made ready for effective energetic and practicable action?" The writer worried that the convention was being planned without such deliberation, and that those gathered in Albany would thus "come together strangers, not only personally, but without any defined, understood and adjusted policy." His criticism could be applied to many other conventions as well, with much of the work needed for effective collaboration—"a general correspondence, to gather statistics, prepare documents and reports," in his estimation—following from rather than preceding the meetings.

Still, those who attended the conventions played an important role in *defining* the community in whose name they gathered. As stated in the official publication of the 1835 convention, held in the Wesley Church of Philadelphia, "It is in view of these mighty evils that exist in our country, which are truly national, that has caused us to meet in annual convention for six successive years to take into consideration the best method of remedying our present situation by contributing to their removal." In effect the conventions created a national community to deal with national evils by transforming individuals into representatives "from half the states of this Union" to give voice to "the collected wisdom of our people." The 1835 meeting, for example, called for the formation of an interracial "National Moral Reform Society" devoted to four "rallying points" familiar to the cause of black uplift: "Education, Temperance, Economy, and Universal Liberty." Later conventions would emphasize the importance of the conventions themselves as the means by which blacks could benefit from their community's history of struggle and achievement.

❖❖

While the national conventions were important in shaping a national community, perhaps the most important gatherings were state and local. Many of these conventions were inspired by and connected to the national meetings, but often they were organized specifically to address local or regional concerns, and often they reinforced the activities of religious, fraternal, and social organizations. In 1842, for example, John

Britton, a barber in Indianapolis, Indiana, organized a meeting held at the Bethel AME Church of that city to plan for a state convention later that year. While churches provided both the site and the society for collective action, fraternal orders and other associations similarly offered the benefits of established affiliation, philosophical orientation, and collective experience. Through these other organizations, African Americans had worked out a means of self-determination and self-reliance—everything from moral ideals to historical affiliations to practical experience with economics and the law. The state conventions enabled individuals to initiate a process by which various members of the community could combine their experience to make both symbolic and practical statements to blacks throughout the state and to the national conventions, from as far south as Baltimore to as far north as Canada.

Although they were often linked to the national conventions, at least through common delegates and leadership, the state conventions benefited from grassroots community activism. What is generally considered the first statewide gathering was the August 1840 Convention of the Colored Inhabitants of the State of New York. It was planned to address the state's obstruction of black voting rights, something that most African Americans in New York had enjoyed until 1821. Similarly, blacks in Pennsylvania addressed their disfranchisement at the State Convention of the Colored Freemen of Pennsylvania, held in Pittsburgh in August 1841. Detroit hosted the Michigan State Colored Convention in 1843.

The combination of a revitalized national convention movement through the 1840s led to an increase in state-level activity by the end of that decade. In 1849 state conventions were held in Ohio, New Jersey, and Connecticut, and during the 1850s blacks met statewide in Maryland (1852), Illinois (1853), Massachusetts (1854), and California (1855). The movement extended even further through the Civil War, with conventions in Kansas (1863), Louisiana (1865), Virginia (1865), Missouri (1865), and South Carolina (1865). Although they operated independently of one another, this proliferation of state conventions demonstrated the progress of a sense of common cause, of a national community of African Americans that provided a framework for organized action on the state level. The proceedings of conventions, both state and national, were usually printed and published. They included speeches or declarations designed to reach the broader public but also documents that emphasized, in their dry attention to the "minutes" or "proceedings" of the convention, the process of formal debate, committee work, and resolutions central to organizing a community of often diverse philosophies and interests.

But while the conventions did much to promote statewide and national organization, communication, and cooperation, many of their resolutions and proposals did not reach far beyond the meetings themselves. One could say, though, that to some extent the convention itself was the point—a public and publicized affair, a highly visible gathering of African Americans and their white allies, a display of organization and, in most of the conventions, either unity or disciplined disagreement and debate. This awareness of the visibility of the event is recorded in the proceedings of the first of the California conventions, where one delegate, J. B. Sanderson of Sacramento, stated the case that applied to virtually all the conventions: "We are scattered over the State in small numbers; the laws scarcely recognizing us; public sentiment is prejudiced against us; we are misunderstood, and misrepresented; it was needful that we should meet, communicate, and confer with each other upon some plan of representing our interests before the people of California." The need for a combined response to such conditions was clear, but the same social environment that allowed those conditions also raised the stakes for the collective response represented by the convention. "Perhaps no subject is attracting the attention of the public more," Sanderson added, "than the efforts which the colored people are making to elevate themselves; the public eye is upon us." The challenge was to present a unified face to a doubting public—and to respond to an oppression that was so assumed among most white Americans as to be virtually invisible or at least unquestioned.

Moreover the unity offered by the conventions was a unity of order, not of opinion or perspective. Shortly before Sanderson's remarks at the California convention, another delegate, John C. Wilson, offered his sense of the situation at the gathering, noting that "men are differently constituted, and while some seem scarcely moved by the mightiest subjects, others will feel an intensity of excitement upon subjects the most trivial. The same God that made a diversity of colors, hues, kinds and conditions, has seen proper to make minds of different orders and diverse temperaments." At conventions through the years, African Americans frequently had reason to be reminded of the force of "minds of different orders and diverse temperaments." Disagreements could be fierce and occasionally divisive, even causing breaks of several years in the convention movement. Many blacks, though, seemed to recognize that the work of the conventions was not essentially disrupted or undermined by disagreement, however rancorous. The conspicuously ordered unity so characteristic of the conventions was important not only as a response to white criticism of black character but also to members of black communities themselves, whether those in attendance or readers of press reports. Disagreements were also signs of the vitality and democratic potential of African Americans. Through the conventions they not only resolved disputes, they also exposed them, and in the process presented to the world and to themselves the image of a diverse and dynamic community with a range of strategies for responding to the challenges they faced.

While the state conventions were highly visible and perhaps more politically effective than the national meetings, still it was through the national events that a black community was most forcefully imagined and organized as a collective entity, a political presence, in American cultural life. The first national meeting, held in 1830 largely in response to oppressive legal measures in Ohio, was quite explicit about its mission. The pamphlet that recorded its deliberations was entitled *Constitution of the American Society of Free Persons of Colour, for Improving Their Condition in the United States; for Purchasing Lands; and for the Establishment of a Settlement in Upper Canada, also the Proceedings of the Convention, with Their Address to the Free Persons of Color in the United States*. Could conditions in the United States be improved? Or would a community established in Canada offer hope of a better future? What mattered most was that the future, whether in the United States or in Canada, would be self-determined—as was clear in the convention's response to white-led schemes for removing blacks to Africa under the efforts of the American Colonization Society. "However great the debt which these United States may owe to injured Africa," the convention delegates announced, "and however unjustly her sons have been made to bleed, and her daughters to drink of the cup of affliction, still we who have been born and nurtured on this soil, we, whose habits, manners, and customs are the same in common with other Americans, can never consent to take our lives in our hands, and be the bearers of the redress offered by that Society to that much afflicted country." While emigration schemes, those promoted by black leaders as well as the American Colonization Society, would continue to play a key role in convention deliberations, never in question were black claims to citizenship and its rights, and the importance of collective self-determination.

Insisting on their rightful place in the United States, blacks contrasted the clarity of their claims with the rhetorical gymnastics required to promote emigration. At the second national convention, held in Philadelphia in 1831, delegates decided that the Declaration of Independence and the Constitution should be read at every convention, "believing, that the truths contained in the former are incontrovertible; and that the latter guarantees in letter and spirit to every freeman born in the country, all the rights and immunities of citizenship." In sharp contrast to these incontrovertible truths and guaranteed rights were the arguments and strategies launched by the American Colonization Society—what the 1833 convention referred to as "that great BABEL of oppression and persecution," a tower of absurdities that had "been reared so high, that the light of heaven, the benevolence of true philanthropy, and the voice of humanity, forbid its further ascent." "The confusion of tongues has already begun," they asserted, "which speedily promises its final consummation."

A good part of that tower of Babel was built on the shifting foundation of race—the association's attempt "to establish, as a primary belief, that the coloured child, that is, the child not white, no matter how many generations he may be able to trace in a lineal ascent, is an African, and ought to be sent to the land of his forefathers—Africa." The convention noted that by the same logic, after emigrating to Africa "the colonists may be again compelled to migrate to the land of their fathers in America." The 1834 convention addressed the same concerns but noted that, however absurd, the logic proved compelling to a great many Americans, and concluded that "as long at least as the Colonization Society exists, will a Convention of coloured people be highly necessary."

Such arguments make clear the larger aim of these conventions: to improve the condition of free blacks while protesting slavery. At the third annual convention, for example, held in Philadelphia in 1833, delegates considered an ambitious program—the prospect of a manual labor school for black youths, the subject of emigration to Canada, the efforts of the American Colonization Society, and methods for dealing with the effects of alcohol in the black community. Equally important, the delegates assigned a committee to determine the status of initiatives launched by earlier conventions. All these efforts were then summarized in a "Conventional Address" to "the Free Coloured inhabitants of the United States," published with the convention's proceedings.

Attempts to create a school were a constant theme through the conventions, though this early attempt failed. But by and large the delegates were able to inform themselves and the broader public of encouraging successes, often measured by the creation of new organizations. One resolution passed at the 1833 convention, for example, was that "this Convention earnestly recommends the formation of Phoenix Societies in every State, after the form, and on the principles of the Phoenix Societies of the City of New York," an attempt to promote literary societies, discussed later. The convention's address to the broader public extended this recommendation, noting that "societies for mental improvement, particularly among the females, have been established in several places, and a manifest improvement has marked their progress."

A report on temperance, in turn, argued that the remedy for the problems created by alcohol consumption "is the simple principle of voluntary associations, on the plan of INTIRE [sic] ABSTINENCE." The committee noted that, due in part to recommendations of the preceding year's convention, a number of blacks were "more or less under the influence of Temperance Societies" and further were "members of societies connected with the different Churches and Sabbath Schools, and of other societies in almost every section of the country." The committee recommended, accordingly, an extension of this principle: the creation of "a Conventional Temperance Society, to be styled THE COLORED AMERICAN CONVENTIONAL TEMPERANCE SOCIETY." While delegates certainly recognized that each of the societies they invoked had specific purposes and did productive work, to some extent this proliferation of societies was a mark of progress. The report on temperance stated, for example, that the creation of a "conventional temperance society" "will promote unity of feeling and action, which in this work are of intrinsic importance." One great purpose of the conventions, in short, was to promote the organization of other conventions and of numerous societies, and thus to promote community through voluntary associations.

This proliferation of conventions eventually took shape, especially in the late 1840s and after. Numerous state meetings began regularly to complement the national events. But such developments followed predictable challenges of organization and unity that caused a break in the national convention movement from 1835 to 1843. Ideological differences and regional jealousies were primary causes. By the mid-1830s the African colonization movement no longer seemed an immediate threat, but many blacks did not agree that it should be completely rejected. From the beginning, conventions had dealt with the issue of black emigration to Canada—a continuing theme, since a great number of blacks, many of them former slaves, had established communities in Canada. In 1851 the North American Convention convened in Toronto and voted to encourage blacks to emigrate to Canada. By this time other blacks were advocating emigration to other regions as well—to Central America, Haiti, and parts of Africa. Such developments complicated the anti-emigrationist rhetoric that many convention delegates had once employed. But African Americans found themselves split on other concerns too—some arguing for broad-scale reform through moral persuasion, looking beyond issues of race and even nationality, and others arguing for more practical responses to racist practices and attitudes that characterized black American life. Moreover tensions persisted between certain black communities—especially in Philadelphia and New York—over matters of leadership and the direction of the convention movement. These tensions were inspired in part by the identities those communities assumed (and guarded jealously) as a result of their own local organizational efforts. Few were ready to allow the national convention movement to supplant the authority they had painstakingly established through local efforts.

Eventually the persistence of slavery and of racial discrimination, the denial of rights and the removal of rights once possessed, and the ongoing need for an organized force to deal with such concerns at the national level, to act as a nation within a nation, argued for the renewal of the national convention movement. In 1843 African Americans met in Buffalo in the first national gathering since 1835, and before the end of the Civil War conventions followed in 1847 (Troy, New York), 1848 (Cleveland), 1853 (Rochester, New York), 1855 (Philadelphia), and 1864 (Syracuse). State conventions also grew. Scattered throughout the mid-1840s and the 1850s, state conventions were convened in New York, Pennsylvania, Indiana, Michigan, New Jersey, Connecticut, Maryland, Illinois, Massachusetts, and California. Some states held only one or two conventions during this time while others (New York and Michigan) met with greater regularity, but over time conventions were established as a primary means for African Americans to organize their efforts and speak with a unified voice to the American public. In the 1860s the meetings continued, and during and after the Civil War spread to the South and West.

While the years brought many changes, a central theme remained consistent—the need to provide African Americans with uplift while countering the white community's assumptions of black inferiority. As David Walker complained in his 1829 *Appeal*, blacks were too accepting of their situation. Martin Delany would echo this lament in his 1852 manifesto *The Condition, Elevation, Emigration, and Destiny of the Colored People of the United States,* that blacks, "as a body, . . . have been taught to believe, that we must have some person to think for us, instead of thinking for ourselves"—to the point that "the most ordinary white person, is almost revered, while the most qualified colored person is totally neglected." Such concerns were front and center at the conventions, featuring a body of men representing a community that was in danger of failing even to recognize the need for such representation. As the delegates at the 1848 national convention in Cleveland expressed their concern, "The doctrine perseveringly proclaimed in high places in church and state, that it is impossible for colored men to rise from ignorance and debasement, to intelligence and respectability in this country, has made a deep impression upon the public mind generally, and is not without its effect upon us." White Americans were being persuaded while black Americans were being degraded, a process that made for a perfect circle of futility.

Breaking that circle was what the conventions tried to do, though their efforts often amounted to repeated arguments for a collective organization. As the delegates at the 1855 convention in Philadelphia put it, "Years of well-intended effort have been expended for the especial freedom of the slave, while the elevation of the free colored man as an *inseparable priority* to the same, has been entirely overlooked." In this plea they gave voice to a common concern, that white abolitionists were more concerned about the sins of slavery than about those who suffered the force of those sins, and more concerned with abstract freedom than with the recognition of humanity and fundamental equality that gave the concept of freedom meaning and purpose. Free blacks needed to turn this equation around, grounding the mission of moral reform not in bringing an end to the sin of slavery but in working toward the realization of actual freedom. "It is equally obvious," the 1855 delegates continued, "that since the work of elevation of the Free People of Color is (so to speak) the lever by which the whole must rise, that work must now receive a vigorous and hearty support from all of those upon whom it has a claim."

This mission would extend beyond the hope and finally the reality of emancipation. As Frederick Douglass declared at the 1864 meeting in Syracuse when accepting his election as convention president, "The cause which we come here to promote is sacred. Nowhere, in the 'wide, wide world,' can man be found coupled with a cause of greater dignity and importance than that which brings us here. We are here to promote the freedom, progress, elevation, and perfect enfranchisement, of the entire colored people of the United States; to show that, though slaves, we are not contented slaves, but that, like all other progressive races of men, we are resolved to advance in the scale of knowledge, worth, and civilization, and claim our rights as men among men." For this work, many believed, conventions were invaluable. According to the proceedings of the 1864 convention, when asked, "Why need we meet in a National Convention?" Douglass "showed its necessity from the state of feeling in the country toward the colored man; to answer the question, as we pass to and from this hall, by the men on the streets of Syracuse, 'Where are the d——d niggers going?'" Such unadorned racism at the site of the national convention defined both the conditions and the importance of the work to be done.

Perhaps the greatest achievement of the conventions was to spread this sense of mission, inspiring others to meet with similar determination. Even before the Civil War the convention spirit was spreading beyond the relative safety of the North, prompting resolutions of unity and self-determination in numerous gatherings across the nation. In Maryland, for example, an 1852 convention of the "free colored people" resolved, in effect, to relocate itself in time—that is, to resist the pressures of the history forced on African Americans and to insist upon being free citizens of the age. "The present age," they announced, "is one eminently distinguished for inquiry, investigation, enterprise and improvement in physical, political, intellectual, and moral sciences." Noting that "among our white neighbors every exertion is continually being made to improve their social and moral condition, and develop their intellectual faculties," the convention delegates observed, "We, the free colored people of the State of Maryland, are conscious that we have made little or no progress in improvement during the past twenty years, but are now sunken into a condition of social degradation which is truly deplorable." The delegates' resolution rested on a two-pronged moral conviction: first, that continuing in their present circumstances was "a crime and transgression against our God, ourselves and our posterity"; and, second, that "it is a duty which mankind, (colored as well as white,) owe to themselves and their Creator to embrace every opportunity for the accomplishment of this mental culture, and intellectual development, and general social improvement." Several resolutions were designed to address this moral crossroads, but the underlying point was a belief that "an organization of the friends of this just and holy cause is absolutely necessary for effecting the object so much to be desired." Through conventions, African Americans gathered together to acknowledge and define the terms of their situation, to identify its root causes, and to work toward a possible resolution—to create a community capable of promoting those virtues and achievements that the broader culture seemed just as determined to undermine and obstruct. They met, in short, to redefine themselves, to take control of the means by which they would be known to the world and to themselves.

❖

Such collective self-definitions remained a challenge, for the black community's response to the pressures of a surrounding white culture often revealed tensions within the community. There remained, too, the ongoing challenge of speaking to and for a scattered community. To be sure, in creating a formal structure for their meetings—including the rituals of conducting a meeting, selecting delegates and electing officers, and establishing rules for the proceedings—African Americans gave structure to the "free people of color" invoked in the title of the early conventions. But that title itself ignored many people who were not free. When the conventions were renewed in 1843, the Buffalo meeting became "the national convention of colored citizens." The 1847 meeting in Troy was a convention "of colored people, and their friends." Thereafter meetings were of "the colored national convention," inclusive of the enslaved, with the friends of colored people relegated to an assumed role.

As the convention titles indicate, defining the black national community was a difficult endeavor. The proceedings of the conventions made clear that maintaining a sense of community was more difficult still. Colonization plans were opposed in part because they seemed "calculated," as the 1832 convention had it, "to distract and divide the whole colored family." An 1832 committee argued that "any express plan to colonize our people beyond the limits of these United States, tends to weaken the situation of those who are left behind, without any peculiar advantage to those who emigrate." Other divisions also seemed threatening. The 1834 convention delegates expressed their concern that "the present form of society divides the interest of the community into several parts. Of these, there is that of the white man, that of the slave, and that of the free coloured man." These divisions went to the heart of the challenges addressed at these conventions—an attempt to reform, in effect, "a community of castes, with separate interests!" While convention minutes and addresses to the American public made clear the view of delegates that the moral reform of American society must begin by addressing the conditions of black life, they did not view this cause as separate from the concerns of the larger American community. They operated in the belief that a "civilization is not perfect, nor has reason full sway, until the community shall see that a wrong done to one is a wrong done to the whole; that the interest of one is or ought to be the common interest of the whole." What the system of slavery and its corresponding program of racial prejudice and discrimination revealed, for African Americans, was a fundamental, systemic failure in American society. It threatened not just blacks but the security of the nation.

Their mission was broad-scale moral reform, but it began by trying to establish the accomplishments, the determination, the capabilities, even the basic humanity of those of African origins. The authors of the 1834 "Declaration of Sentiments," addressing this mission, commented on "the downfall of Africa from her ancient pride and splendour," and looked to the day when the struggle against slavery and prejudice in the United States would spark a global religious sentiment that would reach back to Africa. "If our presence in this country will aid in producing such a desirable reform," they declared, "although we have been reared under a most debasing system of tyranny and oppression, we shall have been born under the most favourable auspices to promote the redemption of the world." This vision of African Americans as martyrs to a larger cause led those in 1834 nearly to embrace their oppression and argue against an acceptance of partial success in the United States. "Let us not lament," they stated, "that under the present constituted powers of this government, we are disfranchised; better far to be partakers of its guilt." Accordingly they counseled fellow blacks to "refuse to be allured by the glittering endowments of official stations, or enchanted with the robe of American citizenship," but instead to "choose like true patriots, rather to be the victims of oppression, than the administrators of injustice." This view was reiterated the following year at the 1835 convention, at which delegates imagined that America was "to be the instrument through the providence of Almighty God in blessing other portions of the peopled earth," a destiny that required the nation to "first purify her own dominions." In such statements convention delegates attempted to put old history in a new frame—placing themselves in the context of a providential saga which would eventually prove to be their glory.

But such visions of destiny struggled against the effects of present conditions, often provoking divisions within the black community. One effect of racial discrimination was that many blacks could find work only in service occupations, as domestics and other servants. Such concerns had been noted before—for example in one of the earliest conventions, the 1831 meeting in Philadelphia, at which an official statement declared that "it has been a subject of deep regret to this convention, that we as a people, have not availingly appreciated every opportunity placed within our power by the benevolent efforts of the friends of humanity, in elevating our condition to the rank of freemen. That our mental and physical qualities have not been more actively engaged in pursuits more lasting, is attributable in a great measure to a want of unity among ourselves; whilst our only stimulus to action has been to become domestics, which at best is but a precarious and degraded situation."

While not new, such statements tread on delicate territory, since many at the convention were engaged in menial labor. Tensions surfaced at the 1848 national convention in Cleveland, at which Martin

Delany proposed a resolution denouncing any acceptance of the servile condition of blacks. Delany, who had studied to be a doctor and had enjoyed success as a newspaper editor, believed that African Americans suffered from their own acquiescence in the skewed operations of the national economy. Four years later in *The Condition* he lamented that blacks were consumers, not producers—of houses and clothes, of wares and services. ". . . We deliberately wait until they have got them in readiness, then walk in, and contend with as much assurance for a 'right,' as though the whole thing was bought, paid for, and belonged to us." Clearly this was what Delany had in mind when he pressed his resolution against the toleration of such conditions at the 1848 convention. "The houses we live in are built by white men," the 1848 proceedings state, adding, "the clothes we wear are made by white tailors—the hats on our heads are made by white hatters, and the shoes on our feet are made by white shoe-makers, and the food that we eat, is raised and cultivated by white men." Delany's conclusions challenged the convention movement: "Now it is impossible that we should ever be respected as a people, while we are so universally and completely dependent upon white men for the necessaries of life. We must make white persons as dependent upon us, as we are upon them."

But many at the convention either occupied service positions or represented those who did, and some in attendance took offense at Delany's comments. One member, J. D. Patterson, objected to Delany's statement that "he would rather receive a telegraphic dispatch that his wife and two children had fallen victims to a loathsome disease, than to hear that they had become the servants of any man." A discussion ensued, in which Frederick Douglass suggested, "Let us say what is necessary to be done, is honorable to do; and leave situations in which we are considered degraded, as soon as necessity ceases." The delegates then determined that "the Convention was composed of Printers, Carpenters, Blacksmiths, Shoemakers, Engineer, Dentist, Gunsmiths, Editors, Tailors, Merchants, Wheelrights, Painters, Farmers, Physicians, Plasterers, Masons, Students, Clergymen, Barbers and Hair Dressers, Laborers, Coopers, Livery Stable Keepers, Bath House Keepers, Grocery Keepers." The dispute was resolved, but this was only one of several signs that divisions in the black community would find their way into this body that claimed representative authority.

The spirit of Delany's resolution was nonetheless acknowledged in the form of a resolution against "a portion of those of our colored citizens called barbers" who refused "to treat colored men on equality with the whites," thereby encouraging "prejudice among the whites of the several States." The delegates resolved to "recommend to this class of men a change in their course of action relative to us," adding that "if this change is not immediately made, we consider them base serviles, worthy only of the condemnation, censure, and defamation of all lovers of liberty, equality, and right." In this resolution and in the general thrust of the convention movement, African Americans asserted a collective identity that extended beyond ancestry or the color of one's skin. To be African American was to live up to certain standards of collective concern and resistance to the racist social order.

Perhaps to pursue this collective meditation on membership within the black community, the convention addressed its own membership as well, passing a resolution recognizing "the equality of the sexes" and inviting "females hereafter to take part in our deliberations." Both before and after this resolution, the communal body at the conventions was decidedly male. The 1848 *Proceedings* included a brief excerpt from a speech by Mrs. Sanford, tracing women's historical degradation from Eve and regeneration through Christ, born of a woman. She insisted on women's right to "co-operate in making the laws we obey," noting that the demand "is not to domineer, to dictate or assume. We ask it, for it is a right granted by a higher disposer of human events than man." Following the speech, the delegates resumed discussion "on the indefinite postponement of the Resolution as to Woman's Right." Ultimately it was passed "with three cheers for woman's rights." Still, men saw no reason why black conventions should alter the gender practices of the day, and those women who participated in the conventions were relegated to the sidelines. While accepting that position, women who addressed the conventions reminded men of the seriousness of the responsibilities they assumed if they were to maintain authority over women. Speaking to the State Convention of Colored Men in Columbus, Ohio, for example, Sara Stanley, representing the all-black Ladies' Anti-Slavery Society of Delaware, Ohio, noted that while the men were there to fight for their rights, those rights would yet not be available to women. Stanley advised them to "press on," for "manhood's prerogatives are yours by Almighty fiat." She concluded her speech by quoting "a Spartan mother's fare-well to her son, 'Bring home your shield or be brought upon it.'" Stanley added to the gentlemen of the convention, "To you we would say, be true, be courageous, be steadfast in the discharge of your duty," a duty that women would support "in our fireside circles" and "in the seclusion of our closets."

Even by 1864, when women were invited to play a greater role as speakers before the convention, women's voices are largely missing from the record. The *Proceedings* note, for example, that at one point the convention president, Frederick Douglass, "introduced Miss Edmonia Highgate, an accomplished young lady of Syracuse." Douglass had ear-lier associated Highgate with Anna Dickinson, a white Quaker speaker known for her feminist and anti-slavery views. Apparently addressing a white audience within and beyond the walls of the convention, Douglass declared, "You have your Anna Dickinsons; and we have ours. We wish to meet you at every point." Apparently Highgate was valued more as exhibit than as speaker, for all that is recorded of her speech is that "Miss Highgate urged the Convention to trust in God and press on, and not abate one jot or tittle until the glorious day of jubilee shall come." At that same convention the accomplished activist, speaker, and poet Frances E. W. Harper is treated only briefly. "Mrs. Frances Ellen Watkins Harper was then introduced," the *Proceedings* note, "and spoke feelingly and elo-quently of our hopes and prospects in this country."

Beyond these few references, women's presence at the conventions, and in the community, can be observed more by implication than by design— in comments, for example, on the home and the instruction of children, in mentions of the lack of ownership of one's wife under slavery, or in references to the violations of wives and daughters under slavery. More direct commentary on women's lives and the broader field of women's labor is generally absent from convention proceedings, and somewhat awkward when included. The 1853 convention's Report of the Commit-tee on Manual Labor School, for example, offered detailed recommenda-tions for the importance of the trades for men but seemed at a loss when it addressed women's labor. "The Department of Industry for Females," the report noted, "the Committee cannot, in the short time given them, intelligently settle upon, except in outline." Such vague traces are all that one can detect of African-American women in the communal body. The masculine realms of experience remained the official sites upon which the conventions built the foundations of black community.

Of course the tensions within the black community were in part the inevitable result of being surrounded by a racist white community—even when blacks were among friends and allies. White abolitionists and reformers were a strong presence at the black national conventions, especially in the early years, and for good reason. The interracial alliances formed in the anti-slavery movement were important to the African American leadership, and many blacks found weekly support in such publications as William Lloyd Garrison's *Liberator*. Yet there were always tensions between black and white abolitionists too, however close they might be. White abolitionists, though reviled by many whites, nonetheless enjoyed the privileges and access available to white men in the nineteenth century—privileges that sometimes led to an assumption of the right to claim leadership. White abolitionists gave Frederick Douglass, for example, his start in the anti-slavery movement, leading to one of the most important careers in public service in the nineteenth century. But in his second autobiography, *My Bondage and My Freedom*, published in 1855, Douglass famously complained about the role he was asked to assume in the movement, when he was told to simply tell the story of his life, and with a "plantation manner of speech," and leave the philosophy to his white colleagues. In an 1857 speech, Douglass extended his experience to that of African Americans generally, those involved in the anti-slavery and convention movements and other efforts at self-determination. "I know, my friends," he said, "that in some quarters the efforts of colored people meet with very little encouragement. We may fight, but we must fight like the Sepoys of India, under white officers." And while they proclaimed their support, Douglass asserted, those white officers insisted on their authority. "This class of Abolitionists," Douglass continued, "don't like colored celebrations, they don't like colored conventions, they don't like colored antislavery fairs for the support of colored newspapers." White assumptions of leadership ran deep—indeed, Douglass asserted, as deep as blood, for "they talk of the proud Anglo-Saxon blood as flippantly as those who profess to believe in the natural inferiority of races."

To a great extent, the problem Douglass noted involved the challenge of determining the guidelines for moral reform. As their experience had demonstrated beyond doubt, the Christian churches of the nation were, by and large, more a part of the problem than of a solution, and they both reflected and influenced the ways in which white moral sentiment negotiated the color line. In a resolution passed at the 1843 national convention in Buffalo, for example, the delegates asserted, "We believe in the true Church of Christ, and that it will stand while time endures, and that it will evince its spirit by its opposition to all sins, and especially to the sin of slavery, which is a compound of all others, and that the great mass of American sects, falsely called churches, which apologize for slavery and prejudice, or practice slaveholding, are in truth no churches, but Synagogues of Satan." But that was not all. In the second of this series of resolutions, the conventioneers stated, "*Resolved*, That we solemnly believe that slaveholding and prejudice sustaining ministers and churches (falsely so called), are the greatest enemies to Christ and to civil and religious liberty in the world." This seems fairly clear, but the complexity of the ground it covers is indicated by the resolution that followed: "*Resolved*, That the colored people in the free States who belong to pro-slavery sects that will not pray for the oppressed—nor preach the truth in regard to the sin of slavery and all other existing evils, nor publish anti-slavery meetings, nor act for the entire immediate abolition of slavery, are guilty of enslaving themselves and others, and their blood, and the blood of perishing millions will be upon their heads." This resolution identified pro-slavery activity as both deliberate action and compliant inaction, and made it clear that "the Christianity of America" included both white and black as well as both South and North.

These resolutions then moved to a final statement directed rather clearly to black Americans and theoretically to white Americans as well: "*Resolved*, That it is the bounded duty of every person to come out from among these religious organizations in which they are not permitted to enjoy equality." Like the barbers who refused to attend to black patrons, many black Christians were condemned for failing to meet the demands of being black in the United States, for separating themselves from the larger cause of the community. If even African Americans could fall so low, what of white Americans—even those involved in anti-slavery efforts?

These resolutions were echoed in the 1847 national convention held in Troy, New York, which emphasized that moral degradation had become a structural principle in the United States, undermining the nation's professed ideals. In a series of resolutions the delegates first offered thanks to God for "the signal success" of the anti-slavery movement, pledged themselves "to be faithful to the interests of our enslaved brethren until death," and then turned to two overarching problems, religion and inalienable rights. A resolution on religion declared that "those sects (falsely called Christian Churches) who tolerate Caste, and practice Slave holding, are nothing more than synagogues of Satan." The second observed that "the Declaration of American Independence is not a lie, and, if the fathers of the Revolution were not base and shameless hypocrites, it is evident that all men are created equal, and are endowed by their Creator with certain inalienable rights, among which are life, liberty and the pursuit of happiness." Claiming authority over these ideals—over even the very language of morality and political rights—was a central concern throughout the conventions and the most pressing point behind declarations of sentiment and published addresses to the general public.

In the resolutions that followed, though, the delegates acknowledged the hard work required to transform these resolutions into results. The delegates addressed temperance, the need to continue organizing state and national conventions, the need to publish an address to the public, and the need to "recommend" to blacks across the country "the propriety of instructing their sons in the art of war." As years passed, those attending the conventions knew that moral suasion would not be enough. They looked to the demands for action and even the possibility of physical conflict in the struggle ahead.

By 1855 this drive for practical action was manifest in a renewed effort to protect black workers who suffered discrimination in their various trades by establishing the means for them to borrow money. The published proceedings of this convention include an overview of African-American trades and accumulated wealth in states from New England to the West. For each state are figures showing the number of African Americans working at specific trades along with a separate list of those qualified for such work but either unemployed or unable to apply their training or follow their vocations. "We would recommend our clergy, our teachers, and leading men, and above all our women on whom we must depend for our future leaders," an ensuing document stated, "to inculcate a disposition for trades, agriculture and such of the higher branches of business as are necessary and requisite to develop persistence—our requirement to do something for the advancement of Society from the cradle to the grave!" African Americans must, in short, organize themselves into a community with its own economy, a nation within a nation capable of raising the hopes of rising generations while also sending a message to the white community—"to destroy," as the delegates put it, "the opinion that we raise our children to that sweet stage of life which prepares them for business (16 years) with no other aspirations than to be a waiter."

But if the tensions between black and white America were obvious, drawing boundaries between these two overlapping and highly contingent communities proved impossible, as was emphasized at the 1865 convention held in Syracuse. Two episodes involving Henry Highland Garnet are especially revealing. In the first, Garnet addressed the convention on the racism he had witnessed in the New York City draft riots of 1863. The whites involved in those riots were responding to their sense that the Civil War was being fought for the freedom of blacks, who would then take jobs away from the poorer classes of whites, especially the Irish. Many African Americans were killed during the riots, and their bodies placed on display. Garnet provided an eyewitness account of these events, relating the story of "how one man was hung upon a tree; and that then a demon in human form, taking a sharp knife, cut out pieces of the quivering flesh, and offered it to the greedy, blood-thirsty mob, saying, 'Who wants some nigger meat?' and then the reply, 'I!' 'I!' 'I!' as if they were scrambling for pieces of gold."

But this was not just a story of the "demoniac hate" of racism, for Garnet continued the story of whiteness by describing how various ethnic groups were gathered under the umbrella of whiteness when they emigrated to the United States. Referring "to the nationality of those composing that mob," Garnet "said he could not tell how it was that men crossing the ocean only should change as much as they." Garnet, we are told, "had traveled from Belfast to Cork, and from Dublin to the Giant's Causeway, and the treatment he received was uniformly that of kindness." So how to explain the change upon the arrival of Irish immigrants to the United States? Garnet "attributed the change in the Irish people to the debasing influence of unprincipled American politicians." One might say they were Irish when they left Ireland but became white when they arrived in the United States.

While the delegates could appreciate this story of racial transformation, of the whiteness formed by not being blackness, the other episode involving Garnet at the 1865 convention underscored the difficulty of following those clear divisions with action. The issue involved emigration. African Americans had been warming to the idea of emigration over the years, as their experience in the United States suggested there was little hope of achieving equality there. But the signal difference from the efforts of the American Colonization Society was that these developing plans for emigration were led by black Americans. In 1858, at the suggestion of a white man, Benjamin Coates, a supporter of the American Colonization Society, one of these plans took form in the organization of the African Civilization Society, an interracial organization that elected Garnet its first president. Given the similarity of the mission of each of the movements, Garnet was widely criticized for his involvement with this organization. That criticism reemerged at the 1865 meeting when it was proposed that the African Civilization Society be endorsed as one of many "associations for freedom." Garnet defended himself, declaring his belief in a "Negro nationality." But another delegate, George T. Downing of Rhode Island, called the African Civilization Society "the child of prejudice," noting that the "originators assert that the colored man cannot be elevated in the United States; that black men must be 'massed to themselves' and have a grand fight for a 'Negro nationality,' before they can be respected!" Garnet asked his fellow delegates whether they believed that, "so late in his public life, he had begun to falsify himself by putting himself under the direction, and being made the fool, of white men." He and Downing had long disputed this issue, he added, suggesting that Downing's purpose was to "cripple" Garnet's "influence on this Convention."

Similar disputes may be found in the proceedings and certainly in the background of all the conventions—as, indeed, they arise wherever men and women gather in virtually any official capacity. What is significant about the quarrels that ran through the black state and national conventions is not that there were disagreements and jealousies and competitions for power but rather that the disputes demonstrated just how difficult it was to close the door on white America so as to deliberate the future of black America. Just as Garnet witnessed the transformation of many Irish upon their arrival in New York, African Americans witnessed again and again the limits of interracial alliances in the United States, the boundaries of racial understanding and sympathy. Moreover blacks discovered time and again the challenge of imagining themselves as a nation within a nation, and they struggled to present the conventions as truly representative bodies, speaking *from* and not just *to* the scattered communities of those of African origins in the United States. What the conventions accomplished was the creation of a unified front, an assembly where disagreements and tensions within the community could be aired and brought to order. By promoting the procedural rituals of community, the conventions succeeded in serving as a focal point for a great number of black organizations and an inspiration for the formation of others.

❖

Ultimately, what one encounters in the minutes and proceedings of the conventions are the signs of a developing community, defined by consistent themes but also by an evolving argument, a rising collective voice. At the state level, conventions spread across the country as blacks gathered to announce (to themselves as well as to others) their presence and collective force in the state. But the national conventions tell the story of a different kind of unity, one defined not by geography but by a growing commitment to an ideological community. Over the course of the conventions, African Americans made an important transition. Through all the conventions they faced the challenge of responding to racism, of countering the stereotypes and insults promoted virtually everywhere in white culture while trying to establish their claims to basic rights and opportunities. As the delegates of the 1853 meeting in Rochester put it, "What stone has been left unturned to degrade us? What hand has refused to fan the flame of prejudice against us? What American artist has not caricatured us? What wit has not laughed at us in our wretchedness? What songster has not made merry over our depressed spirits? What press has not ridiculed and contemned us? What pulpit has withheld from our devoted heads its angry lightning, or its sanctimonious hate?" Such complaints may be found in African-American publications from the first years of the convention movement to the end of the century, and indeed beyond. What changed was not so much the situation that blacks faced but rather the collective spirit they gathered in the process of meeting their challenges in organized meetings. In the development of that unified front, familiar arguments began to take form in such a way as not just to answer critics from without but to define a community from within.

The story should begin with perhaps the most important result of the conventions, the fact that African Americans gathered to organize their resistance to an oppressive state. The delegates of the 1832 convention in Philadelphia paused to look ahead at what they hoped would be a movement capable of transforming black Americans from an oppressed people to a real community. "We have a right to expect that future Conventions will be increased by a geometrical ratio," they declared, "until we shall present a body, not inferior in numbers to our state legislatures." This shadow government would be forceful in and of itself, they believed— "the *phenomena* of an *oppressed people*, deprived of the rights of citizenship, in the midst of an enlightened nation, devising plans and measures, for their personal and mental elevation." For this internal nation to work, though, for it to have the global influence implicitly envisioned in this statement, some degree of self-governance would be necessary. This requirement led to one of the other primary themes of the convention movement—the attempt to inculcate certain principles by which blacks should know themselves, principles designed to shape the private lives of this very public community.

The advice offered at the 1832 gathering is typical of what one finds throughout the convention movement: "Be righteous, be honest, be just, be economical, be prudent, offend not the laws of your country—in a word, live in that purity of life, by both precept and example—live in the constant pursuit of that moral and intellectual strength, which will invigorate your understandings, and render you illustrious in the eyes of civilized nations, when they will assert, that all that illustrious worth, which was once possessed by the Egyptians, and slept for ages, has now arisen in their descendants, the inhabitants of the new world." Pivotal to this statement is the complex historical consciousness that the conventions promoted. It was an attempt to claim authority over an ancient history so as to reimagine the present as a significant return, one that would place those of African origins not at the margins but at the center of the civilized world.

Through their public addresses at the conventions, later published, African Americans took seriously this assumed leadership role. They believed their cause was historically important precisely because they were oppressed "in the midst of an enlightened nation." Many blacks viewed their struggle as a continuation of the American Revolution. As those attending the 1835 convention announced, "We plead for the extension of those principles on which our government was formed, that it in turn may become purified from those iniquitous inconsistencies into which she has fallen by her aberration from first principles; that the laws of our country may cease to conflict with the spirit of that sacred instrument, the Declaration of American Independence." The struggle for black rights was here portrayed as a significant return to the guiding spirit of the Revolution, a task of purifying a nation that had fallen from its defining principles. Like many of America's founding revolutionaries, too, blacks viewed their struggle as having global importance, an example to the world. "We believe in a pure, unmixed republicanism," they announced in 1835, "as a form of government best suited to the condition of man, by its promoting equality, virtue, and happiness to all within its jurisdiction."

This was not simply a rhetorical claim. Convention delegates demonstrated an understanding of republican theory, central to which was the belief in a fundamental connection between the character of the republic and the character of individual citizens. It also included an awareness of a republic's inevitable corruption, as government accumulates more power and shifts toward subtle new forms of tyranny, and as civic virtue—succumbing to the republic's own economic prosperity—is displaced by a love of luxury. As the white abolitionist Lydia Maria Child put it in an 1827 handbook for middle-class housewives, "A luxurious and idle *republic*! Look at the phrase!—The words were never made to be married together; every body sees it would be death to one of them." Thus what was most threatening to the stability of a republic were the effects of its own material success upon the character of individual citizens. Accordingly, the conventions promoted principles that balanced immediate needs with broad philosophical doctrine. "We shall advocate the cause of peace," the delegates stated in 1835, "believing that whatever tends to the destruction of human life, is at variance with the precepts of the Gospel." "We shall advocate a system of *economy*," they added, "not only because luxury is injurious to individuals, but because its practice exercises an influence on society, which in its very nature is sinful." And similarly, in that same statement, they pledged themselves to the cause of "universal liberty, as the inalienable right of every individual born in the world," and promised to devote themselves to "the extinction of mental thraldom." They envisioned their struggle, in short, as one taking place as much in the battlefields of the mind as in the fields of labor and social practice. Making clear the terms of this struggle, the 1835 statement emphasized, "We will not stoop to contend with those who style us inferior beings." This was not simply a struggle against oppressors; it was a struggle against oppression itself.

In many ways, then, the African-American convention movement echoed the development of the larger nation, including white concerns for the historical instability of republics. The difference was that blacks believed they had discovered—and, indeed, embodied—the weakness in the national development. But in their attention to the character and deportment of African Americans, the leaders of the national conventions were similar to many white observers who believed in a fundamental connection between individual and national character and who valued the United States not simply as a political entity but as an idea, a new way of thinking about human governance.

In the dominant culture this analogy between individual and nation, and even between mind and nation, was particularly attractive to a country struggling for order, self-definition, and empire. This is the cultural mode of nationalism that Joel Barlow, for example, had in mind when, in his 1792 *Advice to the Privileged Orders in the Several States of Europe* (a title which itself views Europe as a potential union of states), he identified a "*habit of thinking*" as "the *only* foundation" for a sociopolitical system. "The *habit of thinking*," Barlow explained, considering primarily the doctrine of equality, "has so much of nature in it, it is so undistinguishable from the indelible marks of the man, that it is a perfectly safe foundation for any system that we may choose to build upon it." Indeed, "it is the only point of contact by which men communicate as moral associates."

This mode of national self-conception inspired George Bancroft—who once referred to America as an "empire of mind"—to write a history of the United States which begins with the earliest precolonial adventures and ends (in a supplement to the original ten-volume work) with the writing of the Constitution—the point being that "America" was an idea that evolved through the ages and was finally realized in the United States and institutionalized in the Constitution. Similarly, in an 1818 letter to Hezekiah Niles, John Adams asserted that "the real American Revolution" was the "radical change in the principles, opinions, sentiments, and affections of the people," a change that took place "before a drop of blood was shed."

If the nation was a mode of thought, an intellectual method, a revolution of principles, opinion, sentiments, and affections, the fundamental duty of republican citizens was to learn how to use their minds "correctly," to organize their critical approach according to the demands of moral law. Promoting a national community, then, required an attempt to influence not *what* but *how* people thought, and to convince that community that it was the *how*, not the *what*, upon which ideological, social, and moral unity would depend. Involved is a conception of public address similar to Thomas Jefferson's, as presented in *A Summary View of the Rights of British America* (1774), of "the language of truth." For Jefferson, this language is a narrative "divested of those expressions of servility which would persuade his majesty that we are asking favors, and not rights." In other words, it is a language which itself represents a communal consensus, which asserts its distinctiveness by insisting upon its epistemological authority, and which therefore makes much of the substance of the "asking" seem like merely rhetorical questions, there to validate the author's basic position and to limit the reader's possible responses. This is the language to which the conventions were devoted, and establishing and publicizing that language and the mode of thought it represented was a primary aim of the convention. Throughout the convention movement, African Americans declared their faith in what they called, in 1835, "the omnipotence of Truth." They worked to craft a "language of truth" suited specifically to the situation of African Americans. In 1834 the delegates declared that "under whatever pretext or authority laws have been promulgated or executed, whether under parliamentary, colonial, or American legislation, *we declare* them in the sight of Heaven wholly *null* and *void*, and should be *immediately abrogated*." Such words would require a revolution. It was slow in coming, but throughout the convention movement one can observe the sort of revolution that John Adams remembered before the American Revolution, one of intellect and sentiment, of principle and method.

Of course, this would need to be a revolution without as well as within the developing African-American community—a transformation in white minds and sentiments as well as in black—though throughout the convention movement blacks argued that such a revolution should not be necessary. At the 1853 convention the delegates addressed the broader public as members of the same ideological community, greeting them as "fellow-citizens" and noting that their cause was originally defined by white America. "We cannot announce the discovery of any new principle adapted to ameliorate the condition of mankind," they declared, adding,

> The great truths of moral and political science, upon which we rely, and which we press upon your consideration, have been evolved and enunciated by you. We point to your principles, your wisdom, and to your great example as the full justification of our course this day. That "ALL MEN ARE CREATED EQUAL": that "LIFE LIBERTY, AND THE PURSUIT OF HAPPINESS" ARE THE RIGHT OF ALL; that "TAXATION AND REPRESENTA-TION" SHOULD GO TOGETHER; THAT GOVERNMENTS ARE TO PROTECT, NOT TO DESTROY, THE RIGHTS OF MANKIND; that THE CONSTITUTION OF THE UNITED STATES WAS FORMED TO ESTABLISH JUSTICE, PROMOTE THE GEN-ERAL WELFARE, AND SECURE THE BLESSINGS OF LIBERTY TO ALL THE PEOPLE OF THIS COUNTRY; THAT RESISTANCE TO TYRANTS IS OBEDIENCE TO GOD—are American principles and maxims, and together they form and con-stitute the constructive elements of the American government.

On one hand, the conventions simply confirmed American principles and devoted themselves to the argument that "we are Americans, and as Americans, we would speak to Americans." On the other hand, they felt they had to shout to be heard by Americans, and they had to explain even so basic a statement as "we are Americans." And so they did: "By birth, we are American citizens; by the principles of the Declaration of Inde-pendence, we are American citizens; within the meaning of the United States Constitution, we are American citizens; by the facts of history, and the admissions of American statesmen, we are American citizens; by the hardships and trials endured; by the courage and fidelity displayed by our ancestors in defending the liberties and in achieving the independence of our land, we are American citizens." These ties of principle, deep experi-ence, and the tests of history, though, were not enough. African Ameri-cans would turn again and again to such arguments throughout the convention movement, quoting from the Declaration of Independence, publishing their own declarations of rights (and of wrongs committed against them), and continually making the case that they had a right to be recognized, that they had suffered wrongs that would dwarf those used to justified the American Revolution.

So it was that the conventions became increasingly devoted to an imagined nation within the fallen nation—a reapplication of the principles and rights used to justify the formation of a separate country forged in revolution. To reach the point where they would be recognized as part of the larger nation—recognized in rights and opportunities as well as in their presence in the cultural landscape—blacks needed to imagine themselves first as a nation within a nation, an organized collective engaged in revolution against an oppressive force. As the delegates declared at the 1843 convention in Buffalo, "The oppressed in all ages of the world have emerged from their condition of degradation and servitude in proportion as they have exerted themselves in their *own cause*, and have convinced the world and their oppressors that they were determined to be free." These exertions, many blacks believed, required the work of the convention movement, the means by which a scattered collective could be made a self-determining community. "The history of the present and the past," the Buffalo convention asserted, "establish the great truth that it is as much impossible for any people to secure the enjoyment of their inalienable rights without organization, as it is to reach an end without means. Acting in accordance with this truth, the oppressed people of England, Ireland and Scotland, have banded themselves together in their respective nations to wage unceasing war against the green-eyed monster, tyranny."

African Americans similarly needed to band together. In renewing the convention movement in 1843 after a break of several years, those organizing the Buffalo gathering asserted their sense of purpose: "Since we have ceased to meet together in National Convention, we have become ignorant of the moral and intellectual strength of our people. We have also been deprived of the councils of our fathers, who have borne the burden and heat of the day—the spirit of virtuous ambition and emulation has died in the bosoms of the young men, and in great degree we have become divided, and the bright rising stars that once shone in our skies, have become partially obscured." As much as anything else, the convention movements brought together in a concentrated event information

about the black community, evidence of black accomplishments, and opportunities for black leadership.

Particularly since the convention leadership and attendees endorsed
both the principles of the American Revolution and the doctrines of
Christianity, how might these black organizations distinguish their cause
while working toward an imagined nation free of racial distinctions? For
many blacks, this challenge involved the distinction between how white
America imagined itself and how it had developed over the years, between principle and practice. To some extent, too, a gap existed between
national institutions (the products of revolutionary habits of thought and
governing methods) and the nation's people, who had, in effect, fallen
out of the habit of being American. The delegates at the 1843 Buffalo
convention announced, for example, "We must profit by the example of
our oppressors. We must act on their principles in resisting tyranny. We
must adopt their resolutions in favor of liberty." These sentiments were
echoed at the 1848 convention in Cleveland, during which delegates advised the black community "to occupy memberships and stations among
white persons, and in white institutions, just so fast as our rights are se-
cured to us." Recognizing the need for clarification, they added, "We say,
avail yourselves of *white* institutions, not because they are white, but because they afford a more convenient means of improvement." Similarly,
those attending the 1855 convention declared, "This republic is yet in its
infancy, and we must grow with it—let us follow in the footsteps of the
whites in this respect, as the only tangible ground—we must use similar
means to reach similar ends, notwithstanding disabilities. If we can live
in this country, bidding defiance to its wicked laws, we can do anything
that prosperity requires at our hands."

The challenge was thus to see past white dominance so as to value
those institutions essential to a republican community while also re-
maining vigilant against the racist guards at the institutional doors. This
struggle would ensure that black America would establish not only its
equality but also its superiority in a nation that had abandoned all principle for the sake of slavery and racial control. The effort would require
African-American adaptations of one institution above all: education.

6

Breaking "The Chains of Ignorance"

ANYONE VISITING Dimond Library at the University of New Hampshire is likely to notice a painting placed at the right of the doors as one exits—a portrait of an African-American woman. An adjoining plaque identifies her as: "Elizabeth Ann Virgil. The first African-American woman to be graduated from the University of New Hampshire, Class of 1926. Her achievements symbolize the courage and self-confidence to be the first in any endeavor. She is an inspiration to future generations of UNH students."

The University of New Hampshire was established in 1868 as the New Hampshire College of Agriculture and Mechanic Arts. Its first female student was admitted in 1891, and even at the beginning of the twenty-first century the university was still struggling to attract a substantial number of black students. Thus the school has reason to commemorate Virgil's achievements, and anyone who stops to look at the portrait is likely to reflect on the challenges of being among the first to break the color line at any university. Indeed, it is often by such individual achievements that African-American progress has been measured—a history told in stories of significant firsts, the lives and achievements of pioneering individuals, brave souls who experienced the isolation and often the abuse that comes from breaking through the boundaries of social convention. From the nineteenth century to the present, African-American history has been regularly related through books comprised of biographical sketches. A prominent theme in many of those profiles is the story of how an individual overcame the odds, broke the barriers, and received an education in schools once closed to blacks.

There were many such individuals in the nineteenth century, each one a story not only about a person transformed by education but also an educational system transformed—or, at the very least, agitated—by an individual who was simply determined to receive an education. There is, after all, a reason why various schools and civic organizations continue to commemorate these important firsts. One might be hard put to discover the first white male to be enrolled in many of the nation's colleges and universities, since those institutions were established, after all, for white males. But one can often find, in libraries and other academic halls, in books and on websites, the names of the first African American or Native American or white woman to attend the institution.

The first African Americans to receive baccalaureate degrees from U.S. colleges and universities—all of them male, since black women had a double obstacle to negotiate—were pioneers indeed: Alexander Twilight at Middlebury College (1823), Edward Jones at Amherst College (1826), John Russwurm at Bowdoin College (1826), and Edward Mitchell at Dartmouth College (1828). In some cases the institutions themselves experienced important changes because of their decision to admit blacks. Intense protests erupted, for example, when Ohio's Oberlin College first admitted blacks, but Oberlin would soon become an important center for African-American education. At times students and faculty were behind the protest against admitting blacks, though at Dartmouth College student petitions helped reverse a policy that had denied consideration to black applicants.

But behind the list of firsts that so often represents African-American progress is a longer record of those who faced severe trials in their efforts to achieve an education. Some indication of these intertwined stories—of collective struggle and isolated achievements—can be found in the way success stories are related in nineteenth-century books devoted to black history. In one of the most important historical works written by an African American before the Civil War, William C. Nell's *The Colored Patriots of the American Revolution*, published in 1855, readers encounter a comprehensive portrait of black contributions to the nation, emphasizing but not limited to military history. At the close of this book, Nell mentions "a colored girl in Portsmouth, N.H." who had been recently granted a high school diploma, and then Edwin Garrison Draper's graduation from Dartmouth College in 1855. It is as if Nell wished to include these achievements but did not know how to fold them into the larger story. For he knew that there was no larger story of educational progress to tell, and the individual tales were themselves complicated.

Consider, for example, the story of one of the most prominent black leaders of the nineteenth century, Martin Delany. Delany had studied medicine with Dr. Andrew N. McDowell in Pittsburgh and eventually wished to continue his medical education. Some medical schools were in fact admitting blacks, but mostly students who were destined for emigration to Liberia. Delany wanted to pursue a medical practice in the United States. He applied to the University of Pennsylvania but was rejected, and then he was denied by various other institutions. When he applied to Berkshire Medical College in Pittsfield, Massachusetts, which had accepted other blacks, he was again turned down when he told the dean that he did not intend to move to Liberia after receiving his degree. Finally Delany was accepted at Harvard Medical School—but after a semester and various student petitions and resolutions, the faculty voted to dismiss him and two other black students who had been admitted.

African-American writers like Nell, Delany, William Wells Brown, and others told the stories of individual achievements, as we continue to do today, because they understood the importance of education in the struggles of African Americans to improve their condition, both individual and collective. Even these stories of individual breakthroughs became narratives of important community progress. After graduating from Bowdoin College in 1826, for example, John Russwurm helped establish and edit the nation's first black newspaper, *Freedom's Journal*, a paper that did much to encourage the development of the African-American community and to mobilize black activists of the time. After graduating from Dartmouth College in 1841, Thomas Paul, Jr., became a teacher and headmaster of Boston's all-black Smith School, formerly the African School, one of many influential schools. But while they recorded such stories with pride, blacks were not satisfied with individual achievements. By 1860 only roughly thirty African Americans had received degrees from colleges. Community leaders, grassroots activists, and parents alike understood the limits of such numbers, and they knew that the community required efforts at every educational level, long before their children could be prepared for college.

❖

African-American leaders recognized that education was the key to their liberation from white racial control and to their self-definition as a people, and they knew as well the effects of a lack of education. It was not simply that individual ambitions were thwarted; the problem was that African Americans found it difficult to achieve a *systemic* approach to collective uplift—the social process by which those with a measure of wealth and influence create opportunities for others. Moreover the effects of a denial of education extended over generations, in many cases encouraging blacks to believe that the racist characterizations of their character and abilities were grounded in reality and that the occupations available to them were all they could reasonably hope for. As David Walker put it in his *Appeal*, "Ignorance, my brethren, is a mist, low down into the very dark and almost impenetrable abyss in which, our fathers for many centuries have been plunged."

The process by which their subjugation was perpetuated was clear, and African Americans addressed this process in their earliest writings. In a statement written in response to allegations that black Philadelphians had taken pecuniary advantage of an outbreak of yellow fever, including charges that "some of them were even detected in plundering," Absalom Jones and Richard Allen responded with their own history of the event, but they included a statement about how education both contributed to and reflected white racist views. "We believe," Jones and Allen observed, "if you would try the experiment of taking a few black children, and cultivate their minds with the same care, and let them have the same prospect in view, as to living in the world, as you would wish for your own children, you would find upon the trial, they were not inferior in mental endowments." To Jones and Allen the problem was systemic, extending far beyond the availability of equal schools, and involved prospects for living in the world. In a white supremacist culture, with both government and social opinion against them, African Americans could not hope for much from education. They would need to create their own opportunities.

The needs were great. As Maria Stewart remarked in an 1832 lecture, there can be "no chains so galling as the chains of ignorance." While many African Americans valued and promoted education, many others lacked even basic literacy. In 1807, for example, of forty-nine members of the AME Bethel Church in Philadelphia, only eighteen could sign their own names. From 1813 to 1815 that city's black mariners demonstrated a much lower literacy race than the city's white mariners, with only 28 percent able to sign their names as opposed to 50 percent of their white brethren. In the Beech and Roberts settlements in Indiana, black farming communities, only 20 percent of residents aged forty or older could read or write in 1850, the consequence of their upbringing, such as it was, in the Old South.

These communities were determined that their children and grand-children would have a different experience, and in all areas where education was accessible, the benefits of such opportunities were clear. But Jones and Allen's understanding of education as a systemic enterprise remained all too relevant, for even when educational opportunities were made available, black children often were unable to take advantage of them. At the time most children of a lower social class, black and white, became either indentured servants or apprentices, to allay expenses and to prepare them for an occupation. So black children were at the mercy of their masters, who were often white, if they wanted time away from work to attend schools available to them. While this was a problem for white children as well, such limitations were more keenly felt and their effects more serious in the black community, where social mobility had strict limitations. The stakes were high, and everything depended on accessing or creating the means by which black children and adults alike might acquire an education. Walker advised readers of his *Appeal*, "Remember, to let the aim of your labours among your brethren, and particularly the youths, be the dissemination of education and religion."

Even though leading blacks agreed on the importance of education, they often disagreed about how to manage it, and upon what principles. Various writers for the *Anglo-African Magazine*, published in 1859, agreed that the approach to education must be particularly suited to black children. "We are too apt to take the precepts that are taught to the ruling race in this country," argued M. H. Freeman, "and apply them to ourselves without considering that different traits in our character, either natural or acquired by our different circumstances, require an entirely different treatment." What, then, would that different treatment be?— or, as Freeman asked, "What then is an education?" "It is certainly not," he continued, "as many seem to suppose, merely a large collection of facts laid up in the store-house of memory, whence may be brought forth at any time and in any quantity things new and old. Nor is it a mere knowledge of languages, mathematics, histories and philosophies. The various sciences, each and all, may be used as a means of education, but they are not the education itself. Education is the harmonious development of the physical, mental, and moral powers of man."

For Freeman, what followed from this quite reasonable concept of education was that education was part of a larger system, and that blacks needed to play a role in every part of that system if their children were to be properly educated. In part this meant they would be inspired by the opportunities for which they were preparing and reassured as to their chances of claiming those opportunities. "We need the educating power of wealth," Freeman argued, "of civil and political honors and offices for our children, for these are the means that first develop in the children of the other race, that due self-respect and self-reliance which must lie at the foundation of any just and harmonious development of mind."

In the *Anglo-African Magazine*, Freeman's article was followed almost immediately by one from the clergyman Daniel Alexander Payne, in which Payne cautioned that "knowledge is more to be desired, and really more valuable than gold." "Give your child gold without knowledge," Payne argued, "and this will be the self-evident proof that you wish to curse him." Payne was as impatient with alternate priorities as Freeman, exclaiming at one point, "Don't tell us that you have educated him as well as enriched him. For there is many an educated fool. Give him *first of all*, that *knowledge* which will *qualify* him to make a *right proper* and *beneficent* use of gold, or give him no gold at all."

In the same issue Frances Ellen Watkins echoed Payne, arguing that "our greatest want is not gold or silver, talent or genius, but true men and true women." For Watkins, to accept the belief that wealth was the primary source of power and public status was to miss the point of the historical moment in which African Americans, and the nation generally, found themselves. "Leading ideas impress themselves upon communities and countries," and the nation needed a "Moses in freedom" who could guide the people through to a new understanding of the character and responsibilities of liberty.

Underlying these differences of opinion about the relative value of wealth was a common understanding that black children needed something more than the acquisition of knowledge and vocational training. Their education must address the mechanisms of racial discrimination. As the Reverend Amos Gerry Beman argued, in that same issue of the

Anglo-African Magazine, "we need teachers for our youth who can, aside from their prescribed text-books, speak to them of their condition, and inspire them with noble ideas of self-respect, development, and enterprise." This approach to education would involve discussions of "all the great questions of humanity, which now agitate the world," and would include "the science of political economy" so as to "show the people how to secure their highest welfare."

For Freeman, such an approach would be secure in its principles and revolutionary in its results. "Teach your child to look upon slavery and prejudice," Freeman argued, "in the light of reason and revolution, and you at once strip this boasted land and its lauded institutions of its grandeur and its glory, and reveal at a glance its true character. Its flaunted freedom and equality, a stupid failure—its high sounding republicanism, a pitiful oligarchy of men-stealers and women-whippers, its religion a shameless inconsistency, and an arrant hypocrisy, lifting its hand red with a brother's blood to Heaven, and mouthing its impious prayers in the face of the great Jehovah, while it tramples on God's image, and traffics in the souls of men." Exposing the American system for what it was, Beman and others argued, would clear the ideological, discursive, and practical space for black children to imagine a nation conceived but not yet born, one in which "the colored race," as Beman had it, could realize its position as "an element of power in the earth, 'like a city set upon a hill.'" Educational reform would amount to a revision of history, replacing the nation's myths—drawn from the moment when Puritans imagined their colony to be a city on a hill, an example to the world—with the nation's reality as embodied in the black community.

Then as now, though, to imagine such an approach to education was to rediscover that racial difference was not biological but systemic, not a matter of individual attitudes but of historical practices that had been institutionalized in virtually every realm of American society. Ideals of education continually faced an entrance exam administered by market forces. James McCune Smith, in his reflections on citizenship, spoke for both his own time and ours in commenting on the state of education:

> Young America, as instructed in the Ward Schools of the City of New York, and we fear throughout the land, is forced to *cram*, into the *dates* of every sanguinary conflict of the Revolution, the *numbers* slain, and the *event* of the battle; it is pitiful to hear school boys

complain of their inability to remember these dates; thus filling the young mind with the *dates* instead of the *principles* of the Revolution, generally a hatred instead of a reverence for that great event. A School History, sound on the principles of liberty which lay at the root, and culminated in the result of the American Revolution, would be entirely too Anti-slavery to command *the market*. So the South not only buys our goods, but saps the principles of our youth, and gains command of the next generation. WILLIAM GOODELL owes it to the cause to write and print, a "Constitution of the United States with questions and answers for the use of schools."

One is reminded of the regular news features in our own time which sound alarms about the decaying state of education by noting that students cannot identify a president, a Civil War general, or other facts from our nation's past. But one needn't look far to see a systemic ignorance about "the *principles* of the Revolution," or to see the alliance of market forces and what we call the educational system. Such were the concerns of many African Americans who could see all too well the ways in which their children were being prepared for their position in the American system.

To be effective, education would have to address both the effects of a repressive past and the promise of an uncertain future. The mission was amply stated in an 1839 article entitled "Elevation of Our People," which appeared in the important newspaper the *Colored American*. Education, the writer emphasized, was by no means a simple or unidimensional task, for the work of elevation would need to encompass the various effects, material and psychological, of a history of oppression: "To raise up a people to intellectual, social, and moral life, long having been kept down, oppressed, and proscribed, mentally, socially, and legally; whose education has been entirely neglected, and thought either not proper, or possible by others, and by themselves thought to be out of their power; whose claims have been regarded as though they had none, and against whom has been every man's hand, and whose disposition and habits, social and moral, have been formed under those circumstances, is a work, than which there is none more honorable and God-like." As in all other endeavors, blacks could scarcely afford to trust this mission to existing institutions. They would need to organize their own educational societies and organizations, and in the process define themselves as a people.

As a writer for *Freedom's Journal* put it in a February 1828 issue of that paper, "We are sure we speak the sentiments of our brethren generally, and especially, the enlightened part, when we say that we are prepared to enlist our means, efforts and influence, in the encouragement of any National Society, whose object is African Education." National societies remained elusive, but local and regional efforts were impressive—and, as with other African-American organizations, through local and regional efforts blacks built national alliances.

❖

While African Americans recognized the importance of education, efforts to translate their desires into social practice were continually frustrated. Southern attempts at education were clandestine or tenuous. In the North, blacks struggled through the antebellum years for access to the public schools, but progress was slow. In Boston blacks petitioned the state legislature in 1787 for educational access and resources, complaining that they "now receive no benefit from the free schools." Forty years later little had improved, and the complaint was repeated in the first African-American newspaper, *Freedom's Journal*, in 1827—and then again in 1860, when H. Ford Douglas, a former slave and now a powerful abolitionist speaker, declared, "The state lays its iron hand upon the Negro, holds him down, and puts the other hand into his pocket and steals his hard earnings, to eradicate the children of white men; and if we sent our children to school, Abraham Lincoln would kick them out, in the name of Republicanism and antislavery!"

African Americans had long protested a situation that amounted not only to taxation without representation but also taxation without access to those benefits paid for by taxes. While some white schools admitted black students through the years, by and large they found themselves either wholly excluded from public education or restricted to separate schools. At private schools the situation was little better. Charles B. Ray, who would become a recognized leader in the black community, was met with a hostile reaction when he was admitted to Wesleyan in 1832, and after protests by the students he decided to withdraw.

Two cases in particular came to symbolize the blacks' situation in seeking quality education. The first involved Noyes Academy in New

Hampshire, which in 1835 admitted twenty-eight white students and fourteen African Americans. (Abolitionists had been involved in planning the school, and they lobbied the trustees for these admissions.) The reaction to this interracial initiative was so great that a town meeting established a committee to abolish the school in "the *interest* of the town, the *honor* of the State, and the *good* of the whole community, (both black and white)." The committee's method was surprisingly direct. With the aid of men from neighboring towns and close to one hundred yoke of oxen, the school building was torn from its foundation.

Less direct, but equally dramatic, was the case involving a young white Quaker teacher, Prudence Crandall, who in 1831 established a girls' boarding school in Canterbury, Connecticut. When she admitted a black girl the following year, many white parents removed their daughters from the school. The Connecticut legislature thereupon passed a law prohibiting the establishment of "any school, academy, or literary institutions, for the instruction or education of colored persons who are not inhabitants of this state." Crandall refused to submit to this law and was arrested. In a high-profile case that involved prominent abolitionists as well as other interested parties, Crandall was eventually found guilty by a jury, though an appellate court later reversed the conviction on a technicality. But attacks on the school, including stoning and an attempt to burn it down, continued, and eventually, in 1834, Crandall left both the school and the state. Although famous, these cases were neither isolated nor unique, with racial control, and not just discrimination, sometimes a conspicuous if complex concern.

In the South the education of African Americans was of special concern, since an educated black populace represented a direct threat to both the stability and the very justification of the slavery system. Such concerns were only aggravated by the advent of notorious slave rebellions such as those of Gabriel Prosser in Virginia (1800), Denmark Vesey in South Carolina (1822), and Nat Turner in Virginia (1831). For the white slaveholding class, education raised the possibility of inspiration, communication, and organization central to such rebellions. Nat Turner, for example, was inspired by his readings of the Bible, and schools and churches alike provided blacks with opportunities to meet. Moreover from the nation's founding African Americans had realized the value of such documents as the Declaration of Independence and the Constitution, which they often turned to their advantage. After the American Revolution and the establishment of the Republic, blacks in all regions petitioned both Congress and state legislative bodies for recognition of their rights. In one of the earliest of those petitions to survive, four black men protested a North Carolina law that called for the capture and reenslavement of those who had been freed. Asserting that laws forbidding the manumission of slaves were "a stretch of power, morally and politically, a Governmental defect," and suggesting that such laws were "a direct violation of the declared fundamental principles of the Constitution," the petitioners asked "for redress of our grievances." The subsequent congressional debate over whether to accept this petition suggested that this was not the first such case, for Representative William Smith of South Carolina argued that "the practice of a former time, in a similar case, was that the petition was sealed up and sent back to the petitioners."

Revealing, too, is another petition to Massachusetts in January 1777. In this entreaty, the writers' struggling style only emphasizes the extent to which the language of natural rights and religion had become available to African Americans. The key phrases of this document, so conspicuously defining its purpose, speak of the influence of the Bible, the Declaration of Independence, and the numerous pamphlets published before the American Revolution to justify the colonies' break from England:

> The petition of A Great Number of Blackes detained in a State of slavery in the Bowels of a free & Christian Country Humbly sheweth that your Petitioners apprehend that they have in Common with all other men a Natural and Unaliable Right to that freedom which the Grat Parent of the Unavers hath Bestowed equalley on all menkind and which they have Never forfeited by any Compact or agreement whatever—but that wher Unjustly Dragged by the hand of cruel Power from their Derest friends and sum of them Even torn from the Embraces of their tender Parents—from A populous Pleasant and plentiful country and in violation of Laws of Nature and of Nations and in defiance of all the tender feelings of humanity Brough hear Either to Be sold Like Beast of Burthen & Like them Condemned to Slavery for Life—Among A People Profesing the mild Religion of Jesus A people Not Insensible of the Secrets of Rational Being Nor without spirit to Resent the unjust endeavours of others to Reduce them to a state of Bondage and Subjection your honouer Need not to be informed that A Live of Slavery Like that of your petitioners

Deprived of Every social privilege of Every thing Requisit to Render Life Tolable is far worse then Nonexistence.

In this document the petitioners connect their own experience to the discourse of "Bondage and Subjection" that was so great a presence in the pamphlets, sermons, and essays written to define and justify the American Revolution. Just as those pamphlets led to the defining document of the American Revolution, so too did the language of such publications influence blacks determined to argue against the perpetuation of slavery in a land that professed devotion to self-evident truths of liberty and natural rights.

As these examples suggest, African Americans of every state of the young Union, both free and enslaved, recognized the value of education. Many understood that the nation's guiding documents—religious as well as political, from newspapers to the Bible—were being interpreted so as to preserve the system of slavery and promote racial prejudice. They understood as well that such documents held the key to the glaring philosophical contradictions central to the slaveholding nation, and that education might therefore offer a key to both liberty and the recognition of African-American rights. These would be manifest in such small but important things as written passes that enabled escapes from slavery to such grand enterprises as essays and histories written in defense of the black cause. Frederick Douglass, for example, credited the acquisition of literacy not only with his eventual escape from slavery but also with a newfound sense of power over his enslavers while he was still a slave. Famously, Douglass had learned to read in part by working with a school textbook, *The Columbian Orator*, which included debates over slavery, and along the way he encountered references to abolition and abolitionists. Noting that "there was HOPE in those words," Douglass offered his reading of the grounds for optimism:

> I had a deep satisfaction in the thought, that the rascality of slaveholders was not concealed from the eyes of the world, and that I was not alone in abhorring the cruelty and brutality of slavery. A still deeper train of thought was stirred. I saw that there was *fear*, as well as *rage*, in the manner of speaking of the abolitionists. The latter, therefore, I was compelled to regard as having some power in the country; and I felt that they might, possibly, succeed in their designs. When I met with a slave to whom I deemed it safe to talk on the subject, I would impart

to him so much of the mystery as I had been able to penetrate. Thus, the light of this grand movement broke in upon my mind, by degrees.

Douglass spoke confidently of his readiness to engage in religious debate over the fundamental realities of his life: "With a book of this kind in my hand, my own human nature, and the facts of my experience, to help me, I was equal to a contest with the religious advocates of slavery." Among the various benefits of education, then, was its ability to provide isolated and oppressed individuals with a sense of community, for through books and newspapers one could feel connected to a world of like-minded people who represented the possibility of a fundamentally different world.

Important in the North long after slavery was largely abolished there, such benefits were especially needed in the South, and many blacks rose to the challenge by establishing informal and usually clandestine schools. These attempts met with great resistance. Representative was the case of Alphonso Sumner, a black barber in Nashville, Tennessee, who operated the first of a series of underground schools for African Americans in the area between 1833 and 1837. Eventually accused of writing letters to aid runaway slaves, Sumner was whipped and forced to leave the area, but other schools rose in place of the one he established. Similarly, an enslaved man known as Joe held class for a small group of slaves in Kentucky, but in 1816 the trustees of his area, Greensburg in Green County, put an end to the school by threatening all participants with whippings if they continued to attend any classes.

In its session of 1834–1835, the North Carolina legislature attempted to pass a bill prohibiting free blacks from educating their own children or arranging for their education. That bill failed, but a similar law passed the Georgia legislature in 1829, making it unlawful for anyone to educate blacks. Those who did, white or black, would face a five-hundred-dollar fine and imprisonment. Moreover the law criminalized the circulation of pamphlets, papers, and other materials capable of inspiring or otherwise encouraging slave rebellions—perhaps a reaction to *David Walker's Appeal*, published in 1829 and smuggled into the South where it outraged the governor of Georgia, among many others. The punishment for the distribution of such publications was death. In 1842 Georgia intensified such measures, making it illegal to sell or distribute books, pamphlets, writing paper, ink, or other writing materials to blacks, unless the blacks in question had written permission to obtain such materials from a white guardian or slaveowner.

Not all educational attempts in the South were marked by racial divisions, however, for many whites encouraged and supported education for free blacks and slaves. Particularly active in the South were the Quakers, known also for their lead in anti-slavery work. Quakers offered basic literacy lessons to slaves in North Carolina as early as 1771, and by 1816 they had established a school for blacks in that state that offered limited but valuable lessons. In spite of Georgia's legislation, local officials in the state did not interfere with Mary Woodhouse's school for about twenty-five or thirty free and enslaved black children, which she operated in her home during the 1850s. Woodhouse offered two years of basic reading, writing, and arithmetic, after which the students could continue on in another school run by Mary Beasley. There were many such efforts, some the product of an individual's ingenuity and some a more communal affair, some strictly underground and others treated like an open secret by regional citizens. The many slave narratives published before the Civil War often include important stories of how the author, who eventually managed to escape from enslavement, first or later acquired literacy, sometimes considered the very pathway to liberation and self-determination.

In Kentucky some African Americans, both enslaved and free, were able to obtain an education primarily through schools associated with religious institutions. In some of them both black and white teachers offered basic education to black children in independent classes, small groups, or even individually, with classes held in the evenings or on Sunday afternoons. In Frankfort a day school for black children was established in 1820, and another was begun before the Civil War in Lexington, led by the black educator Jane Washington. In Lexington, too, the First African Baptist Church ran a successful school in the 1830s, taught by a white man from fees paid by the students. In Louisville education for black children was first provided in 1829 by the Reverend Henry Adams of the First Colored Baptist Church. Adams taught children individually at first, but by 1841 he was running a school large enough to require four teachers. Similarly William H. Gibson, Sr., who himself had been taught by private tutors in Baltimore, responded in 1847 to a call for teachers from the Fourth Street Methodist Church.

Within a year after his arrival in Louisville, Gibson established his own school, which served between fifty and one hundred students. Other black schools came and went throughout Kentucky, and in 1850 African American children were attending school in fourteen of the state's counties. Of these children, the majority were free, and of that majority only 12 percent were attending schools by 1850—but such numbers were important all the same in a slave state.

In the North, opportunities for education were generally more available—but, as the example of Prudence Crandall, the Noyes Academy, and numerous other attempts indicate, resistance to black education was often fierce. African Americans were admitted to some schools, but in most areas schools quickly were identified by the community as either white or black. Beyond such attempts to assure the segregation of the races in the schools, many white Americans resisted black education on the grounds that an educated black populace promoted an increasingly integrated society, including competition in the labor force. That such unequal public education, when it was available at all, did not prevent state and local governments from taxing African Americans continued to be a sore point for blacks, who regularly complained about taxation without representation. Many black activists devoted themselves to exposing and resolving such glaring contradictions in public policy, working to integrate everything from public transportation to public schools. But such efforts often led to a labyrinthine process by which states both recognized and put off African-American claims to educational access.

Instructive is the example of Michigan, one of many states in which blacks supported schools through their taxes that their children were not allowed to attend. When the state legislature considered a school for African Americans, it was met with insistent protest, and the measure was finally adopted only after an amendment was added to the bill prohibiting whites from attending the black school. Legislators were not worried that the black school would exceed the white schools in funding or other resources; rather, they feared that educational proximity would encourage social interaction, and that educational equality would encourage notions of social equality. In Detroit the black community responded to this situation by funding their own private school—while continuing to support the public schools through their taxes. The city established a school for African Americans in 1839, but it never opened. Eventually, in 1842, the state established free public schools, and blacks in Detroit were given a tax-supported school—but instead of a new school the board of education appropriated the school that had been established by the black community, firing its teacher and replacing him with a white teacher. Again concerned parents responded by organizing their own school, hiring the fired teacher, Reverend William Monroe. When the private school failed, Monroe was hired to teach the public school. He was forced to end his teaching career in 1856 for health reasons, and white teachers of questionable competence were again hired. After various relocations, the school was established in adequate housing and led by a white principal, John Whitbeck, under whose leadership the school flourished.

Tensions complicated the development of even one of the most famous and successful schools, the African Free School of New York City. Established in 1787 by the New York Manumission Society, before it became part of the city's public school system it had graduated such notable future leaders as the abolitionist and minister Henry Highland Garnet, the pharmacist and writer James McCune Smith, the engraver Patrick Reason, the actor Ira Aldridge, and Alexander Crummell, one of the most formidable intellectuals of his day. In spite of such successes, the school was plagued by all the racial discords of the time—which the school had been designed, in part, to address. Some believed that the school's mission was to prepare black children for equal citizenship, but many white Americans were opposed to such ideals of equality and preferred to think that the school should prepare black children for the subservient social roles they were expected to assume. For many years the school was run by a black principal, John Teasman, but clashes with the Manumission Society led to his dismissal in 1809. He was replaced by Charles C. Andrews, a white man who was finally forced out in 1831, in part due to the anger of black parents over the educational philosophy promoted by the school. Many of the school's lessons and activities echoed the racist assumptions and stereotypes of the day. And education for girls was limited when it was available at all. Yet the school educated some of the most formidable black leaders of the nineteenth century.

Such racial politics were not uncommon. They marked the experience, for example, of a highly regarded black teacher in Philadelphia, Sarah Mapps Douglass. Douglass taught in a female academy sponsored by the Philadelphia Female Anti-Slavery Society, considered one of the first interracial women's anti-slavery organizations, though most of its members were white. Douglass requested the formal separation of her academy from the parent organization in 1840, noting her appreciation for the organization's financial support through the years but declaring her preference that the school be controlled by African Americans. While the specific issues that led Douglass to her decision are uncertain, she was clearly responding to the faltering interest in black education among the predominantly white organization. She and other prominent blacks wanted control over the school in part to ensure that the students would receive an appropriate as well as an adequate education—that is, an education that represented the values and goals of the African-American community that Douglass served.

As the example of the African Free School suggests, even the best-intentioned attempts to educate black children were beset by all too predictable problems, but such attempts were indeed made. In Portland, Maine, what locals called the "Colored School" was established in 1827, one of only ten black schools in the country and one of only five in cities that funded black schools. But the school was a response, in part, to the refusal of whites to accept the black students in the public schools. Philadelphia offered public schooling for black residents as early as 1822, only a few years after "universal" public education was made available to white students. By 1838 the city boasted roughly twenty-five schools for black children, though only nine of them were free. Thus education was gradually becoming available to all students who could afford the time and clothing to attend, but even in the best situation education was available primarily to wealthier blacks who could afford to fund schools through their taxes while also paying for their children to attend private schools. Of the roughly three thousand school-aged African-American children in Philadelphia in 1838, for example, only seventeen hundred were enrolled in school. Attendance largely declined over the years because of worsening economic conditions and the city's violently racist environment. Some schools disappeared quickly for lack of enrollment and attendance; at other schools, black and white teachers and administrators came and went, and tensions between the white-led organizations that sponsored some of the schools and the needs and desires of black parents were not at all unusual.

Regardless of such obstacles, African Americans pursued educational opportunities wherever they could be found—either created or otherwise cobbled together. Schools became part of churches almost as soon as black-run churches were themselves established, and parents and community leaders continued to pressure school boards and others for access to public education and proper schooling. Benevolent societies, too, were important to black education. The Brooklyn African Woolman Benevolent Society, for example, was devoted to educating black children, and in 1815 its charter president, Peter Croger, established Brooklyn's first school for black children and adults in his home. In 1827, when black children were denied access to the local public school (so as to accommodate more white children), the Woolman society raised money to build a school, church, and library.

Such efforts were not unusual. Private schools were established in Boston, as in Philadelphia and New York, toward the end of the eighteenth century—at first meeting in private homes and later in churches. Buffalo and Cincinnati similarly relied on private school efforts until laws allowed for black public education (in some cases with separate school boards) closer to the mid-nineteenth century. Public schools reached San Francisco and Sacramento in 1854. Of course, beyond even the availability of schools, and the concerns of time, clothing, and other resources for the children who wished to attend them, there remained questions about the resources available for the schools themselves, the social philosophy they promoted, the lack of access to higher education, and the resignation, among many students, that the rudimentary education available to them would amount to little in a white supremacist culture seemingly determined to limit opportunity for blacks. In this as in other areas of life, African Americans needed not simply access but community if they were to deal with the challenges they faced.

❖

African Americans were not silent in the face of deliberate attempts to bar their educational progress. The *Anglo-African Magazine*, for example, published numerous articles on education, often exposing the conditions under which many blacks were being educated. In "American Caste, and Common Schools," J. Holland Townsend discussed both Prudence

Crandall's attempt to educate black children in her Connecticut school and the remarkable response to the Noyes Academy in New Hampshire. But Townsend devoted most of his article to schools in the West, particularly California, where he found the situation all too familiar.

In black newspapers, pamphlets, and books, education also was a frequent and pressing topic. Reports often described how racial prejudice either corrupted the educational process or otherwise affected the lives of black pupils and teachers alike. One famous case resulted in a book, William G. Allen's *The American Prejudice Against Color. An Authentic Narrative, Showing How Easily the Nation Got into an Uproar*, published in 1853. Allen, a black scholar, was a faculty member at New York Central College in McGrawville, New York, a school founded in 1849 by the American Baptist Free Mission Society. In addition to enrolling African Americans, the college also admitted young white women, one of whom became engaged to Allen. Allen was forced to leave the school, which by the end of the 1850s was bankrupt. In his book Allen identified himself as "a refugee from American despotism." He was especially critical of those who had at one time seemed allies, white abolitionists who could not accept an interracial relationship.

Among the primary forums for debating and promoting the cause of education was the black national convention movement, itself inspired in part by a desire to provide education to black children. At the beginning of the convention movement in 1831, prominent white abolitionists proposed the establishment of a college "for the liberal education of Young Men of Colour, on the Manual Labor System." The idea was to offer a broad education while also preparing students for "a useful Mechanical or Agricultural profession," and in that way to address the "present ignorant and degraded condition" of free blacks and "elevate the general character of the coloured population." The idea never led to a school, but debates over education continued to be a central concern at the conventions. At some of them, black leaders argued over the assumption that African Americans were necessarily consigned to manual labor and service occupations. At other conventions leaders worried about what kind of education blacks were most likely to receive. In 1853, at the Colored National Convention in Rochester, for example, the Committee on Social Relations and Polity noted the importance of "schools adapted" to the needs of black males (education for females was addressed in a separate report). The committee observed of the black male student that "neither schools nor educators for the whites, at present, are in full sympathy with him; and . . . he must either abandon his own state of things which he finds around him, and which he is pledged to change and better, or cease to receive culture from such sources, since their whole tendency is to change him, not his condition—to educate him out of his sympathies, not to quicken and warm his sympathies." African Americans attending the conventions recognized the value of education, but they understood too the difference between educating and changing young minds.

Such distinctions were not easily resolved in practice. Debates among blacks over the relative value of receiving a broad education or learning a useful trade persisted long after the Civil War—characterizing, for example, a major difference between the approaches of W. E. B. DuBois and Booker T. Washington at the century's end. At the 1855 convention a committee reported on the proposal of an industrial school, noting that the needs of the black national community were too dispersed and too diverse to be met by any single initiative. "Our people are widespread as are the free states of this Confederacy," the report noted, adding that "their wants are varied as their localities, and all demand that their requirements should be equally cared for." The report focused on the needs of "the masses," arguing that "the masses" of any country and any people "cannot be deeply learned," and can be "in fact only partially developed." Accordingly, the report counseled, "These are foundation facts with all peoples, so must it be with the colored people of these United States. We must begin with the tillage of the earth and the practice of the mechanical branches, with whatever learning we may have, or the best we can now get." Those attending the 1864 convention thought differently, arguing that "there are two great principles in operation in this world. One is that of progression; the other, that of development: one is the body of success; the other is its soul: the one makes us scholars merely; the other makes us MEN,—and *that*, and that only, is the pearl for which we are seeking." "It is not the thought-gatherer who makes his mark in the world;" the 1864 report asserted, "but it is the thought-producer who is the man of mark and value. Development means persistent culture of our latent powers; and we need it. Slavery and ignorance, liberty and light! It is the mind, not the dollars, that makes the man."

Whether focused on dollars or minds, on the masses or the elite, on manual labor or classical education, African Americans at the conventions agreed that educational opportunities must be created for black children, and that existing educational forums remained either closed to or dismissive of African Americans. Thus the conventions recognized that education was essential to the formation and maintenance of a black community, which in turn was necessary to the development of black children in a white supremacist culture.

Beyond the conventions, many individual blacks were actively engaged in efforts to desegregate public transportation and public schools. The two concerns were related. Just as many black children found it difficult to attend school because they needed to work or because they lacked proper clothing, others could not get to school in areas where public transportation was unavailable to them. In *The Negro in the American Rebellion* (1867), William Wells Brown related a story about the daughter of the prominent Philadelphia black activist William Still. "I was much amused," Brown reported,

> at seeing his little daughter, a child of eight or nine years, and her cousin, entering the omnibus which passed the door, going towards their school. Colored persons were not allowed to ride in those conveyances; and one of the girls, being very fair, would pay the fare for both; while the dark complexioned one would keep her face veiled. Thus the two children daily passed unmolested from their homes to the school, and returned. I was informed that once while I was there the veil unfortunately was lifted, the dark face seen, and the child turned out of the coach. How foolish that one's ride on a stormy day should depend entirely on a black veil!

In this tale of fair complexions and public fares, Brown captured the challenges faced even by children of elite black families. Such prominent blacks as Sojourner Truth, Frederick Douglass, and William Still protested, sometimes in writing and sometimes in person, such restricted access to transportation.

There remained the challenge of actually entering the school, and here too black activists worked for equal access. Boston offered an instructive example of such work. In 1849 a member of Boston's black community, Benjamin Roberts, challenged in the courts the segregation enforced by the Primary School Committee—bringing suit based on a statute that allowed for damages to anyone illegally excluded from public schools. The court unanimously rejected Roberts's argument on the grounds that Boston did in fact provide for the education of black children, albeit in segregated schools. In response, Boston's black leaders formed the Equal School Rights Committee and focused on legislative appeals. Within five years Boston's Public Instruction Committee recommended that separate schools be abolished. Following that recommendation, in 1855 a legislative committee proposed a bill to prohibit schools from denying access based on either race or religion, a bill soon passed and signed by the governor. Boston's black children entered the city's schools in September 1855—and without the community violence that many expected to follow from integration. Other cities were more cautious, or at least used the veil of community resistance to avoid the steps that Boston had taken. From New England to other areas of the North, integrated classrooms were common in rural areas, though such classrooms remained predominantly white. But in such cities as New York, Philadelphia, Cincinnati, Providence, and New Haven, educational officials approached the issue by trying to improve the schools set aside for black children rather than moving toward full integration.

Although access to education varied according to locale, and though local communities worked to address those conditions that most directly affected them, African Americans recognized that the problem was nationwide, and that they could best address educational needs through combined action. The need, one might say, was to both create and represent a coherent black community. A writer for *Freedom's Journal* could say, as in February 1828, "We are sure we speak the sentiments of our brethren generally, and especially, the enlightened part, when we say that we are prepared to enlist our means, efforts and influence, in the encouragement of any National Society, whose object is African Education." The writer could also suggest the proper balance of power in joint efforts by white and black Americans, asserting that "all coloured men possessing wealth, education or influence would rejoice in the privilege of uniting all their abilities with those of the white population, in any plan, that would raise the standard of education among our colour, reserving to themselves at the same time, the privilege of educating their own children according to their respective views." But questions of appropriate representation were raised within the community as well. An August 1827 correspondent to *Freedom's Journal*, for example, who identified herself only as "Matilda," could remind the editors of the importance of "the education of females," noting at the end of her short say, "I merely throw out these hints, in order that some more able pen will take up the subject." Although calls for a national approach to black access to the schools were regularly raised, the practical work of education remained a local concern, usually serving both boys and girls, men and women, though in different forums.

Perhaps the most influential black self-help efforts in education were the numerous literary societies they organized. When Sarah Mapps Douglass called for more active participation in anti-slavery efforts in 1832, she did so before the recently formed Female Literary Society of Philadelphia, addressing her audience as "my sisters." When the important early black feminist and activist Maria W. Stewart announced that same year that "the frowns of the world shall never discourage me," she did so before the Afric-American Female Intelligence Society of America. Such societies provided a great many black leaders with forums for honing their skills as public speakers; they offered access to educational resources to many black children and adults; and they furnished the means by which a wide range of communities might realize themselves. Some societies were informal groups, others were highly organized associations; some were large enough to support libraries and reading rooms while others gathered at odd times to discuss books. Many societies offered a program of lectures at which both members like Sarah Douglass or important guests could speak to a thoughtful and interested audience—and often these remarks were later published in supportive newspapers, such as the *Liberator*, or in pamphlets. Indeed, many orations—probably the most important of black writings from the nineteenth century—are still available because they were recorded by literary societies.

African-American literary societies were everywhere, and most offered educational programs. By and large, Philadelphia was the site of some of the earliest literary societies, but communities in other cities quickly followed suit, and literary groups developed in such cities as New York, Boston, Albany, Rochester, Cincinnati, and Pittsburgh. Groups appeared in the South as well. In Charleston, South Carolina, for example, the Bonneau Literary Society encouraged literacy among its members while Baltimore's community was served by the Phoenix Society and the Young Men's Mental Improvement Society for the Discussion of Moral and Philosophical Questions of All Kinds. In 1827 in New York City the African Mutual Instruction Society was organized to encourage young men to study literature and science. There too the Philomathean Literary Society, formed in 1829, hosted debates among its members along with weekly lectures. The Pennsylvania Augustine Society was formed in Philadelphia in 1827, followed in 1828 by the Colored Reading Society of Philadelphia, which offered a library with classics and works by "our best English writers" as well as "books treating . . . the subject of Ancient Modern and Ecclesiastical History, [and] the Laws of Pennsylvania." The group's library also carried a subscription to important newspapers, such as the *Genius of Universal Emancipation*, an important early anti-slavery paper, and *Freedom's Journal*, the first newspaper published by and directed to African Americans. Most societies were reserved for men, but women responded by forming their own groups, such as the Female Literary Society of Philadelphia, organized in 1831, or the Minerva Literary Association in that same city, formed in 1834.

While these societies supported many activities, their central mission (and the source of their lasting influence) was often to provide a library for members while also encouraging them to add to it their own writings. In many cases the records of these groups give us a glimpse of a significant body of writing—including original plays performed in the societies—that has not yet been found, but many orations have survived, along with evidence of a broader devotion to literature, the sciences, and the arts. In Boston, for example, the future black activist and historian William C. Nell, an important advocate for the integration of Boston's public schools, benefited greatly from literary societies and was apparently also a playwright, though his dramatic compositions have not been found. In the 1850s Nell helped form the Attucks Glee Club. In 1833 William Whipper, a founding member of Philadelphia's Colored Reading Society, established the Philadelphia Library Company of Colored Persons, modeled after the Library Company of Philadelphia, organized by Benjamin Franklin in 1731 for "literary and scientific discussion, the reading of original essays, poems, and so forth." By 1838 the Library Company's collection included more than 600 volumes available for its roughly 150 members. Similarly, in New York, the Phoenix Society was formed in 1833, devoted to the belief that the "condition" of African Americans could "only be meliorated by their being improved in morals, literature, and mechanic arts." While Philadelphia's Colored Reading Society was open to free black males, New York's Phoenix Society was more ambitious still in its community service. Dividing New York's black communities into wards, the society sought to "make a register of every colored person" so as to document whether "they read, write and cipher." In this way it hoped to attract both children and adults to school and planned to "establish circulating libraries in each ward for the use of people of colour on every moderate pay,—to establish mental feasts, and also lyceums for speaking and for lectures on sciences." Among the society's goals was to raise ten thousand dollars for a manual labor college, a project never realized. New York's Phoenixonian Literary Society, in turn, hosted weekly debates and recitations as well as annual lectures open to the public, offered by both members and guest speakers from other cities speaking on such topics as "Astronomy," "Duty of Young Men," "Patriots of the American Revolution," and "Music—Its Practical Influence on Society."

In 1839 one black writer declared, "We consider these institutions as of more importance than any others in the present age of societies and Associations." Certainly there was reason to think so. Although the literary societies could not address the full range of educational challenges that blacks faced before the Civil War, they were important educational and community centers. Through the literary societies African Americans read, lectured, and performed their way into a sense of community—with deep historical ties to the various national and cultural streams that fed into black life and character. In the literary societies African Americans made manifest their desire for education, and there they debated, lectured, and read their way through the issues that were pivotal to their educational activism—the schools they created and sustained, and the public schools to which they claimed the fundamental right of taxpayers. Moreover through the literary societies African Americans looked for ways to address the needs of a community often relegated to manual labor and regularly degraded in public forums. There they could find and practice their individual and collective voices, looking for outlets to reach a broader community—forums provided by the black press.

7

"Our Warfare Lies in the Field of Thought"

TO TRANSFORM THEMSELVES from a scattered collective of people united only by a common experience of oppression into a coherent and influential community, African Americans would need a press of their own. The call for this asset was one of the most frequent and fervent pleas in the black community. To some extent the eagerness was a response to the characterizations of blacks one would regularly encounter in almost every public forum, depictions that were promoted and hardened into racist assumptions and stereotypes through newspapers and magazines controlled by white Americans. To some extent, too, blacks sought to overcome the narrow representation they received through newspapers controlled by white allies. Some of their most dependable friends in the white community were more interested in the anti-slavery cause than they were in the broader and varied interests and needs of a self-contained and self-sustaining black community of readers and writers, intellectuals and students, parents and children, professionals and laborers. Through newspapers and magazines of their own, African Americans could speak to a geographically scattered and ideologically diverse community, allowing readers to define themselves in terms not limited to the evils of slavery and the weight of oppression.

Beyond all else, though, black newspapers and magazines were the natural product of every other forum through which African Americans organized themselves. Just as mutual aid societies helped foster the development of black denominations and churches (and vice versa); as churches provided both the space and personnel for schools and literary societies; as fraternal orders extended from and fed into the development of black religious and educational life; as the convention movement both drew from and encouraged the development of all these organizations, so black newspapers and magazines too were a natural outgrowth of concerns for community.

Some literary societies developed their own magazines, and with the development of black religious denominations came associated publications. Important community members who were affiliated with both the fraternal orders and the churches—for example, David Walker—became important promoters of early black newspapers. Virtually all these organizations and societies were already involved in other publications—in the form of pamphlets especially, recording important orations, convention proceedings, and other notices of the organization's ongoing work—and to some extent the turn to newspapers was a natural development. But newspapers were especially important, for through their pages African Americans could encounter a host of writers, articles that reached across geographic boundaries and through history, examples of the representation of black concerns in other publications, and the news of the day made relevant to the special circumstances of African American life.

The advantage of a focused and dedicated press was clear, but the challenges of maintaining that press were daunting. For all their obvious advantages, many black newspapers and magazines struggled for their existence, and a great many newspapers were short-lived. The need to sustain a particular publication was frequently its chief topic of concern, including regular—and sometimes desperate—calls for subscribers and appeals to readers. One might say that the black press suffered from problems it was designed to address—the working conditions and poverty of many black communities, the lack of education among many who might otherwise become subscribers, the conditions that made it difficult for those of African heritage to transform and realize themselves as a potentially powerful community, and the simple lack of time that many blacks, struggling for their existence in a hostile environment, experienced. But if many papers left the scene quickly after their arrival, many more took their place. They often served a community beyond those who could read, for newspapers and magazines often found audiences through readings conducted in the societies, churches, and schools that blacks attended.

It is no surprise, then, that through newspapers and magazines we have some of the best glimpses of African-American literary production, ranging from fiction and poetry to essays, orations, scientific explorations, theological musings, historical surveys, journalistic exposés, philosophical treatises, satiric commentaries, and even musical and dramatic compositions. In the pages of these newspapers, too, are notices of other black publications, advertisements for black businesses, and reports on the meetings of fraternal orders, conventions, anti-slavery groups, literary societies, mutual aid societies, religious gatherings, political rallies, and the dire situation of black education as well as the achievements of black students. Through the pages of these newspapers and magazines we witness the development and organization of African-American communities and see a broader community forming across regions. To the various organizational efforts already examined, black newspapers and magazines offered something essential: a community forum, where the voices of various communities, including disputes as well as common commitments, could come together.

❖

It would be difficult to overstate the importance to the black community of African-American newspapers and magazines before the Civil War. Even without these publications we would have a wealth of historical records—books and pamphlets, poems and essays that appeared in white-run anti-slavery papers, letters and other documents that managed to survive the vicissitudes of history to find their way into private collections and public archives. But many books, essays, poems, proceedings, letters, advertisements, and more were published in African-American newspapers and magazines, and often appeared nowhere else. Some of the novels written by influential blacks in the nineteenth century (for example, those of Martin Delany and Frances E. W. Harper) as well as works by otherwise little-known writers (Julia C. Collins, author of one of the earliest published novels by a black woman, for example) are available to us today only through the periodicals that remain. In many cases these novels exist in incomplete form because we have not yet found all the issues of the newspaper or magazine in which they originally appeared. In thinking of the importance of the press, one might reflect on Henry M. Turner's comments in his introduction to William J. Simmons's 1887 collective biography (a series of biographical sketches) of African-

American men, *Men of Mark: Eminent, Progressive and Rising.* "Little as the common observer may regard it," Turner observed, "we men who gather up the fragments of our labors, acts, achievements, sayings, songs, oddities, peculiarities, fun, speeches, lectures, poems, war struggles, bravery, degradation and sufferings, and preserve them for the future, now while they are within reach, will stand out as heroes in the day to come." They would be recognized as heroes, Turner suggested, because their work was part of a larger struggle not simply to tell the story of the past but to gather the materials necessary for the moral work of the future. "The future orator, statesman, minister, poet, journalist, ethnologist, as well as the historian," Turner wrote, "will from these gather materials to build towers heaven-reaching that will monument the grandeur of our race, and still grander struggles that lifted them from the barren plains of the contempt of the world, to the majestic heights that we are destined to scale in God's Providence." This was precisely the work that the editors and writers for black newspapers and magazines performed, and we continue to benefit from the materials they made available to the historical record. Without this record we might well be overwhelmed by the partial and biased representations, or outright misrepresentations, of African-American life by white Americans of the time.

Such misrepresentations were a primary force behind the ongoing calls for a black press. In 1827 an editorial from the first issue of *Freedom's Journal* announced the primary mission of the newspaper—to be the voice of the community, and thereby to exercise some influence in the representation of African-American character. "We wish to plead our own cause," the editorial stated, for "too long have others spoken for us. Too long has the public been deceived by misrepresentations, in things which concern us dearly, though in the estimation of some mere trifles; for though there are many in society who exercise towards us benevolent feelings; still (with sorrow we confess it) there are others who make it their business to enlarge upon the least trifle, which tends to the discredit of any person of color; and pronounce anathemas and denounce our whole body for the misconduct of this guilty one." In 1853 blacks amplified this mission in the proceedings of the Rochester national convention, emphasizing that black uplift required responses to white characterizations. "What stone has been left unturned to degrade us?" the convention members asked. "What hand has refused to fan the flame of prejudice against us? What American artist has not caricatured us? What wit has not laughed at us in our wretchedness? What songster has not made merry over our depressed spirits? What press has not ridiculed and contemned us? What pulpit has withheld from our devoted heads its angry lightning, or its sanctimonious hate?" In 1859 the editor Thomas Hamilton continued this cause in his opening "Apology" for the *Anglo-African Magazine*, emphasizing the systemic nature of those misrepresentations. "The wealth, the intellect, the Legislation, (State and Federal,) the pulpit, and the science of America," Hamilton asserted, "have concentrated on no one point so heartily as in the endeavor to write down the negro as something less than a man."

Throughout the black national conventions a constant concern was the influence of the press in promoting and maintaining a system of white supremacy by controlling the images of black character and negotiating the cultural politics associated with the system of slavery. The 1843 "Report of Committee Upon the Press" is representative in its summary of the influence of white publications. "Your committee entertain the common views entertained of the power and influence of the press," the report noted,

> for good or for evil; they believe that much of the existing good, as well as of the evil in the world, owes itself to the press as an instrumentality, and that most of the peculiar evils to which we of this country are subjected, if not brought into existence, are now sustained by the power and influence of the press; that slaveholding, in this country, finds now, as it ever has found, support and a grand means of defense, in the influence of the newspaper press; that that peculiar and unhallowed sensibility, so prevalent in this country, called prejudice against color, has become wider spread, and firmer fixed, by the views and sentiments which sustain it, having been taken up and palmed off upon the reading public by the press.

The truth of this claim need hardly be established. Simply to report on national or regional politics was to present a social realm in which black Americans were marginalized, rendered invisible, brought to visibility as a problem to be solved, or otherwise degraded. At a time when blackface minstrelsy was the most popular form of entertainment, and (later) when Uncle Tom shows aided in the transformation of *Uncle Tom's Cabin* into a warehouse of commercial images of black identity and experience, the white press brought race into its pages for entertainment, for purposes of political or ethical self-positioning, and as a commercial necessity.

While the presence of racial politics was sometimes subtle in the white press (the usual assumption of whiteness being the nonracial norm), more often it was direct and even blatant. Readers of the white-run *Democratic Review* could find articles that provided models of reflection on racial concerns—for example, "Do the Various Races of Man Constitute a Single Species?"—that effectively sectioned off race from the mainstream of concerns. A decade later readers of *Putnam's Monthly* encountered such articles as "Uncle Tomitudes," "Negro Minstrelsy—Ancient and Modern," and "About Niggers." Some publications were more forceful still in their portrayal of blacks as a separate concern and an inferior race. The *Southern Literary Journal, and Monthly Magazine*, for example, included an editorial feature, "From Our Armchair," which included, among other topics, the "Natural History of the Negro Race." It argued that "It is very questionable whether the abolutionists [sic] in their efforts for the emancipation of the Negro race, are not attempting a thing, physically and morally impossible—if by emancipation be meant, enabling them to be republicans. . . . Of this republican liberty in government we believe the black race absolutely incapable." One African-American newspaper began precisely because of the handling of race concerns in a white publication, the *New York Sun*. In 1846 the *Sun* published a series of editorials arguing for limitations on existing black rights of citizenship. When Willis A. Hodges, an African American, wrote a reply, he found he could get it published only by paying to print it as an advertisement. When his submission was changed by the *Sun*'s editorial staff, Hodges protested, but he was told that "the *Sun* shines for all white men, and not for colored men."

If he wished to represent the views of African Americans, Hodges was told, he would need to start his own paper—and the representatives at various national conventions agreed. As the 1843 "Report of Committee Upon the Press" argued, "if one class of the people ought to have a press absolutely under their control, it is that class who are the prescribed, and whose rights are cloven down." The advantages of establishing an identifiably black newspaper were many, the report argued, for it would "have a tendency to unite us in a stronger bond, by teaching us that our cause and our interests are one and common, and that what is for the interest of the one, or a point gained in our common cause in one section of the country, is for the interest of all, or a point gained by all. Besides, being the organ of the whole, it would necessarily chronicle the public measures of the whole, and thus become a medium to enable us to learn about, as well as from each other." A black press was viewed as vital to the formation of an African-American community, providing a record of the experiences that joined people who might not recognize their common bond, and a forum through which individuals separated geographically, economically, politically, and socially could discover their common cause.

Although the conventions debated the practicality of a single, national press for African Americans, the belief in the importance of some sort of black press, singular or multiple, was emphasized again and again. It was stated plainly in a prospectus for a "quarterly anti-slavery magazine" that appeared in the *Colored American* in 1838: "The pen or the sword must soon decide whether or not slavery is to remain one of the elements of our republic. But all those who prefer the mode of argument to that of brute force, it cannot but be deemed important that there should be a periodical in which all questions pertaining to slavery may be settled in the light of thorough investigation." Increasingly the press was viewed as both pen and sword. Some sense of the power associated with the press is revealed in the 1847 debates on establishing a national press in which Henry Highland Garnet is reported to have expressed his belief "that the most successful means which can be used for the overthrow of Slavery and Caste in this country, would be found in an able and well-conducted Press, solely under control of the people of color." Garnet quoted the lines from Byron's *Childe Harold's Pilgrimage* that were quoted regularly in black orations and publications (and that Martin Delany used in the masthead for his paper the *Mystery*): "Hereditary bondman, know ye not, / Who would be free, themselves must strike the blow?" And with Byron's brave words behind him, Garnet himself pressed forth, arguing that "the establishment of a National Printing Press would send terror into the ranks of our enemies, and encourage all our friends, whose friendship is greater than their selfishness." Many at the 1847 convention agreed. The "Report of the Committee on a National Press" put forth the position that "we struggle against opinions. Our warfare lies in the field of thought. Glorious struggle! God-like warfare! In training our soldiers for the field, in marshaling our hosts for the fight, in leading the onset, and through the conflict, we need a Printing Press, because a printing press is the vehicle of thought—is a ruler of opinions."

The 1848 "Address to the Colored People of the United States" asserted more simply that "it is easy to see that the means which have been used to destroy us, must be used to save us." Black newspapers and magazines, in short, were important in the related goals of resisting political oppression, responding to racist representations, and working toward the definition and "uplift" of a community only tenuously aware of itself beyond the common condition imposed by racism, exclusion from citizenship, and the effects of slavery.

There was reason to believe in the power of an African-American press, if only because anti-slavery newspapers inspired such heated response from a public opposed to abolitionist agitation. White anti-slavery editors had famously suffered the wrath of the public. In 1835 William Lloyd Garrison was threatened and paraded in public humiliation by a white mob (including "gentlemen of property and standing"); in 1837 another white mob murdered the white abolitionist Elijah Lovejoy in Alton, Illinois, and dragged his printing press into the river. This was evidence of the power of the press in a double sense, for these were not only attempts to silence the anti-slavery press but were also viewed as effects of the power of a racist and pro-slavery press. The *Colored American*, for example, reacted strongly to the murder of Lovejoy in an article presented under the dramatic headline "An American Citizen Murdered!! The Press Destroyed!!! The Spirit of Slavery Triumphant!!!" Implicitly connecting this event to Garrison's earlier ordeal, the article asked, "Who are guilty in this matter? Is it the poor ignorant, sunken and abandoned wretches who consummate the work planned out by 'gentlemen of property and standing?'" The people, the article continued, "know not what they do. But the Press, which from the commencement of the Anti-Slavery controversy, has kept alive by base misrepresentation, the worst passions of the human heart, and pointed at abolitionists as fit subjects for the assassin's dagger—the press—Political and Religious, by baptizing itself in all manner of abominations, in order to oppose the progress of pure principles, is guilty of this crime." Such power had to be resisted, and the *Colored American*, like other black periodicals, regularly reprinted and commented on articles first published elsewhere, noting their misrepresentations and biases.

This is not to say that the black press operated independently of white support. Most early black newspapers and magazines relied heavily on white backers and featured writing by whites. Frederick Douglass established the *North Star* and subsequent publications with the aid of white Europeans and Americans, whose help he relied upon heavily through the years. And whites were as significant a presence on the page as they were behind the scenes. The *Mirror of Liberty* featured more work by white writers than by black, and Douglass's periodical designed for European circulation, *Frederick Douglass' Monthly*, similarly included work by such prominent white abolitionists as Gerrit Smith, Lewis Tappan, Wendell Phillips, and Charles Sumner more frequently than it presented writings by black authors. It also included as a regular feature a series of "Letters from the Old World," sent from England by Mrs. Julia Griffith Crofts. But with alliances came significant tensions. Douglass, for example, when he founded the *North Star*, met with resistance from Garrison and his allies, former friends who now viewed Douglass's decision to form his own paper as a betrayal to Garrison's cause and its organ, the *Liberator*.

Thus black newspapers and magazines existed in a necessary but sometimes uneasy alliance with white supporters, and blacks themselves were sometimes torn by the argument that a specifically black press would only weaken the alliance necessary to oppose the force of the mainstream press. Still, the importance of a specifically African-American paper in promoting the full range of black rights was regularly reestablished— and was emphasized during the Civil War when the 1864 convention found reason to complain about those publications most closely associated with the black cause. "The weakness of our friends," the convention declared through its "Address," "is strength to our foes. When the 'Anti-Slavery Standard' representing the American Anti-Slavery Society, denies that society asks for the enfranchisement of colored men, and the 'Liberator' apologizes for excluding the colored men of Louisiana from the ballot-box, they injure us more vitally than all the ribald jests of the whole proslavery system." The collective voice of the black community clearly could not be fully represented in the pages of publications edited by whites. An article in the *Colored American* stated the case strongly in an appeal to its readers for financial support in 1838: "As to the necessity and importance of our paper;—This point hardly needs an argument. *We* have a place and a part to act in the great contest now waging between liberty and slavery—the powers of light and the powers of darkness. The interests of *three hundred thousand colored freemen*, for themselves, and as the true representatives of the enslaved, not only require, but equal justice to friends and enemies, demands that *we should give our testimony*; and pour our entreaties and rebukes in the ears of this guilty nation." This article was one of many that appeared regularly in appeals for support of the African-American press, from its earliest days to the post–Civil War years.

In the pages of black-run newspapers and magazines, readers would find the subjects and themes that quickly became central features of African-American collective self-definition. The presses included articles on the history of slavery, the American Revolution, the War of 1812, the Haitian Revolution, and African and European civilizations; their writers presented famous cases of rebellion and rescue, including pieces on Denmark Vesey, Nat Turner, Madison Washington, and John Brown, in addition to important events in the anti-slavery movement; they provided biographical sketches of black achievement, from Phillis Wheatley to Richard Allen to Toussaint L'Ouverture; and they offered samplings from the documents of organized resistance and communal struggle, from anti-slavery meetings to local and national black conventions. Thus they presented both a history and an ongoing account of a community's grand and small, international and local, collective and personal interests. Although some attempts at black publications lasted no more than a year or two, they were part of the effort to establish a community defined by something other than anti-slavery concerns.

❖

A comprehensive history of pre–Civil War African-American newspapers and magazines would be impossible to write. But a selective overview of these publications can suggest the process by which individual efforts became the working networks that ultimately constituted the black press.

Just as we can be sure that there were many benevolent associations, churches, schools, and literary associations as well as proposals for fraternal lodges and conventions that remain undiscovered or have been lost to the historical record, it is certain that many African-American newspapers and magazines, both planned and actually published, remain unknown to historians. Consider, for example, the quarterly publication *Afric-American Repository*, proposed in 1854 at the National Emigration Convention of Colored People, held in Cleveland. The black poet James Monroe Whitfield was to edit the magazine, which would be published by the Afric-American Printing Company, but no evidence of its publication has yet surfaced. Even many papers that were well known in their time are available to us today only in incomplete form, with important issues missing.

It is useful to remember that many black periodicals employed white editors and sometimes featured more white writers than black. Too, many African-American writers found forums for their work in white-run publications—for example, in such anti-slavery newspapers as Benjamin Lundy's *The Genius of Universal Emancipation*, which began in 1821 and ran until 1839, or especially in Garrison's *Liberator*, which ran from 1831 to 1866 and frequently published both essays and creative works by African Americans, including items in the paper's "Ladies Department." Although Frederick Douglass would eventually be recognized as the most prominent black newspaper editor of his time, more blacks subscribed to the *Liberator* than to Douglass's papers, which relied heavily on white subscribers. Moreover the concerns of the African-American press extended far beyond periodical publications. The first known black publishing company was the African Methodist Episcopal Book Concern, established in 1817, which concentrated at first on church and denominational publications, such as hymnals or doctrinal books, but would become an increasingly important black publishing center. Still, a highly selective view of specific black newspapers and magazines offers snapshots of a broader and more complex field of publications.

The story begins in 1827 with what is generally regarded as the first African-American newspaper, *Freedom's Journal*, edited by John B. Russwurm and Samuel E. Cornish. *Freedom's Journal* published everything from international events to ancient history, from biographies of prominent people of African heritage to notices of births, deaths, marriages, and other important moments in the lives of its immediate community of readers. The first issues of the weekly paper were printed in the basement of an AME Zion church in New York City, and the influence of the church and other black organizations was evident in its production. Among its founders were David Walker, a Prince Hall Freemason, and Richard Allen, founder of the AME church. Its contributors included some of the most influential activists of the time, including David Walker, author of the infamous *Appeal*. Subscriptions indicate that the newspaper's reach extended as far as Canada, Haiti, and England—and it was known in the American South as well, where blacks might be punished simply for possessing a copy. When on July 4, 1827, the New York legislature emancipated slaves in that state, *Freedom's Journal* was widely celebrated for playing a role in that decision—and among the celebrations was one in Fredricksburg, Virginia, where free blacks toasted the newspaper and took encouragement from New York's action.

Disagreements over editorial policy plagued *Freedom's Journal*, particularly Russwurm's support for black colonization in Africa. When Cornish left the paper, Russwurm's editorials in favor of emigration caused the paper to lose important support. Cornish moved on to found *The Rights of All* in 1829 and later joined with one of the most important black newspaper editors of the nineteenth century, Philip A. Bell. In 1837 Bell founded the *Weekly Advocate* in New York City, but he soon decided that the paper needed a title that would identify the community it was intended to serve. Renaming his weekly paper the *Colored American*, Bell appointed Cornish its first editor, and the paper ran until 1842.

William Whipper, one of *Freedom's Journal*'s readers and a prominent community leader, would later establish a newspaper of his own. Whipper published the first issue of the *National Reformer*, a monthly paper, in Philadelphia in 1838 under the motto "'God hath made of one blood all nations of men for to dwell on all the face of the earth.'—Acts, xvii, 26." The paper appeared under the auspices of the American Moral Reform Society, of which Whipper was a founder, and it addressed a broad range of issues important to the black community. Like *Freedom's Journal*, the *National Reformer* thus grew out of other organizational efforts, including Whipper's participation in literary societies and the convention movement, his service as first secretary of Philadelphia's Reading Room Society, and his position as a charter member of the Philadelphia Library Company of Colored Persons. He did much of the writing for the paper and featured notices of organizations and movements that he supported. But the *National Reformer* also included contributions by at least a few prominent African Americans, including Daniel Alexander Payne, who would soon become a major figure, and a bishop, in the AME church; the educator and activist William Watkins; and Henry Highland Garnet, then still studying for the ministry but already becoming known as an anti-slavery speaker. All three were involved in the American Moral Reform Society.

The paper took a broad approach to moral reform, which Whipper viewed as "the corner stone of the temple of universal freedom and eternal justice," covering everything from temperance to economics, anti-slavery to education, and it reprinted essays on such topics from other periodicals or pamphlets. But unlike Bell, who appealed explicitly to the black community, Whipple—who opposed the use of racial designations in the titles of black organizations—sought to reach a broader readership. He announced the paper's pages, "We have been of *no* sect, creed, or complexion, for the sake of all *sects, creeds,* and *complexions.* . . . The rights for which we are contending are the rights of universal man, and we shall not wait to inquire whether the oppressed are white, red, black, or brown, before we have bestowed on them our sympathy. . . . We here publicly renounce all COMPLEXIONAL ALLEGIANCE."

Another important periodical appeared in 1838 as well, leading some to identify that year as a fortuitous moment in the development of the black periodical press. David Ruggles's the *Mirror of Liberty* was published in New York City from 1838 to 1842. Like other magazines, the *Mirror* covered a wide range of topics, organized into such sections as the Poet's Mirror, Correspondence Mirror, Ladies Mirror, Political Mirror, Death's Mirror, and Reform's Mirror. The motto of this quarterly publication, both edited and published by Ruggles, was "Liberty is the word for me—above all, liberty," a cause to which Ruggles devoted his life. He had worked as a traveling salesman in the grocery and newspaper businesses, but he became well known as both a journalist and an activist for the anti-slavery movement. Like Whipple, he had also been involved in other organizations, particularly literary societies, having been one of the founders of the New York Philomathean Society and a member of the governing board of the Phoenix Society and the New York Garrison Literary and Benevolent Society.

In the *Mirror of Liberty*, Ruggles promoted his mission through essays opposing slavery, racial inequality, and African colonization. Many of the paper's writers were white—indeed, white contributors considerably outnumbered black contributors—but Ruggles insisted on his and his paper's own liberty as well, annoucing *Mirror of Liberty* as "a free and independent journal" whose editor was "an unmuzzled man, who goes for freedom of speech and the liberty of the press." Ruggles was active in efforts to aid fugitive slaves, and he used his paper to offer news of his activities with the New York Committee of Vigilance, reporting also on kidnappings of fugitives and relevant court cases. And Ruggles promised to take the paper further still, noting his intention to publish what amounted to a local directory of people who supported slavery, "furnishing the names and residences of all members of the bar, police officers, city marshals, constables, and other persons who lend themselves in the nefarious business of kidnapping; and the names of slaveholders residing in [New York] and in Brooklyn."

Black churches and denominations were especially important to the history of the African-American press. An outgrowth of church interest appeared in 1841 with the monthly *African Methodist Episcopal Church Magazine*, published in Brooklyn and edited by George Hogarth, an AME pastor and missionary. Many of the magazine's pages were devoted to denominational concerns—the proceedings of conferences, reports and editorials on religion, communications from individual churches—though they also included poetry and essays, most often religious in nature. Most of the contributors were AME ministers, though others, including William Whipper, were also represented. In focusing on church activities the magazine explored an important center of African-American life and community organization, a concern made more explicit by a series of travel-inspired articles about life among blacks of various communities. The *Church Magazine* also included essays on reform attempts (some of them controversial) within the church, including Daniel Payne's arguments for raising the educational level of AME ministers.

Such concerns were echoed in other publications, including what is perhaps the most famous African-American anti-slavery paper of the time, Frederick Douglass's *North Star*. In a letter published in a January 1849 issue of the paper, Mary Ann Shadd, who would found the *Provincial Freeman* newspaper in Canada in 1853, complained about "the influence of a corrupt clergy among us, sapping our every means, and, as a compensation, inculcating ignorance as a duty, superstition as true religion—in short, hanging like millstones about our necks. . . ." Although Douglass's paper is generally considered an anti-slavery publication, it covered a wide range of topics, as did other anti-slavery papers. Such attention to community needs was especially important to Douglass. He had been a close associate of Garrison, whose *Liberator* was viewed with reverence by its many black readers. As Douglass rose to prominence, he came to believe in the need for another paper, one published by an African American. He established the *North Star*, published in Rochester, New York, and subsequent publications with the support of white Europeans and Americans, whom he relied upon heavily through the years. Whites were also important contributors to the paper. The first issue was published in November 1847 with a masthead that proclaimed, "Right is of no Sex—Truth is of no Color—God is the Father of us all, and we are all Brethren." Douglass often struggled to keep the paper operating and did much of the writing for it. The *North Star* remained influential, eventually merging with the white abolitionist Gerrit Smith's *Liberty Party Paper* in 1851 to become *Frederick Douglass' Paper*. This lasted as a weekly publication until 1860 and was then published monthly for another three years.

Douglass's paper has received a great deal of scholarly attention, in part because of his personal prominence. Scholars have been relatively silent about a publication with an equal claim to influence, the *Repository of Religion and Literature and of Science and Art*, published from 1858 to 1863 under the editorial guidance of Daniel Payne. In contrast to the *African Methodist Episcopal Church Magazine*, the *Repository* was directed to a broader public and was itself an outgrowth of literary societies formed within the AME denomination. During the years of its existence the *Repository* moved its offices frequently, claiming as its home Indianapolis, then Philadelphia, and finally Baltimore. A magazine devoted to religion, literature, science, natural science, the arts, music, biography, and poetry, the *Repository* attempted "first, to diffuse useful knowledge among our people—second, to cultivate and develop their latent talents, and elevate their intellectual, moral, and religious character." Like Douglass and like many other editors of his day, Payne drew from a number of different writers but also wrote a great many of the magazine's articles himself. Although its editorial board included some of the leading African Americans of the time, men and women, the magazine also encouraged new writers, often printing speeches or essays they had presented at the meetings of literary societies. Included in its pages were a Mothers' Department, a Young Ladies' Lecture Room, a Children's Room, a Monthly Book Table that included notices of other publications, and the Church's Monthly Record. As was customary in nineteenth-century publications, the *Repository* published many pieces in series format so that readers would be encouraged to follow developing essays, biographies, or philosophical explorations from issue to issue, covering everything from religion to travel to natural history.

One of the most important black newspapers published before the Civil War, the *Weekly Anglo-African*, had both broad and deep roots in the newspaper business. When the *Colored American* discontinued publication in 1841, it was replaced that same year by the *People's Press*, a weekly paper founded by Thomas Hamilton. The *People's Press* was short-lived, but Hamilton continued to gain experience by working for a number of other papers, including the *National Anti-Slavery Standard* and the New York *Independent*. Drawing from that experience, he formed the *Weekly Anglo-African* in New York City in 1859, along with a sister publication, the monthly *Anglo-African Magazine*. The weekly paper, Hamilton made clear, had a clear mission: "We hope to supply a demand too long felt in this community. We need a Press—a press of our own. . . . Our *cause* (for in this country we have a cause) demands our own advocacy." The paper presented a wide range of subjects, including original literature by black writers. It ran until 1861, when it was transformed by George Lawrence, Jr., and the white abolitionist James Redpath into a platform for the cause of emigration to Haiti and renamed *The Pine and Palm*. Soon, however, Hamilton's brother Robert rejuvenated the *Weekly Anglo-African*, with Thomas working as business manager, and the paper continued from 1861 to 1865, often featuring the military experience of black soldiers in the Civil War.

As important as the *Weekly Anglo-African* was its monthly sister publication, the *Anglo-African Magazine*. Although the magazine lasted only a year, it was the original publishing site for important early black works of fiction, social commentary, and science writing. Hamilton's hopes for the magazine were ambitious: to collect statistics and other information about African-American educational, economic, social, and legal life; to record the biographies of leading figures of African heritage in the United States and around the world; to highlight the work of other black publications; and to provide a forum for "the rapidly rising talent of colored men in their special and general literature." The magazine was intended to be a showcase and forum for black intellectuals and writers, and its contributors constituted a virtual Who's Who of early black leadership. It published one of the earliest short stories and chapters from one of the first novels written by blacks—Frances E. W. Harper's "The Two Offers" and Martin Delany's *Blake, or The Huts of America*. Besides Delany and Harper, readers of the magazine could find the writings of Amos Gerry Beman, Edward Wilmot Blyden, Robert Campbell, Mary Ann Shadd Cary, Frederick Douglass, Sarah M. Douglass, James Theodore Holly, John Mercer Langston, J. Sella Martin, William C. Nell, Daniel Alexander Payne, James W. C. Pennington, Charles B. Ray, James McCune Smith, George B. Vashon, and William J. Wilson. When Hamilton issued a bound edition of the first volume of the magazine, he could claim with considerable justice, as an advertisement had it, that the *Anglo-African Magazine* "contains more facts and statistics of the colored race than any other publication extant."

Among the *Anglo-African*'s articles, representing the wide range of its concerns, were Robert Campbell on "Struggles for Freedom in Jamaica" and "Effects of Emancipation in Jamaica," and Martin Delany on "The Attraction of Planets" and on "Comets." Edward W. Blyden, addressing the effects of international politics on the situation in Liberia, contributed "A Chapter in the History of the Slave Trade." A. J. R. Connor provided the words and music to "My Cherished Hope, My Fondest Dream." James McCune Smith wrote "On the Fourteenth Query of Thomas Jefferson's Notes on Virginia." George B. Vashon's "The Successive Advances of Astronomy" might be followed by James Field's "The Shadows of Intemperance," which would carry a different philosophical tone than Robert Gordon's "In the Constitution of Man There Exists a Religious Element." An article on "Chess" noted the Egyptian roots of the game and was followed later by a review of *The Book of the First American Chess Congress*.

Another monthly periodical from roughly the same period was aimed at a quite different readership. In 1858 Frederick Douglass announced his plan to publish a monthly magazine "for all the British subscribers, in lieu of the weekly which they now receive." Where the *Anglo-African Magazine* is fascinating precisely because of the range of its writers, subjects, and views, *Douglass' Monthly* served primarily as a forum for Douglass's views and causes. Still, it covered a broad scope of events and concerns, including regular political reportage (including reprintings of important speeches by Abraham Lincoln and others), news of anti-slavery activities in the United States and abroad, eulogies of important white abolitionists, reprintings (under the title "Southern Gems") of advertisements for slave sales and rewards for recaptured fugitives, and historical accounts of important events in the anti-slavery movement. The monthly's international appeal was in bringing together a broad range of activities, from the Rochester Ladies Anti-Slavery Society to the Irish Ladies Anti-Slavery Society, including reprinted articles from both British and American sources. Many prominent blacks contributed to *Douglass' Monthly*, including James McCune Smith, Daniel Payne, Alexander Crummell, Jermain Wesley Loguen, J. Sella Martin, John Willis Menard, Martin Delany, Henry Highland Garnet, and George B. Vashon. Still, *Douglass' Monthly*, unlike the *Anglo-African Magazine*, had no commitment to a black-authored magazine, for it was dominated, beyond Douglass's own writings, by the work of such white abolitionists as Gerrit Smith, Lewis Tappan, Wendell Phillips, and Charles Sumner.

When Daniel Payne wrote for *Douglass' Monthly*, he expressed his concerns about the educational aims of what became the longest continuously printed African-American newspaper, the *Christian Recorder*. Established in 1852 by the AME Book Concern and long eclipsed in scholarship by Douglass's and Garrison's anti-slavery papers, this important periodical is now increasingly recognized as an especially rich source for understanding black literature, history, and community development. The weekly included regular departments devoted to Religious Intelligence, Domestic News, General Items, Foreign News, Obituaries, Marriages, Notices, and Advertisements. It was in the *Christian Recorder* that Frances E. W. Harper published, serially, the novels that would lead twentieth-century scholars to identify her for a time as the first black female novelist. In fact that distinction belongs to Julia C. Collins, who published *The Curse of Caste* in the same magazine before Harper's fiction appeared. Like the *Repository*, the *Christian Recorder* was devoted to a broad sweep of concerns, including religion, morality, literature, and science. Like the black church itself, the AME's major organ served as a community forum, publishing articles and works of literature of interest to its readers but also working to develop the community. During the Civil War the *Recorder* broadened its coverage, traveling to the South with black soldiers to provide an important forum that black communities could not find in the mainstream press. In addition to publishing firsthand accounts of battles, the paper promoted and facilitated black recruitment in the Union Army, published black soldiers' letters to their loved ones at home, and reported on other concerns important both to those engaged in the war and those watching its progress from a distance. A regular correspondent for the *Christian Recorder* beginning in 1862, Henry McNeal Turner (later a bishop in the AME church) continued to write for the paper when he became the army's first black chaplain in 1863, reporting on everything from battles to race issues to church affairs from his perspective in the Union lines. Through such correspondents, the *Recorder* extended its attention to the South to include reports on church burnings, white supremacist terrorist organizations such as the Ku Klux Klan, and related items. After the war, too, the paper served as a major formation center for families separated under slavery and trying to reunite. The *Recorder*, in short, was both comprehensive and adaptable, adjusting its outlook to account for shifts in history and culture while providing a stable and consistent voice and presence throughout the black community.

As should be clear from these examples, most black publications developed almost organically from other organizations or from other publication attempts. As soon as literary societies appeared, for example, their members began to submit writings to established newspapers and magazines. The Female Literary Society of Philadelphia, whose members formed the organization in 1831, soon were sending poems and other work to Garrison's *Liberator*. After the Demosthenian Literary Society was established in 1837, its forty-two members began to discuss the possibility of a weekly paper, and in 1841 they inaugurated, for one thousand subscribers, the *Demosthenian Shield*. In that same year the *African Methodist Episcopal Review* also started publication. And out of David Ruggles's failed paper, the *Mirror of Liberty*, came the *Genius of Freedom*, which also failed. Addressing the need for a paper that did the work of the *Mirror of Liberty*, Willis Hodges, whose letter to the *New York Sun* had convinced him of the need for a paper friendly to black interests, partnered with Thomas Van Rensselaer and in 1846 began publishing the *Ram's Horn*, with the motto, "We are men, and therefore interested in whatever concerns men."

Wherever free black communities formed, periodical publications emerged. In 1843, for example, a bimonthly and bilingual magazine, the *Literary Album, Journal of Young People*, began publication in New Orleans and was so successful that it soon became a semimonthly. The *Semi-Weekly and Daily Creole* (later the *New Orleans Daily Creole*), began publication in the city in 1856. This was followed by the *Union*, published in New Orleans starting in 1862, and the first black daily newspaper, the *New Orleans Tribune*, in 1864. In Paterson, New Jersey, in 1851, Alfred Gibbs Campbell established the *Alarm Bell*, a monthly paper devoted to temperance issues but actually covering the broad range of concerns that characterized virtually all black periodicals. In the West, Judge Mifflin W. Gibbs started the first African-American newspaper, the *Mirror of the Times*, in 1855 in the Bay Area. That paper was followed in 1862 by San Francisco's *Pacific Appeal*. Such publications served black communities in numerous ways, not the least of which was to announce the presence of the community to itself as well as to others.

In many ways the press was the most democratic of the various associations formed by African Americans before the Civil War, for through it many voices and views came together. In its articles and the letters and other notices it printed, the press gave voice to a wide swath of people who made up the black community, some prominent and some not. Some publications reflected the editorial biases of the organizations from which they grew, and each newspaper and magazine was also controlled by a dominant editorial voice, even if aided by an editorial board. Some individuals, such as Frederick Douglass or David Ruggles, maintained strong editorial control. In many cases editorial or ideological disagreements, often sharp, arose between editors, as was the case with John Russwurm and Samuel Cornish of *Freedom's Journal*, or with Douglass and Martin Delany of the *North Star*, or with Henry Bibb, editor of Canada's *Voice of the Fugitive*, and Mary Ann Shadd, editor of Canada's *Provincial Freeman*.

Influential editors often left to form new papers. Philip A. Bell, once chairman of the board of associates of the Philomathean Society, edited the *Colored American*, but over the years he edited or was prominently involved in a number of other papers, including *Struggler* (New York City,

1835), the *Weekly Advocate* (New York City, 1837), the *Elevator* (Philadelphia, 1840s), the *Pacific Appeal* (San Francisco, 1862), and the *Elevator*
(San Francisco, 1865). One of Bell's contributors to the *Colored American* was William Whipper, among the founders of the Philadelphia Library Company of Colored Persons, who went on to edit the *National
Reformer*. John Russwurm, the controversial editor of *Freedom's Journal*,
because of his views on colonization, moved to Monrovia, Liberia, where
he founded the *Liberian Herald*. Delany, a leader of Pittsburgh's Philanthropic Society, founded the Pittsburgh newspaper *The Mystery* and later
was listed with Douglass as one of the editors of the *North Star*. *The Mystery*, meanwhile, was sold in 1847 to the AME church and renamed the
Christian Herald, which was again renamed the *Christian Recorder* and
moved to Philadelphia.

The dedication of these editors cannot be overstated. Producing and
maintaining a newspaper or a magazine was challenging even under
the best of circumstances, and black editors rarely had that luxury. Often the editors found that they needed to write much of the material
for their own papers. Many of them did so tirelessly to fill their pages
while soliciting new material from other writers and reprinting material from other papers. Although Frederick Douglass is known for his
autobiographies—the favorite texts offered in many high school and college classes—a more representative reading of Douglass's life as a writer
would certainly include an extensive collection of his writings for his papers, and the same can be said of many editors.

But even after filling their pages, black editors often struggled to secure enough subscribers to keep the paper in business. Black subscribers to Garrison's *Liberator*, for example, far outnumbered the subscribers
Douglass was able to win over for his paper, in part because of long and
deep loyalties in the black community to Garrison's commitment to the
abolitionist cause. Papers often issued appeals for subscribers, and public
meetings were sometimes held in attempts to raise support for specific
papers, as was the case in New York, Hartford, New Bedford, and Boston when David Ruggles's *Mirror of Liberty* was in danger of running out
of adequate funds, as eventually it did. In these appeals, writers and supporters would often repeat the arguments for a specifically black press
that had been presented at conventions, churches, literary societies, and

other forums—always reiterating that newspapers oriented to the specific needs of the black community were essential to maintaining it.

The link between the press and the community was presented quite
directly in an 1841 article relating to subscriptions for the *Colored American*. A report by a subscription agent, W. P. Johnson, concerned his experiences with "our people in Schenectady": "I saw a great many instances
where the whites had cheated and fooled the poor colored people of their
property. I at one sight saw 13 houses and lots that had a few years ago
belonged to colored people, and they are all gone now but one, and they
have tried hard to get that one." Sounding the *Colored American*'s familiar call, Johnson added, "We should be as careful then to educate our
children as we are to give them bread." "Touching our paper," Johnson
continued, "I found very few who seem to appreciate the great good that
is being produced, or its claims on them. What few I did find, plead poverty. In fact, I am sorry to say that Schenectady is the only place where I
have been and failed to please the people generally in the discharge of my
duties as a professing Christian, and as agent for our journal; and it is the
only place where I have been and labored so hard with so little success."

Johnson's blending of concerns—the loss of property with compla-
cency toward education and religious instruction, his own failure to
make an impression as both "a professing Christian" and "as agent for
our journal"—is appropriate to the aims of the *Colored American* as well
as other black papers. "They have all the means in their hands to do
great things," Johnson notes at the end, "and my prayer to God is that
he will bind them together in love and religion, so that their labors may
be crowned with success." The African-American press could instruct
"our people" in those arts of reading that would protect them from being
"fooled and cheated," not only of their property but of their existence as a
self-determined community.

Such appeals were common in the pages of the *Colored American*
and other black papers. In 1839 the paper published an "Appeal to the
Friends of the Colored American," addressed to the paper's "Brethren
and Friends." "It is now nearly three years since the publication of the
COLORED AMERICAN was commenced as the mouth piece to our people,"
the writer observed, "through which to meet together and compare
views, have a free interchange of opinion, and strike upon some plan,

for the correction of our own errors, the improvement of our social condition, the procurement of civil rights, and to help on the holy cause of universal freedom, in our country and throughout the world." But those years had been a struggle, and "We have now arrived at the darkest point yet, in the history of the COLORED AMERICAN, we confess we hardly know how to get out."

David Ruggles, on the other hand, argued specifically for an anti-slavery press, observing at the beginning of a six-part article, "Though ours is the 'Land of Liberty' *we are slaves* whose condition is but a short remove from that of two millions of our race who are pining in their bloody chains." To emerge from that condition of slavery, nominally free African Americans would need a strong anti-slavery press. Ruggles declared that "our contest is for *freedom*," and insisted that "the PRESS is the weapon which we wield in behalf of our rights, is the engine that will speed us *on* to the full enjoyment of *freedom's* blessings." Subscribing to anti-slavery newspapers was, acccordingly, a "duty," but one too often ignored. Ruggles offered a dialogue in which one after another person claimed that he could not subscribe to the paper—the first because he couldn't afford it, the second because he could not read, the third because he had no time to read, and the fourth because "many of my customers are slaveholders and colonizationists, and they don't like it." Ruggles rebutted each argument, ultimately linking support of the anti-slavery press to the cause of freedom—freedom for the community not quite envisioned or realized by each of the imaginary people who offered excuses for not subscribing.

Ruggles's argument was persuasive, but many blacks believed that it needed to be extended beyond the limited dimensions of the anti-slavery cause, that African Americans would never enjoy "freedom's blessings" as long as they relied on white America to represent their experiences, good and bad. Even within the anti-slavery movement, the limitations of white allies were increasingly clear. As noted earlier, Frederick Douglass in 1855 commented pointedly on the limitations of interracial understanding even in the anti-slavery movement, where he worked closely with white abolitionists. "Our oppressed people," he complained,

> are wholly ignored, in one sense, in the generalship of the movement to effect our Redemption. Nothing is done—no, nothing . . . to inspire us with the Idea of our Equality with the whites. We are a poor, pitiful, dependent and servile class of Negroes, *"unable to keep pace"*

with the movement, to which we have adverted—not even capable of *"perceiving what are its demands, or understanding the philosophy of its operations!"* Of course, if we are "unable to keep pace" with our white brethren, in their vivid perception of the demands of our cause, those who assume the leadership of the Anti-Slavery Movement; if it is regarded as having *"transcended our ability,"* we cannot consistently expect to receive from those who indulge in this opinion, a *practical recognition of our Equality.* This is what we are contending for. It is what we have never received. It is what we must receive to inspire us with confidence in the self-appointed generals of the Anti-Slavery host, the Euclids who are *theoretically* working out the almost insoluble problem of our future destiny.

The usually moderate Douglass was not alone in voicing such complaints. The fact that black communities were forced to develop within a white supremacist culture was a major concern of the African-American press. It was presented with great satiric force by William J. Wilson in an 1860 issue of the *Anglo-African Magazine*—"What Shall We Do with the White People?"—in which Wilson considered colonizing white people elsewhere but concluded, paternalistically, that "in view of the existing state of things around us, let our constant thought be, *what for the best good of all shall we do with the White people?*" An 1859 article in the magazine's sister publication, the *Weekly Anglo-African*, took on the same issues more seriously while grouping Americans together as a flawed whole. Proclaiming that "truly we are a great people," the author went on to characterize that greatness in terms that could not be mistaken:

> Whatsoever we do is right. We have a high notion of ourselves. We can do anything. We can make wrong right, and can right wrongs. We take special interest in toleration, if in that toleration a wrong is involved. Wrongs smartly executed or inflicted please us far more than right doing. Of course, in all this we speak nationally, and not Anglo-Africanwise. We Americans are, so we think, singularly fortunate in having instructors and instruction that lead to these results, and that make us in these days conquer our prejudices, and throw aside old-fashioned notions of right and wrong.

Here the author highlighted the importance of an African American press—a publication capable of adopting the perspective on current and past events needed in order to speak "Anglo-Africanwise" rather than "naturally" as an American. The black press was essential, in other words, not only in speaking to and for the black community but also in its ability to voice opinions forged through the experience of living with the philosophical contradictions and legal labyrinths created and sustained by the white community.

African-American newspapers accounted for this complex racial environment in numerous ways—through editorials and through articles reprinted from white Northern and Southern newspapers—but the purpose was to bring into focus the community shaped by that hostile environment. A frequently repeated word in the headlines of the *Colored American*, for example, was "elevation," as in an 1839 article, "Elevation of Our People." Many pressures were shaping black communities from without, the author warned. "To raise up a people to intellectual, social, and moral life, long having been kept down, oppressed, and proscribed, mentally, socially, and legally; whose education has been entirely neglected, and thought either not proper, or possible by others, and by themselves thought to be out of their power; whose claims have been regarded as though they had none, and against whom has been every man's hand, and whose disposition and habits, social and moral, have been formed under those circumstances, is a work, than which there is none more honorable and God-like." How might the cause of elevation be realized in such an environment? Through the workings of the press, the writer hoped, where people operating in a "humble sphere" could promote a cause that "might fill an angel's heart, and which certainly ought to occupy the minds and attention of men." Among the means necessary for the work would be education, "social as well as literary." But the writer worried too that "the disposition and habits of our people, in most cases, are essentially wrong," and that what was needed was "a reading disposition." "Every man therefore among us," the author concluded, "who is a reader, *merely*, and will avail himself of books and papers, cultivate a reading habit, he will not only by contrast know his own condition better, and see its wants, but will have the means for improvement, become conversant with the world, and prepared to lend an influence, to give a right direction and tone, to the habits of all within his reach."

But here again the terms of the struggle ahead were determined by others. In an 1837 *Colored American* article on the murder of Elijah P. Lovejoy, the author located the heart of the problem in the white press.

"Whither shall we turn our aching eyes?" the author asked. "Where shall we look for a redeeming spirit? To the Press? Gracious Heaven! How has it spoken? Read the New York Gazette, the Courier & Enquirer, the Star and the Sun, and then let us hang our heads in shame. To the pulpit? It is recreant to its trust. With a few noble and splendid exceptions the Pulpit and the Press, have virtually by their silence and actual committal, espoused the side of the oppressor. Truly, 'on the side of the oppressor there is power.'" Lovejoy's murderers were not the most guilty of the parties in this tragedy, the author charged, for they were acting out of ignorance. The guilty party was the force that maintained and encouraged such ignorance: "the Press, which from the commencement of the Anti-Slavery controversy, has kept alive by base misrepresentations, the worst passions of the human heart, and pointed at abolitionists as fit subjects for the assassin's dagger—the press—Political and Religious, by baptizing itself in all manner of abominations, in order to oppose the progress of pure principles, is guilty of this crime." Just as African Americans needed their own press to establish a coherent community for themselves, so they had to confront the reality that the white press too was busily creating a community, one defined by a combination of racist ignorance and deadly force.

❖

African-American newspapers and magazines grew from the many organizations and associations that blacks formed, and the press worked to give both voice and support to those efforts. In the opening "Apology" for the *Anglo-African Magazine*, the editor Thomas Hamilton collected this entire endeavor in a single sentence, announcing,

> In addition to an exposé of the condition of the blacks, this Magazine will have the aim to uphold and encourage the now depressed hopes of thinking black men, in the United States—the men who, for twenty years and more have been active in conventions, in public meetings, in societies, in the pulpit, and through the press, cheering on and laboring on to promote emancipation, affranchisement and education; some of them in, and some of them past the prime of life, yet see, as the apparent result of their work and their sacrifices, only Fugitive Slave laws and Compromise bills, and the denial of citizenship on the part

of the Federal and State Governments, and, saddest of all, such men as
Seward and Preston King insulting the rights of their black constitu-
ents by voting to admit Oregon as a state with a constitution denying
to black men even an entrance within its borders.

The political and social territory covered in this sentence—moving as
it does from depressed hopes to valiant organizational efforts and leading
finally to specific legislative acts and to the terms of Oregon's admission
to the Union—is breathtaking. It mirrors the challenge faced through
the agency of the black press, akin to establishing a new nation, or at least
of reforming the nation in which African Americans found themselves
both included and excluded. "Our cause is something higher," Hamilton
declared, "something holier than the founding of states. Any five hundred men with thews and sinews, and a moderate share of prudence, can
found a state; it is nothing new or wonderful to do. And after we had
founded such a state, our work in the United States would remain to be
done by other hands. Our work here, is, to purify the State, and purify
Christianity from the foul blot which here rests upon them."

This assertion might well serve as a statement of purpose for all the
organizations and associations explored in this book—the challenge of
creating from within a coherent and influential African-American community, in part by reforming the white community that attempted to
shape that community from without.

8

Postscript

THE VARIOUS ORGANIZATIONS that have been the subject of this book were formed during the years when the system of slavery was a defining force in American politics and economics—a force that considerably restricted the lives and communities of nominally free African Americans. Black organizations before the Civil War were defined in large part by the need to respond to the world that slavery made, to determine what "freedom" could mean for blacks at this time, and to create a unified political and social force in the face of the racist assumptions required and promoted by the system of slavery. The need for black community organizers did not end, however, when slavery was officially prohibited by the Thirteenth Amendment to the Constitution. With slavery had come an increasingly defined and insistent set of laws and social practices designed to police the ever-shifting borders of race. These borders determined, with increasing levels of absurdity, who would count as nonwhite, with black Americans always serving as the extreme against which other ethnic groups would be measured. Held outside those borders of social acceptance and equal rights, black Americans found that their lives were not significantly changed by the advent of the Fourteenth Amendment, which established and protected their citizenship, or by the Fifteenth Amendment, which established black male suffrage. True, they had come a long way from 1857, the year of the Supreme Court's *Dred Scott* decision, in which Chief Justice Roger B. Taney declared that African Americans had no rights that white Americans were obliged to respect. But they still faced the world defined by the "separate but equal" doctrine established by the Court's 1896 decision in *Plessy v. Ferguson*. That separate but equal meant separate but *unequal* was clear from the very beginning, and African Americans faced a long struggle for economic access, educational resources, and political representation.

Some of the nineteenth century's most prominent black leaders, men and women who had established their credentials in the anti-slavery and civil rights struggles that preceded the Civil War, found themselves grappling to promote and in some cases even to define their cause after the war. For example, Martin Delany, a prominent and respected leader before the war, found himself ridiculed and denounced as a "nigger Democrat" by the black masses for his collaborations with the white Democratic party (a party hostile to African Americans) in the postwar South. Even the most prominent black leader before the Civil War, Frederick Douglass, had trouble navigating the choppy waters of the postwar years. In those years Douglass held numerous prestigious posts—president of the Freedmen's Savings and Trust Company, federal marshal and recorder of deeds for the District of Columbia, consul to Haiti, and chargé d'affaires for the Dominican Republic—but with each one he discovered a world of concerns that had not been resolved either by the war or by the constitutional amendments passed during the hopeful years immediately following the conflict. When the Supreme Court's ruling in *United States v. Stanley* (1883) furthered the proliferation of Jim Crow laws, Douglass observed, "It is the old spirit of slavery, and nothing else." He would repeat the point ten years later in his "Introduction to the Reason Why the Colored American Is Not in the World's Columbian Exposition" (1893), in which he invoked the standard commemorative rhetoric of progress and principle only to quickly and decidedly deny its application, concluding that American history remained guided by the "asserted spirit" of American slavery.

African Americans who did not enjoy Douglass's prominence were even more greatly plagued by the haunting spirit of slavery. In the South, blacks faced laws designed to replace the system of slavery with harsh economic and legal restrictions that virtually guaranteed their dependence on white landowners, along with the development of a convict leasing system (and a set of laws to feed the system) that historians have characterized as a de facto system of slavery. In the North, African American migrants from the South found themselves lost and manipulated in hostile urban environments, providing a cheap labor force and living in conditions that would eventually become the ghettos or, in current parlance, the inner cities that today symbolize the as-yet-unsolved "black problem" in American life. In the last decades of the nineteenth century and the early years of the twentieth, African Americans who resisted the odds and began to establish successful businesses and local power often faced vandalism, white supremacist terror organizations like the Ku Klux Klan, or even the noose, as lynching became a very open means by which white mobs controlled black lives. Separate but equal quickly devolved into violent separation and enforced inequalities.

To respond to this newly threatening social situation, African Americans applied the lessons of those who had come before, building on existing organizations and developing new ones. After the Civil War, many writers celebrated the success of established black organizations by writing histories of churches, religious denominations, the black press, and fraternal organizations, all subjects covered by black historians in books published in the last decades of the nineteenth century. Other black writers published collective biographies—books that provided biographical sketches of African American men and women who had distinguished themselves in various professional and social endeavors. In all of these books, the authors noted the importance of a record of accomplishment sufficiently durable as to justify a book-length history, and many noted as well that the histories they published would provide material for future historians to reevaluate the place and importance of black endeavors in American life. Fundamentally the authors presented their histories as evidence that African Americans were equal to any challenge they faced, particularly when they joined together in an organized effort.

But as before the Civil War, black Americans often disagreed about what kind of effort was needed and what kind of organization was best suited to the challenge. In the last decades of the nineteenth century, Booker T. Washington emerged as the most powerful and influential African American leader of his time, creating a vast network of political influence, publishing ventures, and educational initiatives pervasive enough to be called the Tuskegee Machine—named after the school, the Tuskegee Institute, that Washington headed and used as his base. Washington's strategy for incorporating blacks into American political and economic life involved compromise and accommodating relationships with white political and economic leaders, compromises that other African Americans found both distasteful and counterproductive. Other leaders would similarly work for interracial alliances but would insist on greater educational opportunities and political independence for blacks, most notably W. E. B. DuBois, who was public in his criticism of Washington and who in 1909 joined with white allies to found the National Association for the Advancement of Colored People (NAACP). DuBois became head of that organization in 1910, and that year founded and began editing its official magazine, *The Crisis*. For many, the difference between Washington and DuBois represented the major split in black political strategies of the time: Washington the man who had struggled "up from slavery," as his autobiography was titled, to work for those unprepared by slavery for the threatening world of tenuous freedom; DuBois the Harvard-educated sociologist who looked to the "talented tenth" of the race to create new avenues for African-American advancement.

Other divisions during these years were even more dramatic. In 1914 Jamaican-born Marcus Garvey founded the Universal Negro Improvement Association, which by 1918 included the organization's official weekly newspaper, the *Negro World*. Garvey's organization promoted black nationalism or Pan-Africanism, devoted to placing those of African heritage into a new understanding of history, making them global citizens of a dispersed nation joined by the common cause of African redemption. Like Washington before him, Garvey created an economic, political, and publishing empire—a vast network of organizations through which a black nation might emerge and a new world history might be written. At roughly the same time, two black leaders worked not to establish a new sense of history but to recover and promote the history they had inherited. In 1915 the educator Carter G. Woodson and Jesse E. Moorland, a minister and civic leader, established the Association for the Study of Negro Life and History (now the Association for the Study of African American Life and History) to encourage the research and promotion of black history, even to the point of providing educational materials that teachers might use instead of those that presented African Americans in a degrading light or omitted them altogether from American history. Their efforts too led to a publishing organ—the *Journal of Negro History* (1916) that continues today as the *Journal of African American History*. Woodson, known as the Father of Black History, would later initiate Negro History Week (the second week in February, encompassing Abraham Lincoln's and Frederick Douglass's birthdays), which has since expanded to Black History Month.

From African Americans rising from the fields of enslavement to those setting out from the halls of Harvard, from leaders calling for a global mission to redeem Africa to those working to intervene in the educational control of African Americans in U.S. classrooms, the network of organizations that worked to join black Americans in a common sense of community was diverse and sometimes fraught with tensions. The story remained the same throughout the twentieth century, a time in which new religious, fraternal, educational, and political organizations proliferated—all promising black Americans the blessings of solidarity and collective identity, but many of them working at cross-purposes with one another. Even with the successes of the civil rights movement in the mid- to late twentieth century, African Americans found themselves engaged in familiar struggles for direction and leadership, still searching for the means to determine their own paths in a nation that had yet to be fully inclusive, still working to promote a vision of nationhood in which all voices were heard and all interests considered with equal respect and seriousness of purpose. In these ongoing struggles, in times of success and in times of frustration, *community* has remained a tenuous but essential goal for black Americans, a matter of working, as did Barack Obama early in his career, to organize black folks.

A Note on Sources

The writings that make up much of the history of African Americans in the nineteenth century are scattered in various archives. The historian's task is to gather the fragments in order to piece together a provisional history, one that might encourage additional research and lead to new and ever more comprehensive histories. This search for historical fragments has been my challenge as well. My primary inspiration for this book has been Frances Smith Foster's call for greater attention to the black press and other nineteenth-century black organizations in her article "A Narrative of the Interesting Origins and (Somewhat) Surprising Developments of African American Print Culture" (*American Literary History* 17:4 [Winter 2005], 714–740). My other guideposts have been Leon F. Litwack's *North of Slavery: The Negro in the Free States, 1790–1860* (Chicago, 1961), which remains an indispensable book on this subject; James Oliver Horton's *Free People of Color: Inside the African American Community* (Washington, D.C., 1993) and (with Lois E. Horton) *In Hope of Liberty: Culture, Community, and Protest Among Northern Free Blacks, 1700–1860* (New York, 1997), which are also essential; and Benjamin Quarles's *Black Abolitionists* (New York, 1969), which offers an examination of African American activism that extends far beyond the anti-slavery movement. More recently, Patrick Rael has edited a collection of essays that brings together some of the best scholars on the subject in *African-American Activism Before the Civil War: The Freedom Struggle in the Antebellum North* (New York, 2008). Another book that, like Quarles's, extends outward from the anti-slavery movement, offering a valuable examination of black (and white) women's activism in the North, is Jean Fagan Yellin and John C. Van Horne, eds., *The Abolitionist Sisterhood: Women's Political Culture in Antebellum America* (Ithaca, 1994). A good study of African-American communities in the late eighteenth century is Sidney Kaplan and Emma Nogrady Kaplan, *The Black Presence in the Era of the American Revolution* (Amherst, Mass., 1989). For a good entrance into African-American social, religious, and political culture in the antebellum South, two books have been especially influential, Ira Berlin's *Slaves Without Masters: The Free Negro in the Antebellum South* (New York, 1974) and Lawrence W. Levine's *Black Culture and Black Consciousness: Afro-American Folk Thought from Slavery to Freedom* (New York, 1977).

The subject of community remains a troubling challenge in the writing of African-American history. It ranges from those who assume the existence of an ideologically or at least historically coherent community to those for whom *the black community* is largely a political or even a theoretical enterprise. At the theoretical end of things, Saidiya V. Hartman's concept of "networks of affiliation" is most valuable. This idea is at the center of her groundbreaking study, *Scenes of Subjection: Terror, Slavery, and Self-Making in Nineteenth-Century America* (New York, 1997). Valuable too is Katherine Clay Bassard's concept of "performing community" in *Spiritual Interrogations: Culture, Gender, and Community in Early African American Women's Writing* (Princeton, 1999). Although they focus primarily on the twentieth century, also valuable are Eddie S. Glaude, Jr.'s *In a Shade of Blue: Pragmatism and the Politics of Black America* (Chicago, 2007) and W. Lawrence Hogue's *The African American Male, Writing, and Difference: A Polycentric Approach to African American Literature, Criticism, and History* (Albany, 2003). Sterling Stuckey looks beyond theoretical concerns in his study of the African roots of black communities in *Slave Culture: Nationalist Theory and the Foundations of Black America* (New York, 1987). Other useful studies are Dylan C. Penningroth's *The Claims of Kinfolk: African American Property and Community in the Nineteenth-Century South* (Chapel Hill, 2003); John Wood Sweet's *Bodies Politic: Negotiating Race in the American North, 1730–1830* (Baltimore, 2003); and Walter C. Rucker's *The River Flows On: Black Resistance, Culture, and Identity Formation in Early America* (Baton Rouge, 2006).

The most detailed accounts of African-American organizational efforts may be found in regional and even local histories, some by professional historians and some by devoted local investigators, including community members involved in recovery and preservation efforts. A good study of this kind, focusing on the Northeast, is the collection of essays edited by David Levinson and published for the Upper Housatonic Valley National Heritage Area, *African American Heritage: In the Upper Housatonic Valley* (Great Barrington, Mass., 2006). Good studies of the North, beyond those noted above, include Lorenzo Johnston Greene's *The Negro in Colonial New England* (New York, 1968); Elizabeth Rauh Bethel's *The Roots of African-American Identity: Memory and History in the Antebellum Free Communities* (New York, 1997); and my own *Liberation Historiography: African American Writers and the Challenge of History, 1794–1861* (Chapel Hill, 2004). For the ever-expanding West in the nineteenth century, useful studies include Joe William Trotter, Jr.'s *River Jordan: African American Urban Life in the Ohio Valley* (Lexington, Ky., 1998); Stephen A. Vincent's *Southern Seed, Northern Soil: African-American Farm Communities in the Midwest, 1765–1900*

(Bloomington, Ind., 1999); Quintard Taylor's *In Search of the Racial Frontier: African Americans in the American West, 1528–1990* (New York, 1998); and John Craig Hammond's *Slavery, Freedom, and Expansion in the Early American West* (Charlottesville, Va., 2007).

Numerous studies concentrate on individual states; some are largely collections of information and discrete stories, others are more developed histories. Particularly important to me in writing this book have been John Hope Franklin's *The Free Negro in North Carolina, 1790–1860* (New York, 1943; Chapel Hill, 1995); Lester C. Lamon's *Blacks in Tennessee, 1791–1970* (Knoxville, 1981); Graham Russell Hodges's *Root & Branch: African Americans in New York and East Jersey, 1613–1863* (Chapel Hill, 1999); Jeffrey J. Crow, Paul D. Escott, and Flora J. Hatley's *A History of African Americans in North Carolina*, published for the Office of Archives and History of the North Carolina Department of Cultural Resources (Raleigh, 2002); the second edition of Marion B. Lucas's *A History of Blacks in Kentucky from Slavery to Segregation, 1760–1891*, published for the Kentucky Historical Society (Frankfort, 2003); H. H. Price and Gerald E. Talbot's *Maine's Visible Black History: The First Chronicle of Its People* (Gardiner, Me., 2006); and Frank Andrews Stone's *African American Connecticut: The Black Scene in a New England State: Eighteenth to Twenty-first Century* (Deland, Fla., 2008).

It would be impossible to account here for all the studies of individual towns and cities, some of them highly influential books and others distinctively local efforts geared toward readers associated with the area or engaged in historical tourism. Philadelphia, New York, and Boston, hubs of African-American organizational efforts, have naturally received a fair amount of attention. Particularly valuable are Julie Winch's *Philadelphia's Black Elite: Activism, Accommodation, and the Struggle for Autonomy, 1787–1848* (Philadelphia, 1988); Gary B. Nash's *Forging Freedom: The Formation of Philadelphia's Black Community, 1720–1840* (Cambridge, Mass., 1988); Craig Steven Wilder's *In the Company of Black Men: The African Influence on African American Culture in New York City* (New York, 2001); Leslie M. Harris's *In the Shadow of Slavery: African Americans in New York City, 1626–1863* (Chicago, 2003); *Courage and Conscience: Black and White Abolitionists in Boston*, edited by Donald M. Jacobs (Bloomington, Ind., 1993); and James Oliver Horton and Lois E. Horton's *Black Bostonians: Family Life and Community Struggle in the Antebellum North* (rev. ed., Teaneck, N.J., 2000). Like the Hortons, Kathryn Grover has been an important pioneer in researching municipal histories, including her study of Syracuse, *Make a Way Somehow: African-American Life in a Northern Community, 1790–1965* (Syracuse, 1994) and *The Fugitives Gibraltar: Escaping Slaves and Abolitionism in New*

Bedford, Massachusetts (Amherst, Mass., 2001). For a good example of a collaboration between a community historian and a historical museum scholar in recovering the history of a town that might not otherwise receive serious scholarly attention, efforts linked (as with many local histories) to the creation of a Black Heritage Trail site, see Mark J. Sammons and Valerie Cunningham, *Black Portsmouth: Three Centuries of African American Heritage* (Durham, N.H., 2004).

A great many nineteenth-century texts relating to African-American organizations are available online and in print. The field has benefited tremendously from general editors Henry Louis Gates, Jr., and Evelyn Brooks Higginbotham in their *African American National Biography* (New York, 2008). Other useful print sources are *Minutes of the Proceedings of the National Negro Conventions, 1830–1864*, edited by Howard Holman Bell (New York, 1969); *Proceedings of the Black State Conventions, 1840–1865*, edited by Philip S. Foner and George E. Walker (Philadelphia, 1979–1980); *The Black Abolitionist Papers*, edited by C. Peter Ripley (Chapel Hill, 1985–1992); *Early Negro Writing, 1760–1837*, edited by Dorothy Porter (Boston, 1971); *Lift Every Voice: African American Oratory, 1787–1900*, edited by Philip S. Foner and Robert James Branham (Tuscaloosa, 1998); and *Prophets of Protest: Reconsidering the History of American Abolitionism*, edited by Timothy Patrick McCarthy and John Stauffer (New York, 2006).

Although much work remains to be done, an important body of scholarship on individual church and denominational organizations is covered in the chapters of this book. One of the best general histories of African-American religion is Albert J. Raboteau's *Canaan Land: A Religious History of African Americans* (New York, 2001). Much of the most detailed and informative work on black religion, though, has been devoted to individual regions, denominations, and churches. See, for example, William J. Walls's *The African Methodist Episcopal Zion Church: Reality of the Black Church* (Charlotte, N.C., 1974); Edward D. Smith's *Climbing Jacob's Ladder: The Rise of Black Churches in Eastern American Cities, 1740–1877* (Washington, D.C., 1988); C. Eric Lincoln and Lawrence H. Mamiya's *The Black Church in the African American Experience* (Durham, N.C., 1990); Henry H. Mitchell's *Black Church Beginnings: The Long-Hidden Realities of the First Years* (Grand Rapids, Mich., 2004); Craig D. Townsend's *Faith in Their Own Color: Black Episcopalians in Antebellum New York City* (New York, 2005); and J. Gordon Melton's *A Will to Choose: The Origins of African American Methodism* (Lanham, Md., 2007). Individual church histories are too numerous to list here, but for good examples of this work see *Many Witnesses: A History of*

Dumbarton United Methodist Church, 1772–1990, edited by Jane Donovan (Georgetown, D.C., 1998), and Mary A. Ward's *A Mission for Justice: The History of the First African American Catholic Church in Newark, New Jersey* (Knoxville, 2002).

The history of African-American fraternal orders is particularly challenging, and many early studies are riddled with errors. Accordingly, it is useful to turn to the emerging work being published in journals. See, for example, Joanna Brooks's "Prince Hall, Freemasonry, and Genealogy" (*African American Review* 34:1 [Summer 2000], 197–216); Brooks's "The Early American Public Sphere and the Emergence of a Black Print Counterpublic" (*William and Mary Quarterly* 62:1 [January 2005], 67–92); Peter P. Hinks's "John Marrant and the Meaning of Early Black Freemasonry" (*William and Mary Quarterly* 64:1 [January 2007], 105–116); and Stephen Kantrowitz's "'Intended for the Better Government of Man': The Political History of African American Freemasonry in the Era of Emancipation" (*Journal of American History* 96:4 [March 2010], 1001–1026). The best study to date of that other largely fraternal endeavor, the convention movement, is Howard Holman Bell's *A Survey of the Negro Convention Movement, 1830–1861* (New York, 1969).

A great deal of research remains to be done on African-American educational efforts. The most comprehensive history to date is Heather Andrea Williams's *Self-Taught: African American Education in Slavery and Freedom* (Chapel Hill, 2005). There are, as well, a few regional histories—for example, Carleton Mabee's *Black Education in New York State: From Colonial to Modern Times* (Syracuse, 1979)—but the best work emphasizes affiliated efforts such as literary societies and other educational sites. On these, see Elizabeth McHenry's groundbreaking *Forgotten Readers: Recovering the Lost History of African American Literary Societies* (Durham, N.C., 2002) and Shirley Wilson Logan's *Liberating Language: Sites of Rhetorical Education in Nineteenth-Century Black America* (Carbondale, Ill., 2008).

Historians have only scratched the surface in studying the African-American press, but they have produced a number of useful books. General studies include *The Black Press, 1827–1890: The Quest for National Identity*, edited by Martin E. Dunn (New York, 1971); Penelope L. Bullock's *The Afro-American Periodical Press, 1838–1909* (Baton Rouge, 1981); Roland E. Wolseley's *The Black Press, U.S.A.* (2nd ed., Ames, Ia., 1990); Bernell Tripp's *Origins of the Black Press: New York, 1827–1847* (Northport, Ala., 1992); Frankie Hutton's *The Early Black Press in America, 1827–1860* (Westport, Conn., 1993); Carl Senna's *The Black Press and the Struggle for Civil Rights* (New York, 1993); Armistead S. Pride and Clint C. Wilson II's *A History of the Black*

Press (Washington, D.C., 1997); Jane Rhodes's *Mary Ann Shadd Cary: The Black Press and Protest in the Nineteenth Century* (Bloomington, Ind., 1998); and *The Black Press: New Literary and Historical Essays*, edited by Todd Vogel (New Brunswick, N.J., 2001). Essential reading in this subject is Jacqueline Bacon's pioneering study of a single newspaper, *Freedom's Journal: The First African-American Newspaper* (Lanham, Md., 2007).

Finally, I wish to acknowledge here the important research of Jeffrey R. Kerr-Ritchie, author of "Rehearsal for War: Black Militias in the Atlantic World" (*Slavery & Abolition* 26.1 [April 2005], 1–34). I could not have written this book without the guidance of Kerr-Ritchie and many other devoted professional and lay historians.

Index

ABOUT THE AUTHOR

John Ernest is Eberly Family Distinguished Professor of American Literature at West Virginia University. Born in Toledo, Ohio, he studied at the State University of New York at Binghamton and at the University of Virginia, where he received a Ph.D. in English. He has also written *Liberation Historiography* and *Resistance and Reformation in Nineteenth-Century African–American Literature*, and *Chaotic Justice*. He lives in Morgantown, West Virginia.